D1079018

Me, My Mother, My Life

A journey through pain and healing

Ayomide Adeniola

authorHOUSE®

AuthorHouse™
1663 Liberty Drive
Bloomington, IN 47403
www.authorhouse.com
Phone: 1-800-839-8640

Published by AuthorHouse   12/11/2012

ISBN: 978-1-4685-8555-1 (sc)
ISBN: 978-1-4685-8554-4 (e)

CONTENTS

Part III
Tomorrow's Hope

Part IV
God Heals

Part V
Walking In Freedom

PERMISSIONS

limited. Word for Today is available free in the UK and Ireland by writing to UCB, Hanchurch Christian Centre, Hanchurch Lane, Stoke-on-Trent, ST4 8RY or by visiting http://www.ucb.co.uk

Get me out of here on dove wings; I want some peace and quiet.
I want a walk in the country, I want a cabin in the woods.
I'm desperate for a change from rage and stormy weather.
Stronger than wild sea storms, Mightier than sea-storm breakers,
Mighty God rules from High Heaven.
Psalm 55:6-8; Psalm 93:4 (The Message Version)

ACKNOWLEDGEMENTS

I would like to say thank you to my publishers for their patient endurance while I took my time to perfect the manuscript. Thanks to my long line of editors—to Graham at Allograph for his mentoring, to Sam and Catherina at Words Worth Reading Ltd for their generous embrace of several rounds of editing; to Jenny at August Editorial for her thought-provoking review and readiness to turn work over quickly. To the other editors who worked on the manuscript, thanks for your honest critique; I believe the book is better for it. A word of thanks also goes to my legal advisers for their candidness.

In addition to this gratitude, I would like to say a few words to the main characters in the story. To my family, whose life history has been made public by it, I do hope that each and every one of you can find a positive way forward because what I realised in writing the book is that there is no shame in the truth, rather, as the Bible says, the knowledge of the truth sets us free, as difficult as that message may seem at this point in time. And specifically, to Mum, precious Mum, did ever a daughter love her mother more than I have loved you? My prayer for you still holds.

To all the other people mentioned in there, whose actions impacted me in negative ways, I would like to say that I bear no grudge and hold no bitterness against you, even though there was a lot of pain and headache as I wrote. My prayer is that you will one day see your actions for what they were.

Finally, but most importantly, I would like to say a word of thanks to God, the Father of all, for the strength He gave me to complete the writing, and I ask Him that He continue to keep everyone mentioned in there by His grace. Amen.

INTRODUCTION

A mother has a special place in the life of a child; mine has always been important to me. She played a significant role in my life as a little girl growing up in less than perfect conditions. Mother has been the primary parent in my life since I was nine years old; we went through the highs and lows of life together. It is, therefore, no great surprise that when I decided to write a book it was about mother and me—although my decision to write a book itself may be the surprise!

Psychologists say that the mother-child relationship determines how we relate to others. This implies that if we have confidence in this one important relationship, we are more likely to be able to relate successfully to others. If that relationship is fractured, the ability to relate to others is broken. What can then go wrong in this much-needed relationship?

For many of us, control is no strange concept. However, we tend not to attribute a lot of our actions or attitudes to our controlling tendencies. We try to exert dominance over people and they in turn try to manipulate us. We have learnt to navigate the muddy waters of life "effectively" and get what we want out of it. We go with the flow, take life as it comes and fight back with wit and doggedness. We are not ones to be beaten.

But there are still many of us who have been practically crippled by the control we have experienced. We are not very skilled at manipulating our way through the issues of life;

neither does shaking off the control from others and taking charge come easily. We are rather mild in personality; we like things black or white with no shady areas.

It is those of us (the latter) who find it difficult moving on from a hurt, because the essence of our very being has been violated. The rule of our world—"I will treat you right, I expect you to do the same to me", has been broken. Such betrayal shakes us to the core.

I am probably more familiar with this latter type of person than the former. I understand what it is to give every ounce of energy within you to being "one" with another individual, only for them to reach out to look after number one. In many cases, they think they are putting their own interest first, but they end up creating a no-win situation from which no one takes anything positive. The hearts of all involved are shattered and great voids are created in their lives that nothing else can fill. When this happens with someone whose life has been enmeshed with yours (someone like your mother), the situation may seem almost irredeemable.

I have always felt a strong connection to my mother, but the older I grew the more I realised it was a rather unhealthy tie. Mum suffered and struggled to keep our family together, and this makes me wonder what, then, was the problem? Why was her utmost not enough for me? Is it due to greed, ingratitude or utter selfishness? No. As human beings, we have the capacity to build and destroy what we have created. Not everyone will be bold enough to admit that they sometimes inadvertently destroy what they create because to do so would seem to show us up as inherently dysfunctional and perhaps evil. Who would own up to that? Not many.

I hope this book will speak to everyone who reads it—those who had vaguely similar situations to mine, those whose situations were far from being similar and those who can see themselves in the pages of the book as I recount some of my experiences. It is my aim that by reading about the problems I faced, the solutions I found to those problems and some of the lessons I learnt along the way, perhaps a daughter or a son, someday, somewhere, might glean an insight that would help them in resolving difficulties with their own parent. Or it may be that a mother or a father would be inspired by the book to shape the nature of their relationship with their child in a positive manner.

The book is written from my Christian faith perspective but it is not intended to be limited to readers who profess Christianity as their religion, faith, way of life or the very essence of their existence. The experiences are in no way different from those that anyone else may have faced, regardless of religious tendencies. These are experiences that come because we are human beings and are fallible. Most of the answers I found came from my relationship with God, and reading about this relationship with God may stir you to want to know more about Him. By all means, please find resources around you that will point you in that direction. For those who are not keen on religion, the resources that helped me understand my situation and helped me to find healing were not limited to those that are faith-based. Some of the books I read were written by psychologists who did not profess a particular faith.

As I wrote *Me, My Mother, My Life*, I came to realise the difficulties attached to writing a biographical piece that presents an unhappy side of life. There were a number of conflicts that I experienced as I wrote the book. The first of those conflicts was in trying to present the details of the narrative as they happened, in order to uphold the integrity of the stories, while at the same time protecting the identities of the people involved. In order to achieve this protection for the relevant individuals, I have changed the names of the characters as well as altered their attributes and the settings of their backgrounds. All of the people mentioned in there and all the experiences told are, however, real.

Another conflict that I experienced was the need to maintain focus and pace of the writing in order to achieve the aim of the book. I considered it important to condense some of the stories in order to direct the pace towards the books ultimate goal.

Lastly, I have never been one to keep a daily diary therefore I found it a challenge trying to recall the order that some of the events happened and their exact timings. It was difficult to remember word for word what different individuals said, but the general order of the conversations stuck in my head and in places I could picture the scenes as they occurred. It is for this reason that the finer details of chronology and dialogue are approximate.

Ayomide Adeniola

PART I

WHEN TROUBLE COMES

1

MOTHER, ONE IN A MILLION

L ife was tough but Mum was tougher.

"Ayo! Have you finished in the bathroom? Yetunde, get in there and have a quick shower while I finish preparing your breakfast. Ayo, did you sweep the living room before you went into the bathroom?"

Mum's lonesome voice echoed throughout our apartment in the stillness of dawn, like it did on many a term-time morning, as she shouted out to me and in the same breath called my dithering younger sister to order. On this occasion, she didn't call me by my full name, Ayomide; she used that variation only when she was frustrated and her words were almost twisting her tongue, or if I had endeared myself to her, in which case she would have called out A-yo-mi-de and the syllables would drag rhythmically and meander out of her mouth like the legato movement of the choir director's hands.

Silly me, I thought I'd grown out of Mum ordering me about, after all I was staring end of school in the face. Not a chance! When I didn't give an answer to her question, Mum assumed the task hadn't been completed and I heard her call out again.

"Ayo, you know you need to be a lot quicker than that."

It was 1987; I was in my penultimate year in secondary school and Yetunde, my younger sister, had gone past the half way mark in primary school. Our days usually started at around 5.30 a.m. I would normally be woken up by a cock that crowed near the boundary wall, between our compound and that of the adjoining house. The nights always seemed to have gone too quickly and the mornings arrived too soon.

Mum was usually up before me. I would hear the clanging of pots and pans as she tried to boil water on the kerosene stove. She had a good command of the mornings; she would handle them with such precise strictness that I couldn't get through those early hours of the day without her classic commands. As Mum would hurry in and out of the kitchen to make breakfast and get me and Yetunde ready for the day, she would also make sure we were fully on board and sailing the morning ashore with her.

"Yetunde! Have you finished your breakfast? Hurry up! You know the Adiguns will leave you behind if you are not on time. How are you going to get to school if they do? Ayo, Make yourself useful and pack my breakfast for me; I will eat it when I get a break at work."

Such a statement as that would mark the beginning of the end for our early morning rush.

Our family of five consisted of Mum, my older brother Olalekan, my older sister Ibidun, myself, the third child, and Yetunde, the lastborn. We lived in our hometown, Ile-Ife, which we simply called Ife. The town was in Oyo State, southwest Nigeria, about one hundred and seventy kilometres northeast of Lagos. Mum was strict and hard working. She was a managing nursing sister, managing the consultant outpatient department within the large Eleyele health centre, which was named after the Eleyele town district in which it was located. Mum was looking forward to becoming a matron and transferring to the big teaching hospital that was on the northeast end of town, along the main intercity road that led to Ilesa, a town about twenty miles from Ife. Mum said she desired to work with the bedside nurses in the hospital, rather than the outpatient care that she was currently overseeing.

Mum took her duties very seriously and made no apologies about the fact that she wanted the rest of us to work hard. Olalekan, at the time, seemed to have been the most ambitious of us four children. He had completed his university studies and was at the tail end of his National Youth Service Corps (NYSC). The NYSC was a one-year work placement by the Nigerian government during which the individual "youth copper" was paid a stipend in exchange for their skills. It was mandatory for every Nigerian graduate and they were usually posted randomly to various states in the country. Olalekan was no exception; he was sent to Ilorin, the capital of Kwara State, which was about a hundred and fifty miles directly north of Ife.

Olalekan had also started to plan for life after youth service. He said he would travel to London immediately afterwards and get a good job there. My older siblings and I had the advantage of being born in England after our parents had met there. Mum and Dad had both been sent, separately by their respective families, to study in England in the sixties. Dad studied for a bachelor's degree in economics while Mum studied nursing; somehow, their paths crossed and our family was created.

Being born in England meant Olalekan, Ibidun and I had the choice of continuing our lives in Nigeria or moving back to London for a different one. It was not a surprise that Olalekan decided he would leave Nigeria for London. He never seemed fully adjusted to the country and the way of life there. He was eight years old when we returned to Nigeria, old enough to have established his own lifestyle it seemed.

Ibidun was still at home even though she had finished her secondary school education about three years prior; she had unfortunately not been able to secure a place in university. I saw her try year in year out to no avail. I did feel sorry for my older sister, but it was difficult for that sympathy to last long—Ibidun was a "tough cookie", and what I mean by her being a tough cookie will be revealed later in this book. Yetunde usually did well in her studies. She had a strong, independent personality, partly bolstered by the fact that she was spoilt by both our parents as their lastborn. And me, I was working hard towards my West Africa School Certificate O-level exams (WASCE), which was due the following academic year. Apart from my impending WASCE there was also the General Certificate of Education (GCE) O-level exams, which candidates could take without being a pupil in a secondary school. The GCE exams were opened to anyone who felt able to take them or who needed to retake some subject they had failed in the WASCE. Mum didn't want to take chances with my WASCE the following year, as in her eyes education was the foundation to a prosperous future. Therefore, in order to give me a taste of what O-level exams were all about, she enrolled me for five subjects in the GCE and they were due in a few months time.

Dad was the only family member missing from our home. My parents had separated when I was nine years old and Dad had conceded that he couldn't look after us, so we all went with Mum. Since the separation, Dad had moved to Ibadan to take up a new job there but kept a residence in Ife, where I went to see him once a month.

Our home was a ground floor apartment, one of six within a two-storey block, which stood right opposite the health centre where Mum worked. The road outside was wide and moderately busy. It led onto the town's main intercity road, which in turn led to other major towns and cities in Oyo State and beyond. The external walls of the block were sprayed with a rough mix of cement and tawny-coloured paint and they grazed the skin when accidentally scraped against. The compound was solidly walled in around the block, with low-level metal fencing and two gates enclosing its front court. A wide spiral staircase wound up from the ground to the first floor, in the middle of the front facade emphasising the asymmetry of the edifice. The whole block was leased by the health centre from its original owner and the apartments were then sublet, fully furnished with brand new items, to qualifying workers within the centre. Mum's senior position meant we were eligible for the accommodation and it was inside it that, for many years, our household's daily life unfolded.

The afternoons were not the same picture of franticness that the mornings usually painted. Evenings could be even better, more relaxed, though not all the time I dare say. Every so often Mum came back from work and took opportunity of the relaxed evening atmosphere to relive gory details of her day, much to our disgust. On a particular evening, Olalekan was home for a week's leave from his NYSC and as we sat in the living room around our bigger and newer dining table, which was in the front right corner of the room, having our dinner of *amala* (cooked yam flour) with okra and beef stew Mum said:

"I was called to the A&E at about 11:30 am."

There was a sense of alert, as everyone seemed to have slowed their pace of eating to hear what Mum had to say.

"This girl had been playing with her brother and climbing a tree when her arm got caught between the branches. She tried to free herself only she somehow hit a stump that tore deep into her flesh, leaving her bone exposed," Mum had continued.

"Urgh, Mummy! Not during, a meal!" It was a chorus of revolt.

"I'm sorry," Mum replied. "It's just that I found it so disheartening, I needed to get it out off my chest. She is such a young child, just ten years old. Hmm." Mum sighed.

"Yes, but not when we are eating," Olalekan insisted.

Olalekan was a voice of authority at home because he was the firstborn and the only male in the house. Mum accorded him a level of reverence which the rest of us lacked. Mum's deference to him didn't seem to matter to me and my sisters because we all held Olalekan in high esteem, and it was fair to say that he earned his respect by being a caring and hardworking brother. He had had his own share of being ordered around by Mum. Now, as a grown man, all gangly at five foot and seven inches, Mum rarely opposed him, and even then not as strongly and fiercely as she would the rest of us.

That evening, Mum didn't seem to have expected such a unified voice from us and I was taken aback by her prompt apology. It was one of the extremely rare occasions when there was an admission of guilt by Mum. But notwithstanding her apology, the image of the vivid description she had given haunted me throughout the rest of my meal. Of course, Mum was forgiven. It never really crossed my mind not to forgive her for anything she did. I wish I could say the reverse was the case. It was not. Mum knew how to pile our offences up.

My mother would say, "Look, your cup is filling up gradually, when it fills to overflowing I will deal with you then."

Trust me, when she was ready, Mum dished out the punishment in full measure, "shaken together and running over". It was unfortunate that many times we didn't know how to stop the cup filling up, by either taking it from underneath the tap or completely stopping the tap of transgression from running. I was the offending party during another dinner table conversation, to which Mum left me in no doubt that she was averse. This time we were seated around the older and smaller dining table which was placed in the make shift dining room outside the kitchen. The original use of the space might have been for circulation between all the rooms in the apartment, but we needed somewhere to put the table which, I was told, was older than me: Mum claimed she had bought it before I was born.

Why I decided to provoke Mum with my unwelcome conversation that evening was not clear, even to me. I was only fourteen going on fifteen; I shouldn't have expected my forty-eight year old conservative mother to take kindly to the talk of boys. But hey, there goes my own adolescent self-assertion. I had helped her make dinner that evening and Mum gave thanks to God for the food before we tucked in.

"This is really good," Mum said as a commendation for my effort in helping her prepare the meal, a compliment which was gratefully received. Ibidun then started the chit-chat. It was about a brother in church who had made pounded yam, the same as I had done that evening only this brother allegedly made it better than I did. I felt a bit slighted by Ibidun; it was as though she was trying to undermine the praise I had received. I was determined to rise above it.

"Yes, you are right, men do have the energy to pound well," I responded.

I had remembered one of my school friends telling me how her male cousin pounded yam. "The pounded yam

9

retains its ivory-like colour and comes out satin smooth like kneaded dough, warm and very light textured," my friend had said. I told my family about the guy and how challenged I had felt, only I told a little white lie and said he was my friend. Mum was displeased. She retorted, "I didn't realise "*we*" are now having boys as friends!" I decided to tease her further and asked what was wrong with it. The look on Mum's face was now taking on a tinge of hatred and I thought I'd better drop it. The rest of our meal that evening was finished in silence.

If I dug deep enough within me to find my motive, I might have found a longing for Mum to engage with me in my little journey of fantasy, and take the opportunity to broach the issue of friendship with the opposite sex with me. I might at the end of it have told her the truth about this so-called friend of mine. It would have been the first such conversation; I had never really had a friend that was a boy and I saw (naively or foolishly) the opportunity to seek some guidance from Mum. Clearly, I was not wise enough in my attempt; she was quite antiquated in some of her approach to life and her response was not at all unexpected.

Notwithstanding Mum's old-fashioned approach to life, she was my hero. Her commitment to provide for us materially never faltered even though she struggled financially. The economic situation in Nigeria at the time was dire; for all we cared, the country might as well have been experiencing a multi-dip recession or a seemingly unending economic trough. The Structural Adjustment Programme brought in by the then military government was biting hard; Mum and her colleagues often didn't get paid for months at a time.

"*This SAP is sapping the life out of people ooo . . . chei! It was only two years ago that we exchange the dollar for less than one naira, now they say you cannot buy one dollar for less than five naira. Un-be-lie-va-ble! Wetin happen for this country for the sake of God?"* Mr Alexander, one of our neighbours, concluded his complaints in pigeon English as the paths of the various adults from the different apartments met outside in the front yard. Inflation and exchange rates had become a frequent topic of discussions amongst the adults and I was beginning to get drawn into the fear that their own anxiety created.

I wondered how I and others in my generation would survive in the future, if in our childhood the economy was that bad. Dad was not very generous towards us either and that made the impact of the country's financial situation even worse. The responsibility fell on Mum to make life work for us (and for herself, I suppose). SAP or no SAP, Mum was determined her children would not suffer or want for anything if she could help it. When she was down to her last pennies, she would put everything in the fridge and cupboards together and would come up with something that filled the whole flat—and the neighbours'—with a mouth-watering aroma and when we ate it, the food was just as delicious to the mouth as its scent was to the nostrils.

When it came to clothes for us to wear, Mum faced the challenge with the same level of potency. She did not let her drive to provide the best for us dwindle. With my own teenage years came a dilemma—being able to choose an outfit or the fabric for a bespoke one. This made my wardrobe something of a major decision. Each time a special occasion loomed, Mum would traipse from market to market with us in her trail. She got frustrated by my "high taste and choosiness" while I, on the other hand, got more frustrated at the merchants' lack of range and eventually we all felt and looked tired. Small beads of sweat would settle on our foreheads after we had paraded through the timber and corrugated iron sheet stalls in the sun.

"Ayomide, you know that I want the best for my children and my struggle is for that best, from what you eat to what you wear. You know I will not be doing this otherwise! It is tiring and you need to make up your mind on time."

Eventually, Mum came to understand that it may take me a while (a long while, actually) to make a choice or more precisely to find what I was looking for, but when I did, I sure was satisfied with it and she was sure to be impressed by it. That knowledge would by and large help her through the frustration. She developed her own tactics for handling the situation—whenever we got to a merchant, she would look me in the eye and if I looked a little bit less than impressed, she was off to the next, no time wasted. If there was nothing I liked in our town, we would travel to the next to look. Ultimately, she got satisfaction out of the end result and I did too, so we were all happy with that aspect of life, or at least we coped well with it.

I loved and appreciated my mother for her effort and admired her determination.

But with a lot of the effort Mum put into bringing us up and providing for us came much bitter nagging. The bitterness pushed me away from her and my withdrawal hurt her. Many a time Mum pondered, and her pondering would lead her to conclude that she was poor because of her children.

"If I didn't have children, I would have built my own house by now," Mum would say.

I could see her point; however, there was not much I could do to change Mum's circumstances. She had a lot of unrealised ambition within her and living in rented accommodation had its own drawbacks. There were the odd moments when a neighbour would get tetchy and offensive because their every whim had not been attended to by the other occupiers of the block. It was difficult to handle such occurrences without a blend of anger and self-pity, especially as there were a lot of other challenges that seemed determined to break one's spirit and you couldn't get away from feeling like a powerless and perpetual tenant. I must confess though, problems like this did not happen often as we had quite friendly neighbours.

There may not have been much that Mum could have done about the rude neighbours, but there was much she did about her own children. Any indiscretion (usually made by me or Ibidun) would attract more than an earful of indignation from my mother. I soon found my own way out, knowing Mum just needed to get things off her chest and that when she did, she felt better for it. Once she started, I would quietly slip into my bedroom and lie on my bed. I was lucky enough to have a room to myself and that protected my privacy.

Once Mum started nagging and I had got a chance to sneak away, for the next five to ten minutes after I had shut my bedroom door behind me, Mum's raging voice would still seep through. I knew well enough to block it out with my daydreams and then it would stop. The trick was to stay still, to allow the air to cool before I showed my face again.

Ibidun was less able to handle Mum's nagging, so one day I gave her my secret, but not more than three days afterwards she turned round and used it against me. In a burst of anger, she told Mum that her infuriating ways were why I always ignored her whenever she scolded me and that I usually left her on her own to bark like a dog. I couldn't believe it! How could I redeem myself? Before Mum had the chance to mull over what Ibidun had said and develop any resentment for me, I followed her straight into her room to explain that I was only trying to get Ibidun to see some sense and stop answering her back. I was relieved after recounting my own version of events that Mum recognised that the comparison to a barking dog was Ibidun's own twist. It was not the way I talked about my mother. Unfortunately, from then on, I could never again get away from Mum's nagging.

"Ayo! Don't you dare go into your bedroom! Come back here at once!" Mum would shout whenever I tried to make a stealthy exit. She didn't seem to have grasped the fact that I found her constant arraignment dreadfully wearisome.

2

AN AMBITION SHORT . . .

I attended an all-girls catholic secondary school, St Mary's Girls High School, about four miles away from home on the southwest side of town. It was a beautifully laid out school with a smooth but dusty approach road from the entrance gate. The road led straight to the immaculately but minimally decorated nuns' convent, forking just about a hundred yards from the convent towards the single-storey principal's office and administration block with its well-kept front lawn. I always admired the beautiful cream and pink convent, its front swathed in beautiful red hibiscus flowers, but only from a distance as no pupil was allowed to go beyond its gates unless invited. All throughout my five years in the school I only entered the convent for a few days in the fourth year, when I played the role of a shepherd as part of the Christmas concert and drama.

The entire cast were called into the convent for rehearsal by Sister Dora, the Italian nun who was putting the production for that year together. She proudly showed us around their mini chapel and altar, where there was a cross with Jesus still hung on it and Mary his mother bowed in prayer.

"We need to approach the son through his mother . . ." Sister Dora explained. Her belief was contrary to the teachings I had been given in my church but I was not going to argue with such a woman of zeal, who had committed all to her faith.

School to me was another thing in life that I had to do, mainly because it was required of me. I liked the beautiful compound and enjoyed the extracurricular activities including the literary debates, which I wasn't particularly good at, though I did manage to win once. There were times when I felt inspired by some of my teachers: their dedication to our success, the passion with which they taught us, and their creative approach to teaching. Those stirrings pushed me towards disparate ambitions for the future, ambitions that didn't translate to clear goals.

"I wonder why she is like that," Mum complained to Pastor Stan, the senior pastor from our church in town, which was called Foursquare Gospel Church, a Pentecostal Church. I stood about five feet away from the door leading from our living room to the dining room, leaning against the sideboard and wondering why I was brought before this committee of elders. Pastor Stan and his wife sat on the armchairs opposite me and Mum sat adjacent to them as they all stared curiously at me.

"Ayo!" Mrs Stan said. "Even our little boy, Soji, he has already started to show some aptitude along the engineering line. Eh! You are about to take your WASCE and you don't know what you want to study in university. What is your favourite subject?" She leaned forward in what seemed an expectation of a satisfying answer, the curiosity in her eyes all the more intense.

Dear me, I don't think anybody had asked me that question before; I couldn't tell them what my favourite subject was—I didn't have a favourite subject. I understood the ones I understood and I was confused by the others. *Wait a minute.* I thought for a second, *the only subject in the latter category was chemistry.* I could almost feel the walls of the laboratory closing in on me anytime we went in there for a lesson. The columns in the chemical-riddled room seemed three times more than the four that there were and the whole laboratory always felt dark. I was never sure whether it was the design of the laboratory, which was painted white, or the confusion in my head that caused the darkness. I enjoyed the fact that I could put a litmus paper in a beaker half filled with acid and it would turn red but the nitty-gritty of it was rather abstract and went right over my head; I knew as much about the elements in the periodic table as I needed to know but I couldn't imagine what many of them looked like and how they impacted on my everyday life. I had lost count of the times when my mind automatically switched itself off the lessons completely; as long as I passed my subjects (and I seemed to have developed a knack for passing them) all that didn't seem to matter.

In order to please my enquiring elders, I concluded that I would study medicine. In any case, I did enjoy my biology classes, and most of my classmates who were taking similar science subjects as me had all expressed their intention to study medicine. It appeared to be the most prestigious career in the country at the time. So, I followed the crowd of aspiring doctors and applied to study medicine in the university.

As my exams approached, Mum knelt beside her bed both morning and night; she prayed for me to get distinctions in all my subjects. The pressure seemed to be directed at God and not me. Nonetheless, I could feel the force of it as she prayed. This was after all the same mother who when she received my first secondary school report, strongly upbraided me for coming seventh out of a total of about one hundred and fifty pupils in my form. I, on the other hand, had been overjoyed at the time because being the seventh best student in my form was for me something of a miracle and it blew me away. Before my parents separated, I hardly knew what school was about. In my early through mid years in primary education, I would get to school one day and there would be exam papers in front of me. Other pupils would seem to have known it was coming but I was always oblivious to its timing. The marks I received in the reports then were not good to put it mildly. I was therefore grateful to God that my performance in secondary school was in stark contrast to those of my primary school days. It was a blow when Mum put me and my great joy down. Never mind—I was determined to try harder next time.

The report next time was only as good, I was seventh again. I thought this must be my place in life. The second year however surprised me, as I came third in my first term's exams. Even then, Mum still scolded me for getting only ninety eight percent in English Language.

What a bore!

The teacher had written a summary of the report, saying it was "worthy of emulation", and my mother said, "Sorry, but I can't see anything worthy of emulation in this." That was it! The camel's back was about to break; she was not going to dictate to me how I should feel about my school report anymore, I was not going to let her! Anger was rising inside me. I was ready to fight back, I was putting on my armour, pulling all my "fighters" together. Then within me, a voice of understanding rose up that said she was scared. She was a single mother struggling to look good to the world, and this was one of the few things in her life that was going right. She did not want to lose it, only she did not know how to keep it by nurturing it, so she resorted to beating it down, forcing it to remain.

The extent of her fear was in no small way exposed as she prayed for me to pass my WASCE with distinctions; she prayed with such apprehension and desperation in her voice. But despite her distressed pleas with God, my mother vacillated between rebuking me for studying too much rather than helping her with the housework and her requirement for me to excel in my studies. Mum would shout whenever she needed something doing while I was shut up in my room studying:

"Ayo! Come out here and do this for me. Other children don't ignore everything around them in the name of an exam. Even those who did Cambridge and Oxford were not this bad."

I would grudgingly and anxiously drag myself away from studying to answer Mum's call, worried that by the time I got back to my books I would have lost my momentum.

As my WASCE drew near, I took to staying back in school to study with some of the other girls in my class, away from the distractions at home: the responsibility for chores, Mrs. Alexander upstairs shouting out to Emeka, the Adekunles' baby two flats away crying, the five-year-old twins from one of the first floor flats running happily around the compound flying their imaginary aeroplanes and attempting an imitation of the engine drone with their high-pitched voices. There was the lure of the snacks in the fridge and pantry and the temptation to join the rare chatter between my sisters and Mum. School was usually over at one forty-five in the afternoon, and we stayed behind until between four and six o'clock. At that time of the day, the school was usually very quiet and we had our pick of classrooms in which to study. Many times we left our first floor classroom, in the two-storey foremost block, and went past the administrative building, through the tree shaded road, underneath the flat canopy of the flame trees, the yellow ones and the red ones, to the year two classes at the rear of the school's compound. It was quieter there and the twitting of birds had a relaxing effect on the mind. One Thursday afternoon my friends and I were a bit tired. Some of them decided they had had enough and wanted to go home to continue studying; others had things to do. I wanted to study more and would have preferred if we had stayed on but they were all clear it was time for them to leave. I was going to be left on my own. I had stayed back alone in the past, but I felt a little uneasy about it that day.

I was disappointed by my friends' decision and I started to whinge to them.

"The thing is Mum could decide that going to the market or somewhere else to do something for the household was more important than my studying."

"Everybody knows I am studying, they know not to ask me to do anything. They cook for me and others do whatever needs doing in the house," was Tomi's reply.

"I wish Mum was like that, get Yetunde and Ibidun to do a bit more," I moaned. "You know what, if she calls me and asks me to buy some kerosene for the stove or anything like that, I will simply turn her down, end of." I declared my intention very loud and clear to the girls as we packed our bags and walked to the junction of the school to get taxis home.

I walked in through the front doors of our apartment and was greeted with unnerving warmth by Mum. She was very nice to me and gave me some food to eat. I sat on the couch in the living room with the plate of stewed beans on my lap and with each spoonful I ate, guilt riddled my mind. I felt bad about all the things I had said at school. I knew I was not to blame; I could not have known Mum would be this nice, it was not like her. Mum came to sit on the chair adjacent. She coughed. I looked up momentarily and continued with my food. As I was about to finish eating she dropped what felt to me like a bombshell.

"When you have finished, I need you to get some kerosene for the stove."

I knew it (or not). This had been too good to be true! Mum watched me as I pouted and frowned.

"Is there a problem?" she asked.

"Why do I have to get the kerosene all the time? Why can't someone else go?"

It quickly turned into a small argument as she asked me what the big deal was in me helping her out in the house.

"I don't mind helping out but I mind you not being considerate of my situation. This, at the end of the day, is a family and the burden of it should not fall on only one person. Others should do their bit too."

She called out to Yetunde and asked her to bring the envelope on her bedside table. Mum had a deliberate look on her face. Almost as though I could read her mind like the pages of a book, I knew instantly what Mum's look was all about. The result of the GCE exams I took in the previous academic year had taken some time to come through but had eventually been released. One of my classmates, Remi, had told us in school that hers had arrived in the post just the day before. I believed Mum's look was all about my grades; the content of the envelope Yetunde was to bring would prove me right or wrong.

Mum handed me the envelope. She practically threw it at me. It was already opened. I took out the contents and just as I had predicted, it was my exam result. I had gained a distinction in English language, a credit in mathematics, and I had failed the other three subjects. I put the paper back in its envelope, slid it underneath my empty plate as I stood up to take it back to the kitchen. When I got near the door, a big grin made its way to my face and I gestured nonchalantly as I grabbed the doorknob. I opened the door, managing to catch a glimpse of Mum through the corner of my eyes. I realised she had seen my action as she had been staring at me all the while my back was turned. She couldn't have been that much displeased with me as she initially appeared to have been, because I caught a smile on her face as it forced its way through her glare.

I was not at all dismayed by the result; I was indeed very pleased with it. I had known many people who were not as fortunate to have passed both English and Mathematics, which were basic requirements for most career paths in Nigeria at the time. The result, as far as I was concerned, merely indicated that I needed to work extra hard to pass my WASCE in a few months time and passing with credits was all I could hope for—I did not have much confidence in myself.

As Mum continued to pray for distinctions in my exams, her prayers wearied me. At the same time as she pleaded with God (literally) I would think and have my own quiet conversation with Him. I would tell God, *This woman has no idea what it is like to go through O-level exams. I don't think she did O-levels in her time; if she did, she would not be praying for all these distinctions. Lord, you know credits all round would do me and just a pass in additional maths, even though I am not bothered about passing it. Lord, credits in the rest would do me.*

Sister Dora, the fervent Italian nun, taught mathematics and additional mathematics. She made my life in school dismal for weeks, when she found out I was not intending to take one of her subjects in the finals. I had to register for additional mathematics when she refused to sign my registration for the mathematics exam. Since I was taking additional mathematics for Sister Dora's sake, it mattered less if I passed or failed it.

When the result came through about three months after I wrote the exams, I found that for reasons unknown to me, it was my mother's prayers that God decided to answer. Well, except for the additional maths, which I failed woefully. The way Mum flung herself on the earthy ground outside the church, rolling around in gratitude to God, showed that the result mattered to her more than it did to me.

We had gone for Bible study and about fifteen minutes to the end of the meeting, Sister Tundun, the sister in my church who taught me physics at school, appeared by the side window next to where I was sitting; she looked in and beckoned me to come outside. Mum saw Sister Tundun's gesture and rushed off her seat on the plain bench adjacent to mine. She hurried after me.

"Well done, my dear," said Sister Tundun. "Seven distinctions!" she exclaimed.

"Sister Tundun, what is it? What did you say?" Mum panicked as she emerged through the church's front entrance.

"Mummy, there's nothing to panic about," answered Sister Tundun.

Younger people called my mother "Mummy" in deference to her. It was part of the Nigerian culture of respect for elders. I called older women Mummy too, especially if they were old enough to be my mother ("Mum" was not particularly used in Nigeria and it was not until later in life that I started to call my mother "Mum").

"Ayo got seven distinctions," Sister Tundun announced to Mum.

"Seven distinctions? Eh, Se-ven distinctions? My Father and my Lo . . . ooord . . . !" Mum shouted.

The next thing we knew she was on the ground rolling back and forth, shouting still. Sister Tundun was stunned.

"Mummy, please get up, please get up."

She couldn't get Mum off the ground until half the church came out to see what was causing the commotion outside. The result, for my mother, was proof that she was as good in bringing up her children as "all those men" out there who criticised her for not having a man in her life to give her children some discipline.

All is well that ends well. My mother was happy, she'd got "her" distinctions; I was happy, I had good prospects and the future was looking bright. We did it as a team, it seemed, even though we did it in the most awkward way. What I needed to do was concentrate on getting into university and put an end to the idle life I had found myself living since finishing my exams a few months before.

Seeing Mum pray with such determination and the fact that she had prayed until she'd received the outcome she was after was an inspiration to me. There was resilience about her. No doubt she flagged sometimes and we had to encourage her, but when push came to shove, she would not settle for less than the best she could afford to have. She did not settle for the difficulty she was facing, whether in her career as a nurse or as a struggling single mother, she kept fighting and pushing on. Her fight was not inspired by covetousness; Mum was not given to hankering after what others have. She was not out to compete with the neighbours, to achieve what they had accomplished. There was a level of contentment with her even though she was far from being complacent. Her battle was for her own destiny.

3

A BREATH OF FRESH AIR . . .

C hristmas of 1989 was fast approaching and I was eagerly awaiting the result of my Joint Matriculation Examination, which, if I passed, together with my O-level result would secure my place in the university to study medicine.

Mum came back from work one afternoon with the news that Saudi Arabia was short of medical practitioners and the country was recruiting high calibre nurses and midwives, especially those trained in the west. It was a great opportunity for Mum. Describing nursing as her calling is not an overstatement. She put her soul into caring for her patients. It was going to be a chance for her to earn significantly more money than she earned in Nigeria; that way she could look after us better. She set out applying for positions in Saudi Arabia and putting the necessary arrangements in place, including moving out of the health centre rented accommodation to a location nearer some of her family members who would be able to keep an eye on me and Yetunde once she had left the country. Mum had very high hopes that her application would succeed. She knew the job she would be offered would not make provisions for her family to relocate with her, so she decided she wanted Ibidun to move to England and join Olalekan, while Yetunde and I stayed back in Nigeria.

Olalekan had returned to London about eighteen months prior: he had made good on his promise of leaving the country immediately he finished his youth service. I could not imagine him trying to struggle through the Nigerian system that had been so unfair to the hardworking civil servants. In the months that he had been living in London, he had sent us countless letters and we received extra large greeting cards on all birthdays and Christmases. We proudly displayed the big cards on the sideboard in the living room, their bold lettering and warm colours belting out their unique messages to their readers *"Happy birthday to a wonderful sister."*, *"God bless you Mother at Christmas."* It was nice when people came in and commented on the size of our cards and how beautiful they were. When we responded to these compliments from our neighbours and friends, you could just feel the sense of collective achievement at having a brother who was doing well for himself.

My results finally came and I managed to gain admission into the university in town, Obafemi Awolowo University (OAU), to study estate management, a five-year course. I had not secured enough marks in the examination to study medicine. In any case, medicine was an irrational choice for me because I couldn't cope with seeing the severely wounded or the critically ill, and I couldn't bear the thought of human dissection. Dr Ola, a member of our church, who was also a lecturer in business management on campus, told me about the estate management program. He and his wife had come to visit us, one Friday evening, after he heard about my predicament.

"I will see what we can do to help Ayo out," he had assured Mum.

I went to see him in his office on campus, two weeks after their visit. His tall, fleshly frame was comfortably settled in an executive chair in the five meters by three meters room. He pushed the papers on his desk, which he had been reading as I entered his office, to one side.

"We have a friend who is an estate surveyor. He's got his own business in Lagos and he's doing really well," he explained.

After a short discussion, he took me on a tour of the Faculty of Environmental Design and Management (EDM) on the northeastern end of the university's campus. The Department of Estate Management was part of the faculty of EDM. The buildings there made the whole faculty look like an afterthought in comparison to the dramatic design of the Business Administration block that we had just left behind. The three-storey Administration building was designed as a cuboid that was held in place by a series of slanted columns, while the faculty of EDM was simply a number of plain, small rectangular bungalows. After a quick look through my prospective faculty, Dr Ola explained to me the process by which I could change my course of study and we walked back into the architectural grandeur of the University's main hub. We stood by the four storeys high Oduduwa Hall and amphitheatre, a work of art in its own right—its hexagonal design was brought to life with various geometric shapes as they defined openings and links from one part of the building to another. The cultural legacy of the building as a performance venue was evidenced by a white splash of what seemed to be African cultural heritage inspired patterns over the natural grey colour of the textured walls. Dr Ola explained what estate surveyors did and it immediately caught my imagination.

"The architects design, the building surveyors and engineers deal with the construction, and the estate surveyors manage the completed structure."

He picked the right location to explain my potential career to me: a roof was being built over the amphitheatre and there was a lot of construction noise, traffic and personnel around. Estate management sounded like a career path I would enjoy, especially as I loved adventure and he told me that a job in the field would involve a lot of travelling. He also said that the remuneration was considerable and that, for me, sealed the deal—I would have enough money to do whatever I liked with!

My change of course was successful and I moved into the halls of residence on campus (which we called hostels) to start my lectures. The excitement of my educational achievements soon gave way to a sense of grave responsibility as the pressure of my modules set in. It was no walk in the park. I lived my student life in a triangle: I woke up to go to lectures and retired to my room afterwards. My evenings were taken up by my Christian fellowship meetings when I was not out in the library revising my lecture notes.

It was a tedious life and estate management didn't seem that interesting after all. I wondered whether my desire to pursue a career in the property industry was sustainable. I became more exposed to other career options as I met students on various courses, and my own choice seemed dull in comparison to theirs. Some of them talked about their vocational preferences with great pride and enthusiasm and my interest jumped around the different faculties on campus. I was sure, however, that I didn't want to be a lawyer—law was for people who could cram cases and dates—and I didn't want anything to do with medicine, not anymore. I thought about other possible changes. There was pharmacy; the girls that I shared a room with were all pharmacy students and they made it seem easy. I considered starting all over again by applying to study for a degree in pharmacy.

My wavering was clearly derived from a confused mind. I remembered soon enough that pharmacy and I were not compatible because chemistry was my least favourite subject and organic chemistry was my weakest point in all the science subjects I had ever taken. I decided to concentrate on making a success of my chosen path and perhaps do a master's degree in business administration so that I could branch out into general management.

It was during my second semester that a letter came to say Mum had got the job in Saudi Arabia that she had applied for. I went home for a brief visit one night when Mum told me the good news. At last! Financial independence! No more nagging or bitterness and reproach to do with money. Mum would finally become happy. Ibidun slid a vibrant Yoruba-language praise cassette into the player, which had been sitting idle on top of the television, and Mum started a thanksgiving dance. She patted her legs together in what almost looked like a waltzing movement and I joined in with my own version of church dance, bending down intermittently in worship of God. Yetunde hopped in from the bedroom and skipped around a bit before doing her own "proper" dance and Ibidun wiggled herself onto the dance floor that was our living room. We had all thrown caution to the wind as we expressed our happiness in singing and dancing when Uncle Deji came in, laughing. Uncle Deji, who was married to my second cousin, Aunty Sheila, lived with his family about four streets away from us and he had dropped by to have a chat with Mum that evening. He had apparently stood in the unlit veranda in front of our ground floor apartment and watched through the living room glass doors as we did our hilarious dances.

"Come in and join us, *Baba Toyin,*" Mum called out to him as he opened the door and walked in.

"I knocked but you didn't hear," he said and side stepped towards me. "Wait till I tell Sheila this," he whispered in my ears.

Even Aunty Sheila admitted she would have done a dance had she been there.

As Mum prepared to travel to Saudi Arabia, Ibidun too made arrangements for her own travel to London. I had a strong feeling that joining Olalekan in London would bring Ibidun her much-needed breakthrough. She had become fairly subdued in the weeks preceding her travel, and not only that—she also sometime seemed a little bit pre-occupied, not in a bad way, as that preoccupation usually seemed accompanied by a touch of serenity. Ibidun travelled to London two weeks before Mum was due to leave Nigeria.

Once Mum had concluded her final preparations, Yetunde and I went with her to Lagos to see her off. We stayed overnight with Aunty Kehinde, a friend of Mum's. She and Mum had worked together at the health centre, and she had become a family friend—Yetunde had been a bridesmaid at her wedding. Aunty Kehinde was such a pretty and affectionate lady with a lovely smile. She had a slim and shapely figure that could not be hidden, even by her modestly crafted nurse's uniform.

We woke up early on the morning of Mum's flight and set out of the house just before dawn. The roads of Lagos were busy even at that time of the morning. It would have been eerily quiet in Ife. Taxi drivers were already out in their ranks and the buses had started running. There were street traders setting up their wares by the roadside, especially those selling various cooked breakfasts. Aunty Kehinde accompanied us to the airport as we didn't know Lagos very well and needed her assistance in getting to our destination promptly. We approached the taxi rank under the Ojuelegba flyover at the junction of her house; she negotiated a fare with one of the drivers and we set off for the airport. She also offered to take Yetunde and I to the bus station to catch a bus back to Ife after we had seen Mum off.

Mum finished checking in and she was ready for the departure gate; we waved her goodbye and left the airport. Yetunde and I then journeyed back to Ife to start life in Aunty Dunmola's house.

4

. . . JUST THE ONE BREATH

Mum had arranged for Yetunde to live with Aunty Dunmola, Mum's younger sister from a different mother, who lived two roads south of our apartment. Mum said I had a choice of living on my own in our apartment or living in my aunty's house with Yetunde, whenever I came home from the university. The excitement of a completely independent life had overshadowed any sense of the reality of living alone in a large three-bedroom flat. By the time I got a slight taste of what it would be like, I ended up not sleeping one single night in there. I found myself agreeing with Aunty Dunmola that it would be a good idea if I came to live in her house. That left our own apartment unoccupied.

Aunty Dunmola was rather sleek and fashionable, with a tall and slightly curvy figure. I thought I was the one guilty of high taste but I was no match for my aunty in that regard. If taste runs in the genes, then I know which ancestry line to trace mine down. She looked a little like granddad, especially with the gap in her immaculately white teeth. She was twenty years younger than Mum, thirteen years older than me and would many times call my mother Mummy. She had a rather mature disposition towards me, which made her a cross between an aunty and a mother figure. She knew how to come down to my level and I could talk to her about many feminine issues that I would not have felt comfortable talking to my mother about. Aunty Dunmola's husband was mostly away from home, working in Lagos, which probably gave me more opportunity to be even closer to her.

It was nice getting to know Aunty Dunmola's four children, John, Matthew, Hannah and Samuel. I helped her look after them when I was home from campus and it made me feel like their younger mum. I learnt to think about their emotional and physical needs, and even though I got it wrong many times Aunty Dunmola would sometimes be gracious enough to point me in the right direction. There was discipline when they needed it and there were cuddles and playtime to show them love and family happiness.

Samuel, her two year old lastborn, liked to be cuddled. He would raise his eyelids to reveal two endearing brown eyes and fix a mischievous gaze on me before saying, "Aunty Ayo, carry Samuel." He had no concept of the first person at the time so he referred to himself as Samuel. He received cuddles even when he didn't ask for them. He was such a cute toddler that my maternal instinct couldn't help but always kick in; I would scoop his small and light frame up in my arms and give him a tight hug.

As my younger cousins grew older, they all got to experience the tough Aunty Ayo who made them pick up their clothes and shoes and would not take no for an answer.

Aunty Dunmola's house was a detached bungalow built on about a quarter of an acre of land. The ground around the house was part hard and part soft landscaped with a paved driveway to the eastern end. There was a well-maintained lawn to the western side of the house, and beyond that there was a box hedging to demarcate the start of a small fruit garden with mango and orange trees. The house was fenced in with a nine foot high block wall and an Alsatian dog barked from behind the fence whenever a stranger approached.

"Ayo, sorry, I can't visit you in your aunty's house. I heard there is a dog there," said Sister Edith, from church.

"He doesn't do any harm; I will be there with you when you visit," I reassured her.

My aunty's dog gained increased popularity with me moving into the house. Unfortunately, he died not long afterwards.

I received the first letter from Mum about two months after her departure. It had been a difficult time for her but thank God, she had managed to get settled into her new life. She also requested that Aunty Dunmola and I look for a new apartment, if we could, and move all our belongings there as a few days before Mum travelled, the landlord of our existing apartment had indicated an intention to let it to one of his relatives.

About four weeks later, Aunty Dunmola and I found an apartment a few streets away, nearer to her own house, and we moved all our belongings there. The apartment, even though nicely and certainly better decorated than the one we had just moved from, had been empty for a long time and had a musty smell. The grass all around was lush and overgrown, the soil underneath softened by the rain of the season. Two other apartments in the block were also vacant and the environment looked generally unkempt. On the morning of the move, I woke up (having arrived home from campus the previous night) feeling weak and feverish, I could feel an unusual warmness in my body. The shifting of boxes and furniture sapped whatever strength I had.

"This place needs thorough cleaning," Aunty Dunmola noted.

I had no energy whatsoever to do the cleaning; I didn't give her a reply.

"Don't worry, it would have to do for now, we can clean it later," said my aunty who couldn't understand the reasons for my sluggishness and had earlier been angry with me because of it. It turned out, a day later, to be the onset of chickenpox. Over the following months, I tried cleaning the apartment one room at a time.

Mum's letters came more frequently and so did her phone calls. She would write and send money home to Aunty Dunmola for mine and Yetunde's upkeep and she would send some extra money to me as my living allowance on campus. It was always nice to receive Mum's letters. She sent us some beautifully designed writing pads and envelopes with which we could write our replies; nothing compared to the art of writing heartfelt letters of appreciation and care for each other. We exchanged pages of them. The distance between us seemed to have increased our fondness of each other, or perhaps it made us appreciate being in each other's lives better. The fact was that I loved Mum. Despite her strictness and nagging, I was strongly emotionally attached to her; when Mum hurt, I hurt. One of the things that guaranteed I would cry was if Mum cried.

Ibidun was doing well in London. She wrote letters to us frequently and sent us tokens of love, just like a "little mother". Olalekan too continued to write to us frequently, and by all indications he was very much a prosperous soul in the country of his birth.

Six months rolled by and it was time for Mum to come home for a holiday. It was exciting to look forward to her first homecoming. I could not wait to see her again. Yetunde and

I prepared ourselves to move back into our apartment for the duration of Mum's stay. I went all out to prepare our new abode for her return. I cleaned the apartment over three days and bought everything I could think of that we would need. Aunty Dunmola notified the landlord of Mum's imminent arrival and he arranged for the compound to be cleaned. The house was now looking a lot more like an inhabited property.

I woke up on the morning of Mum's arrival and made a final shopping list, carefully going through each room, particularly, the kitchen, bathroom and Mum's room, to ensure every needed item was on my list. I was out doing the shopping when Mum arrived. I got back and found her slumped in an armchair, in the living room, sulking. I could not think what had happened in the short time she had been home. I asked her what the matter was—she did not like the place! She said it was dirty. My effort seemed to have gone unnoticed.

"It's not that bad. You know you are coming from a country where all the roads are tarred and your apartment probably sparkled, so it's bound to be a shock to the system coming into this. But it is home, it is where happiness is." I tried to pacify Mum and help her see the brighter side of things. I was resolute that Mum's subsequent holiday home would be better. The apartment would be spick-and-span.

Another six months rolled by and it was time again for Mum to come home. It was my chance to get everything right, from cleanliness to the arrangement of the flat. Unfortunately that effort was just not enough. Mum became more and more insatiable. There was always something to complain about or accuse me of doing wrong. Goodness gracious! Money doesn't buy happiness, does it? I had thought our lack of financial worries would mean love, peace and harmony in the house, but it didn't.

"Ayo," Mum said, "you have been swindling money from me."

I could not be more shocked. I have always been a faithful custodian of her finances—what on earth made her say this? She mentioned some money she had asked me to put in her account. She checked the account and it was not there. I could not remember what happened to the money but I remembered she gave instructions to that effect or similar. The only thing I was sure of was that no matter what had happened, I would not have spent the money if she had not asked me to. I hardly spent all the money she gave me for my personal upkeep, why would I spend the money I had not been authorised to spend?

It was days later when I remembered the instructions Mum gave were different to what we had both remembered. Mum had asked me to put the money in another account, which Aunty Dunmola had opened for her in her absence. Because the account had not been used since it was opened, we had both forgotten about it. I went to Mum to tell her what I remembered and asked her to check the other account for the money but her reaction told me that she had already remembered. I felt disappointed that Mum did not make an attempt to retract her accusation.

Despite all Mum's shortcomings and some of the troubles of our past, I considered my family to be very closely knit. I saw my family as one of the best anyone could have—we had turned the corner. My older siblings in London were doing very well, I was making progress with my studies and working hard to ensure everything in Nigeria was a success: Yetunde's education and the building project Mum started during her second holiday home. That was until . . . I rocked the boat.

5

A NEW LOVE, A
DIFFERENT LOVE

The day was the 3rd of January 1994, and the Sub Saharan Harmattan season was in full swing. Its dry, cold air made its way south from the desert and spread over the country like a blanket in the night, causing cold shivers and chattering of the teeth in the morning. A thick fog took over the air, and as noon approached, the sun, obscured by the fog and the dust-laden desert wind, released its fiery heat. It sucked up every trace of moisture and turned everything under its umbrella brittle dry. Lips were chapped, skin whitened and wrinkled; the smell of the arid air travelled up your nostrils and you could sense it every step of the way. But both the smell of that dry, cold air and its harshness on the skin paled in significance as the yuletide cheer continued to work its way into the atmosphere.

Aunty Dunmola, Yetunde, my cousins (Aunty Dunmola's four children) and I all went to granddad's house for his New Year's party. Granddad's parties were always good to look forward to—generally fun, lots of laughs. In his hey-day, Granddad would do a traditional Yoruba dance with some impressive footwork, like slow tap dancing without the tap shoes. The parties were usually a chance to for me to see many of my extended family members in one place at the same time. This particular party was my last chance to enjoy the seasonal festivities as I was due back into the full flow of campus life that night; I was scheduled to attend a Christian fellowship meeting, where I would be singing.

Granddad looked very well; he was calm, not overly excited as some of us were. There was a level of dignity with which my aged grandfather carried himself. He looked extremely contented and pleased to see his clan gathered together under his roof. He strutted around his complicatedly designed house with its differing floor levels, from one part of the house to the other. I bet anyone would be awestricken to know he designed and built it himself. Granddad moved with the times, he progressively built newer homes for himself, to his taste and in line with emerging styles. This particular one, which had the appearance of a bungalow at the front and that of a two storey building on the eastern side, was the third of such homes.

During one of her storytelling moments, Mum had explained to us that granddad lived in a simpler bungalow, located right in heart of Modakeke, when she was born. Modakeke was Granddad's home town, on the other side of Ife. The boundary between the two towns was marked by the busy main intercity road. Unfortunately, it was more than the road that divided the two communities; there was a long-running feud that dated back to the times of our forefathers. The dispute, at various points in my childhood and adult years, culminated in wars between the two communities and lives were lost. There were rumours of people being beheaded—it was grim. The most diplomatic approach by someone like me, who shared heritage from both communities, would be to take a neutral position, better still if I could avoid talking about it completely.

After Mum and the next two of her siblings were born, Granddad moved to a pale, pink-coloured, three-storey building on the east end of Modakeke. He lived there for many decades, until moving into this more modern and forward-looking building just four years ago.

The design of his new house was carefully planned around every slope of earth under which it stood.

"No need to fill it all in," I had heard Granddaddy say once, when the house was still under construction. "Use the lie of the land to create a new form of space."

How does he manage those flights of steps several times a day? I thought to myself, as I saw my dearly beloved grandfather taking the steps one at a time from his bedroom down into the dining hall and then up into the living area.

We knelt down, all the females, to greet this great patriarch whom I admired so much, and the men prostrated to pay their respect to him—that's part of the ways elders were respected in Nigeria. He looked as handsome as ever. He was my only surviving grandparent; my grandmother, his first wife, had died long before I was born. I heard she died of a strange illness, which presumably was not diagnosed at the time. In all the talks about her life and death, I never heard anyone say how old Nana was when she died. I guessed she must have been in her early to mid forties, when Mum must have been in her early twenties, not a ripe age to die.

Mum talked very highly of her mother: her demure, industrious, and generous nature and her dedication to her husband. At times I wondered how much she would have spoilt me had my grandmother lived long enough to see me born and grow. Dad didn't talk about his own parents; I believe they also died long before he met Mum. I didn't hear about them from his two older siblings either, even though they used to visit us on a regular basis when my siblings and I were growing up. Sometimes I wondered who my paternal grandparents were and the lives they had lived before their death, but I didn't think about them long enough to ask Dad. There were always more pressing issues to occupy my mind.

Several hours at granddad's house and the party was over—back to the reality of life in the university. I returned to the hostel and rushed to get ready for my meeting. There was no light in my room; my roommates—Tilewa, Kike and Rose—were out. I dropped my bag, got a casual outfit out of the wardrobe and spread it out on my bed to iron, when a particularly gentle knock came at the door and in walked a tall, slim, dark complexioned, handsome-looking guy.

Wow, he is handsome—I confirmed to myself in my thought.

"Is Tilewa around?" he asked in a deep hoarse voice.

"No, she's not. Would you like to leave her a note?" I offered him a pen and paper.

He finished his note and returned my pen. "Thanks," he said.

"You're welcome," I replied.

"If you can give her the note and let her know I will call back . . ." He was about to leave, then he paused a bit, turned round and said, "Can I ask what your name is?"

"I'm Ayo, and what's yours?"

"I'm Rex," he replied. "Have you always stayed in this room?"

"Yes, I have, since the beginning of the academic year. Tilewa is my roommate."

"Thanks again, Ayo," he said as he headed for the door.

"You're welcome," I said again and scolded myself for entertaining lustful thoughts. *He's not that handsome anyway, his voice is too rough and he looks a lot older than me*. Those were my second thoughts.

I left his note on Tilewa's table, headed for my meeting, and forgot all about the encounter with Rex.

Two weeks later, I came back from the library late in the evening and there was Rex, sitting on Tilewa's bed as he waited for her to get ready for their outing together. The bed was not an unusual centre of entertainment. The hostels were designed as individual bedrooms along a narrow balcony that spanned the length of the blocks. The balcony's primary purpose was for access into the bedrooms and the kitchen, toilet, and bathroom facilities that were situated at the far end of each floor. There was a big, single-storey common room at the entrance of the hostel that doubled up as an events' venue—not quite the ideal place to entertain personal guests.

I came into the room and found myself being a bit coy. *No, we can't have that; you better shake it off and get a grip*, I told myself. Rex and I exchanged greetings and I joined Kike in making jokes at Tilewa's expense. We were only being mean; we wanted to embarrass her in front of her guest. She eventually got ready and they left.

One week after her outing with Rex, Tilewa woke up from an afternoon nap and said, "Ayo, I have a message for you." The look on Tilewa's face told me the message was of a weighty nature and I wondered who would have given her such a message for me. I decided to tease her all the same.

"Is that a message from the dreamland or a vision from God?" I asked her. "Announcing you had a message for me as you woke up from sleep sounded ominous my dear friend."

My joke was not lost on Tilewa. She replied "Oh, I'll tell you later, I'm not ready for you now," she left the room and headed for the bathroom.

It turned out it was a message from Rex. He would like to invite me on a date. Oh dear.

"What about you Tilewa? You fancy him, don't you?"

"Not really, I like him as a friend," was her reply.

I may have found Rex attractive, but I didn't really expect him to express such interest in me and so quickly. I definitely was not expecting him to invite me out on a date!

"I don't know, Tilewa. Is he a Christian?"

"Absolutely. He attends the Redeemed Christian Church of God."

"Okay, give me some time to think about it."

In the Nigerian Christian culture of the time, an interest from a guy means they consider they would like to marry you at some point in the future. Generally, before they make an approach they would have satisfied themselves of the personality of the woman in question, by becoming friends with her and getting to know her more closely. They would have prayed about the likelihood of a long-term relationship with her and received some guidance from God and possibly older mentors. The stranger that was Rex, asking me out presented me with a challenge.

Rex's tall stature was overwhelming, and I found his husky voice a little bit off-putting, but there seemed to be a lack of "hot-headedness" about him. This portrayal of a charming and gentle demeanour by Rex was a catch. I was very much attracted to him. Not that I had been close to someone I could describe as hot-headed (well, Dad did display a lot of anger; more about that later), but somehow, I knew I would like my man to be equable. Notwithstanding my attraction to Rex, he was unknown to me and I wasn't sure how to go about making my decision on whether to reciprocate his interest or not. Of course, I knew I needed to pray and seek God's guidance. But I needed to be familiar with the person I would be praying about.

Marriage and family were the few things in life that I looked forward to with great expectations, despite my parents' troubled marriage. When my family became *born again* and started to attend the church in town, some of the marriages I saw there seemed enviable. It was the first time I heard husband and wife call each other honeys and darlings, instead of using their first names or making reference to their children's names, for example *Baba Tolu* (Tolu's father), which was a more prevalent way adults in western Nigeria referred to each other. I noticed that some couples from the church expressed annoyance at each other's behaviour, but they seemed to resolve their differences amicably. I daydreamed about what marriage would be like for me; I longed for it, hoping my newfound faith in Christ would afford me a blissful union and I prayed earnestly to God for him to grant me the blessing of a happy one when my time came. Being a wife and a mother became my biggest ambition.

With the interest from Rex, it seemed the time had come for me to start taking steps towards the realisation of my goal and ensure that I made the right choice. I had a good idea what my man would look like and his comportment: not as tall as Rex, he would be light complexioned and besides being gentle and temperate, he would be a good Christian, with whom I could serve God. He would be between three and five years older than me, not a day older. Clearly, Rex only fitted that picture partly.

I agreed to go out on one date with Rex, simply to try and make an initial connection with him, and I insisted Tilewa came along as a chaperone. It wasn't wining and dining in a romantic setting; he had a few items of furniture to shift from his paternal great uncle's house in town and he took me along for a ride. He had two hefty men in the hatchback Peugeot 504, which he explained was borrowed from his aunty for the task; the men in the back of the car had been recruited specially to help him with the heavy duty work. On the way to his great uncle's house, Tilewa had sat in the front passenger seat whilst I sat with the two men at the back. But on the way back, Tilewa and I squeezed into the front seat while the two men sat in the back seat holding on to the tables and chairs that were packed in there with them. How better to get to know a guy than being cramped in his aunty's car with old pieces of furniture and three other people—the light brown vehicle was filled beyond capacity! Actually, I did not expect the outing to be romantic, but I had expected it to be graceful.

It turned out not to be such a bad setting to extract some honest information out of him. I think the extremely informal setting, to put it mildly, was particularly relaxing for him. He had graduated from OAU about ten years prior—he was definitely a lot older than me. He soon ventured into stories about his ex-girlfriends. *I don't like the sound of that,* I thought, and changed the topic and focused on his faith. Apparently, he had only recently accepted Jesus as his personal Lord and Saviour, just two months before my first encounter with him. *That explained it then,* I thought. A mature Christian would have put the wayward days with former girlfriends in the grave, buried in God's forgiveness.

"So what do you think?" Tilewa asked when we got back to our room.

"Thanks Tilewa, he looks to be a pretty settled person. Did you say he's got his own business in Lagos?"

"Oh yes, he has an accountancy practice there, but he is up in Osu mostly. That's where his parents live."

According to Tilewa, Rex had some rapid success shortly after he graduated from university. He had moved to Togo with his Togolese girlfriend, whom he met after his graduation, and had set up an accountancy practice in Lome, Togo's capital city. His relationship went sour and he moved back to Nigeria to re-establish his business in Lagos and in Osu (a small town, about twenty minutes drive northeast of Ife) in order to be closer to his ageing parents.

"I get the impression he would like to be settled in a marriage pretty soon and I am not ready for that yet," I concluded.

Notwithstanding my hopes and prayers for a good marriage in the future, settling down into one just yet was not something I had considered.

A couple of days later, Rex came around to visit Tilewa. We simply exchanged greetings and I went my way. I was sure Tilewa would deliver my message to him. She was well and truly our go-between—not that an intermediary was required, but I suppose the lack of familiarity between Rex and I meant he leant on Tilewa for extra support. About half an hour later, Tilewa met me by the kitchenette and told me she had passed my response onto Rex; he would like to speak to me about it.

"Here comes Ayo who doesn't like me," he said as I approached his deep blue Daewoo Racer, in the car park opposite my block.

"Aw, it's not that I don't like you, there's nothing to dislike about you." I quickly searched my mind for the veracity of my statement. The words had instinctively rolled out of my mouth in sympathy and as an encouragement for Rex. But I concluded it was the truth—I hardly knew him so there was nothing I knew about him that would make him unlikeable. Oh, apart from his husky voice, but that was hardly a reason to turn a potential life partner down.

I explained to him why I did not think it was the right relationship for me. He was eleven years older, his next agenda seem to be marriage and mine was far from marriage. I had kept my third reservation about his maturity as a Christian to myself. Rex appeared somewhat understanding of my reasoning, but his disappointment could not be hidden as disenchantment cast a shadow around his face. He left and I didn't see him again for a while.

Then one afternoon, about two months later, when I was on my way home from campus, I met Rex again by chance. I had got off the bus at the main entrance to the university and started walking the road home. The same road led to Osogbo, the capital of our new home state, Osun State, which the military government carved out of Oyo State in 1991. I saw a blue Daewoo with its bonnet up. Thinking I recognised the car, I moved closer—there was Rex with his head stuck under the bonnet. The car had broken down and he was trying to fix it. He seemed a bit ill at ease about our meeting and attempted an explanation. He told me he had been to the campus to get a transcript of his results in order to send the document with his application for a PhD to some UK universities; he was then heading to Osogbo for a business meeting.

"It's fine, you don't have to explain," I tried to reassure him.

After that encounter, Rex started to visit me each time he came to Ife. He attended my twenty-first birthday party and brought me a gift of a very large hamper that contained almost everything from all aspects of living—a book, a set of audio tapes, a set of *aso oke*—the native Yoruba attire, bottles of non alcoholic wine, ice cream, all sorts. The party was held on a Sunday afternoon in my aunty's living room and I had invited some of my friends from campus to attend. When Aunty Dunmola saw the hamper she got curious.

"Ayo, who is this guy? You need to tell me. We need a chat."

"Oh dear, aunty, I feel embarrassed."

"Hey, there's nothing to feel embarrassed about girl, I just need to know. He seems to like you."

I explained to my aunty that nothing was going on and that he was just a friend, albeit a very generous one.

"And you expect me to buy that?"

"Well . . . actually . . ." I came clean to her. "But please don't tell Mummy because like I said, I am not very keen on him and I don't want her to think there was something going on."

"I am the soul of discretion love, you can count on that." She said in a tongue-in-cheek manner. "Are you going to send the negatives of the pictures from today to Mummy to print? Those pictures printed in Saudi Arabia always come out so nicely."

As naive and unsuspecting as I was, I answered yes. In any case we always sent negatives to Mum for printing, that way, she bore the cost and the pictures, in a sense, communicated our welfare to her.

By this time, it had been two and a half years since Mum had left Nigeria to work abroad and I had three semesters left to complete my university studies. She had continued her six monthly visits home from Saudi Arabia. Those visits were always special to me. I couldn't imagine my life without Mum. Long may my mother live, was my constant prayer to God. Two months after my birthday, she came home for a longer than usual summer holiday and announced that she would not be returning to Saudi but that she was going to move to England to be with my older siblings. I felt greatly relieved at the pleasant news. Mum would be near her family members, no longer on her own in an unfamiliar culture.

For much of Mum's eight-week holiday, Rex was constantly on my mind. Even though he was no more than an acquaintance, I could feel a strange pull towards him. I engaged in prayers to clear my mind of him. I asked God to keep and bless him in all he does and I asked the Holy Spirit to help me focus on the right things so that thoughts of Rex would be far away from my mind. His visits had stopped for the period that Mum was at home as I didn't see the need to introduce him to her—it might tip my mother over the edge if a male friend of mine turned up at her front door. I diplomatically warded Rex off for the duration of Mum's stay. But she noticed him in my photos, because Rex had donned a striking (and not so cheap) tie and die attire for the occasion; his outfit made him stand out amongst my simply dressed university friends. Aunty Dunmola once endeavoured to let discussion about him "slip" into conversations with Mum but I managed to block her attempts.

Rex's visits resumed shortly after Mum left.

As Rex continued to visit me, I got to know him better. He seemed to have grown spiritually more mature than when we first met. He had been baptised in the Holy Spirit and was talking about attending Bible College the following year, because he wanted to know God more intimately. His rate of growth surprised me and his yearning to know God better surprised me even more. I started to think about his proposal of courtship. After a further few months of his visits, I eventually decided to pray about the possibility of a committed relationship with him and to also seek advice from my Pastors, especially as Rex and I had reached a compromise: he was prepared to wait for me to finish my studies, in two years time, and get a job before we started planning a wedding.

I spoke to Pastor Stan and Pastor Olumide for some guidance. Pastor Olumide was one of the co-pastors who worked closely with Pastor Stan in church. Apart from being a pastor in my church, Pastor Olumide was also a friend of one of my uncles, Mum's younger brother; he tended to treat me like a niece and I respected him like my uncle.

Pastor Stan asked me if I had prayed about Rex's proposal.

"Yes, of course I have prayed about it." I explained to him how I had read the Songs of Solomon and felt in my spirit that I needed to look for certain qualities in Rex just as the characters in that book of the Bible found godly traits in each other. He didn't seem convinced. He said I needed to pray more and ask God for a yes or a no. I went back to pray, this time with fasting. At the end of my three days of fasting, as I concluded my prayers, there was like an ocean of peace, blue and immense, that surrounded me, and that for me was a go ahead from God.

Both pastors asked to meet Rex. He saw them separately on a number of occasions over a period of three months, after which they both gave me their respective opinions. Pastor Olumide was particularly sold on the idea. He told me he sensed Rex loved me genuinely and he thought he would make a good husband. I could sense the excitement in his voice as he gesticulated enthusiastically with his hands.

"Ayo, there is a peace that I feel each time I pray about you and Rex. Do you know what, if he says he wants to marry you next year, I do not see a problem with it." He opened his palms and shook them as though confirming there definitely was no problem with an early marriage to Rex.

I was struck by the peace that he felt. It was as though he was confirming my own experience. Pastor Stan, however, had a slight reservation. Even though he said he didn't consider it a red light, he was concerned that Rex seemed astute and had a lot more of life's experiences than I had. His own body language spoke through the movement of his head as he rocked it from side to side in clear ambivalence. I didn't really see how Rex's experience was a problem, especially as he was growing well in his Christian walk. Pastor Stan emphasised that he didn't consider it to be a strong enough reason for him to advice against a relationship with Rex, and he eventually gave his blessings for us to start a formal courtship.

A week later, I went to church for Bible study and met both Pastors Stan and Olumide by the east side entrance. I announced to my pastors that following their blessings, Rex and I were officially in a relationship. I felt a sense of maturity as I spoke.

"Have you told Mummy about Rex?" Pastor Olumide enquired.

The thought of having to tell Mum about him made me a little nervous.

"Erm, no not yet . . ." I responded.

My older and wiser advisors recommended that I address such a delicate issue in a letter.

"A telephone call will not do. Face to face discussion is best, but in the circumstances writing a letter is the better option," they both concurred.

Thank God for that. It would have been a very awkward discussion otherwise, at least from my point of view.

When I got back to my hostel, I picked up my writing pad to write. I could hear my heart beat as I held the pen in my hand, wondering how to start. There was no doubt that this letter would be written with more decorum than I had shown in my life thus far—nothing less than that would be good enough for my mother. I wasn't too sure how much detail Mum would find acceptable. I had heard from friends that parents (in Nigeria, that is) like to research their potential sons—and daughters-in-laws' backgrounds to ensure all would be well with their child marrying into the family. A young man or woman in Nigeria does not just get married to his or her spouse; they both get married to the respective families. The woman would be referred to by every member of her husband's family, both nuclear and extended (as far away as that extension goes) as "our wife" and she would refer to them as her "husbands". The married man, though, is just a son-in-law, not the husband of all members of his wife's family—that would give him too much power! A wife is expected to be submissive, while the husband is expected to take his responsibility and authority as the head of the family very seriously. Considering this cultural context, I thought it might be a good idea to tell Mum all I knew about Rex and his family. But before I got into all of those details, I had to break the news to her that I was now in a relationship with a creature of the opposite sex.

I wrote the initial preamble—how are you, the latest news in town, and everything else that was just about relevant to Mum—then to the real message of the letter. In the Nigerian Christian subculture, we refer to courtship as engagement. The same word is used to describe the traditional wedding, which in most places occurs the day before the "English" wedding with all its trimmings—the white dress, bridesmaids, bouquets, cakes, etc. Mum loved weddings. She loved to be part of the wedding arrangements, especially the traditional weddings, and she loved to hear about the young people in the church becoming engaged because many times she got to be part of the delegates from either the bride's side, receiving those from the groom's family or those from the groom's family taking the *gage* to the bride's family, depending on which of the marrying couple was a member of our church.

After my preamble, I wrote in my letter that I had some good news and that I was engaged to a gentleman named

Rex. I told Mum as much as I knew about his background and about his job as an accountant so that Mum would know that he was educated and that he had some ambition in him. When I finished the letter, I put my pen down, placed my two elbows on my desk and cradled my head in the cups of my hands, my letter laid out before me. I read it over, partly in awe of my seeming transition from a mature girl into a young woman, but mainly to ensure it sounded right and my newest level of maturity was conveyed to Mum in the manner that I had set out to do so. I imagined Mum reading it and giving praise to God for the ways He was helping her twenty-two year old daughter progress through life's critical stages, her face glowing with pride.

I thought it was appropriate to write to my older siblings to introduce Rex to them as well. The letters to my siblings were not as elaborate as the one I wrote to Mum, but I thought they gave enough information for them to feel part of their younger sister's life. I then made a formal announcement to Yetunde, even though she knew Rex already from his visits to Aunty Dunmola's house. It felt a bit strange telling her I was now in a relationship with someone of the opposite sex. I noticed the unease in Yetunde's reaction as she listened to her older sister telling her she now had a love life. I saw her look down to the floor and then turn her face slightly to the side as if trying to avoid eye contact with me. I thought with certain assurance that me and my younger sister would hopefully, with time, get to a place where we could discuss matters of the heart without any awkwardness. Finally, I caught Aunty Dunmola alone in her bedroom and gave her the news. It was important to me that my Aunty understood how highly I placed spiritual guidance in making such a life changing decision as I had made, both from my own direct communication with God and through spiritual authorities like my pastors. My aunty, the "soul of discretion", was as understanding as ever. She listened quietly, smiling relentlessly and looking at me with a little glitter in her eyes. There was no doubt that she was very pleased.

6

MOTHER MAY I?

Six weeks went by after I wrote to Mum, Olalekan and Ibidun, and I had still not received a reply to any of my letters. I did not think much of their lack of reply, because they did not always reply to letters immediately. In the meantime, I was experiencing the happiest times of my life with my new relationship; I had taken the first step towards fulfilling my greatest life ambition of being a wife and a mother and that gave me a sense of contentment. It was good to be able to talk all the time, with Rex, about our various life experiences, the hilarious ones, the ones that weren't so funny, our future life together and what we could achieve as a couple. I thought to myself, these are normal and emotionally healthy conversations. We were not being bitter about anyone. Although, at the beginning, Rex almost wore me out with his own bitterness against his father, but eventually, he seemed to cope with his feelings towards the old man, especially with my eager help:

"I think you need to look beyond all that and focus on what you are able to do for yourself. If your father doesn't build a house for you, build one for yourself."

I had learnt from my experience with Dad that one does not have to depend on people who are not keen to help. There are many other ways that God can provide for our needs.

Rex and I were growing closer each day; we visited friends and family together and had our own special moments. He would, from time to time, pick me up from my hostel and we would go for a car ride around the nooks and crannies of the campus. It was the first time I became aware of the hills that formed an arc around the northern edge of the campus and I got a better appreciation of the vastness of the land on which the university was built; it was big enough to form a small town. Sometimes we sat in the car by a quiet road and talked for hours. I had not realised until then that I had such flair for talking. I carried a little picnic along; he was astonished that I was such a good cook. His amazement surprised me and it made me want to show off my skills even more.

Early one evening, I was going back to my room from the library when I spotted Pastor Olumide's car inside the gates of my hostel. I saw his wife and children waiting in the car and I crossed the road to say hello to them. As I approached them, I saw the pastor coming out of the nearby block.

Pastor Olumide lived in the staff quarters on campus; he was a senior lecturer in public administration and we usually called him Dr Olumide, as he was referred to at work. I walked towards him to say hello, but he apparently had not seen me. As I came close, he stumbled into me. Dr Olumide was a little bit on the hefty side and the collision made me stagger. He was about to give an apology when he realised it was me he had bumped into. His apology turned into confrontation.

"What did you say to your mother? What did you write in your letter?" he asked rather forcefully and curtly. "Just let me get in the car, I don't want that person to see me."

I looked around, but didn't see who it was he had referred to. He seemed a little worked up; it was clearly an awkward moment to have met him. I exchanged pleasantries with his wife as he settled into the driver's seat. After he got his composure, he started to talk in a more familiar tone. He explained that he had received a letter from Mum in which she had expressed a lot of annoyance. He said Pastor Stan had received a similar letter too. Mum had told him in her letter what a brazen girl I was—I had told her I was engaged. I was confused. I wasn't sure what specifically about me being engaged that Mum was angry about; I had thought she would share my joy. I wondered why she would be so disagreeable when the same good news she was pleased to hear about other people was about her.

My own confusion about Mum's reaction was one thing, but I also noticed Dr Olumide appeared to have felt a tad insulted by my mother's letter, and that made me curious. I would have loved to have read it and be able to see what might have annoyed him about it. I briefly recounted the content of my letter to him and I looked at his face, which seemed frozen with surprise as he noticeably wondered what had prompted such an explosive reaction from Mum. He asked me to see him in his office at a more convenient time so we could chat properly.

The joy of my transition into a young woman, looking forward to a happy future, had been in a way tainted by my mother's reaction. When I went to see Dr Olumide in his office, I was a subdued girl who felt she needed to explain her waywardness. I walked timidly up the stairs to the first floor of the Faculty of Administration; this time the architecture of the building was not as enchanting as it had been when I went to see Dr Ola there some six years prior. I had "lived with" the building, like the other ones within its vicinity, for several academic sessions, and as the saying goes, familiarity had bred contempt. The spaces in all those buildings served pure functional purposes—lectures, revision of my notes, administrative tasks such as registration for modules and collecting my results; neither the dull EDM buildings nor the other grander and older ones inspired me a great deal beyond that.

I saw Dr Olumide as I turned in the direction of his office. There was a level of sensitivity with which he treated me, as we approached each other, which turned my confidence level up a notch. His broad smile and gentle pat on the back as he asked, "Ayus, Ayus, how were lectures today? It's tough being a student, isn't it?" were a bit reassuring, and he continued to chat to me about the challenges of campus life until we entered his office.

Once inside, Dr Olumide tried to get to the bottom of Mum's angry reply. He asked what her response to the news had been, and how I was getting on in my relationship. There was not much I could give him by way of an answer to the first part of his query, because the letter he received from Mum was the first I had heard of her feelings about my big announcement. He decided he was going to visit Mum during his next trip to England, which coincidentally would be in four weeks, and give her a good telling off because he really could not see the point of the trouble she was making. He asked me to write a letter of apology to Mum and, to be on the safe side, he requested that he read my letter before I sealed it in case Mum became angry with the second letter as well. Dr Olumide was only trying to keep the peace; I had no option I had to do as I was told. It's one of those things that were part of life in Nigeria: if an elder is angry, the younger person apologises for making them angry—no matter what the fact of the case was. Dr Olumide may have cared about me, but he was not prepared to side-step that principle.

When I spoke to Pastor Stan, he was less forthcoming about my mother's letter: he simply said I couldn't have expected a lesser reaction from her, as I was the third child and I was trying to get in front of my older siblings to marry first, though I was not aware of any rule that indicated my older siblings needed to get married before I could think of starting a courtship.

Dr Olumide went to England for a couple of weeks. On his return, I was one of the first guests to welcome him back home; albeit as anxious as I was to hear whether his meeting with Mum was successful, I thought it would be inconsiderate if I didn't give him a few days to rest. Those few days were about as much as my patience carried me. I went to see him four days after he arrived in the country. When I got off the bus near the junction of their detached bungalow, I walked quickly up the road towards the large oval junction that defined the layout of their street as though the speed with which I would arrive at the house would make a difference to the feedback I was about to hear. All the houses around there were of similar shapes to that of the Olumides'—bungalows laid out in a straight line along the smoothly tarred street and either painted white or finished with brown and grey textured coating. The university, I was told, was developed based on a master plan, and that was why the buildings were well organised—a very different picture to the environment in town; although, in some places in town, the beauty of creativeness revealed itself in the varied designs of the buildings.

I knocked on the door of Dr Olumide's home at about three o'clock in the afternoon; Brother Kunle and Sister Iyabo from church were there with the Olumides and their two children, Bose and Lanre. I sat on the sofa next to Sister Iyabo and chatted with all of them for a while before Dr Olumide excused both of us. He called me aside into Bose's playroom; I realised Bose was already in there.

"Bose, is it okay if I have a quick chat to your aunty in here?" Bose nodded shyly. "Look at her . . . as though butter wouldn't melt in her mouth." Dr Olumide drew his daughter to himself and lovingly patted her head. She shrugged him off and left.

"Look at that, Ayo, it feels only like yesterday when she was a baby growing into a toddler, and you used to plait her hair so beautifully. She's now a girl, huh . . . seven years old. She now tells me to leave the room when she wants to change. Can you imagine that? She started doing that two years ago. I couldn't understand it at first but I learnt; she is growing, and I have to grow with her, I need to respect her privacy. Ayo, God help me."

As Dr Olumide spoke, I recalled in my mind those days when the Olumides lived two houses away from us, opposite the health centre, and they used to drop Bose off for either me or Mum to babysit her. Bose would vigorously resist having her hair done and I would gently rock her to sleep before getting to work on it. Her hair was soft and curly and she had plenty of it. The plaited ends would fall effortlessly and conform to the natural curls, leaving Bose with an exquisite bulk on her head.

We got to the topic of Dr Olumide's meeting with Mum.

"Well, I saw Mummy in her home in London. Ayo, Mummy was very remorseful. She was begging for forgiveness. She even said you were the only one out of her children who didn't give her any problems when you were growing up."

Mother! I thought. She had told me about my special place in her heart several times in the past, but it never really reflected in her behaviour towards me.

"Ah, she sent apologies to Pastor Stan as well." Dr Olumide seemed to have suddenly remembered this somewhat important part. "You know, Ayo, I was astounded. I asked Mummy, 'Why then were you giving her such grief over a joyous thing?' Hun, when she knew you were such a good girl to her. Ayo, honest . . ."

Finally he told me if Mum continued with her attitude, he would take a tougher line with her. Perhaps there was a part of him that did not believe Mum's apology meant she was willing to change her behaviour.

I wasn't sure what to expect from Mum after Dr Olumide's visit to her in London, but it was not long before I found out. A month later, I received a letter from Ibidun encouraging me not to start to think about marriage yet.

> *"Ayo, you see there is still a lot in life that you can achieve. Please don't rush into marriage. You can complete your studies and get a good job. You can even come to London and study more; maybe you can study for a master's degree . . ."*

The tone of the letter gave Ibidun away; it was clearly not something she would have written of her own accord. The unwritten words I could read on the pages of Ibidun's letter were: Mum is nagging and I can't get any peace, so please for God's sake comply with whatever she wants so we can all eat our humble morsels in peace.

It was typical of our exchanges about Mum in those my teenage years. When Mum nagged in the house, we all bore the brunt of it. None of us had any sense of peace. All you wanted was for the "offending" person to fully act in accordance with whatever Mum wanted so we could all experience some calm again. I could imagine clearly the scenes in Ibidun's place in London, how Mum would have almost badgered her to madness about a situation she knew nothing of. Ibidun did not even refer to my letter to her in which I had tried to introduce Rex. Mum's attitude towards my relationship had not changed—but now she showed her disapproval in more covert ways!

A few months into the courtship, Rex started to hint that he would really like to get married the following year. We sat next to each other at a Christian concert on campus, when the compere said, "Turn to the person sitting next to you and say, 'I love you and there is nothing you can do about it.'" Quite hilarious it was, the man was actually trying to promote the idea of loving your neighbour as yourself and had by default created the perfect opportunity for Rex to make his move and let me know he was getting weary of waiting for me to be ready for marriage.

Rex looked me straight in the eyes as we repeated the words of the compere to each other and then said:

"I jolly well can do something about it. We can just ask Mrs Adeniola to throw a party next year."

I saw the seriousness in his eyes and got the message loud and clear. But I knew there was no way it was going to happen. I had my final exams to concentrate on; only after they had been completed would I be able to think about the future. I didn't give him a reply. I smiled shyly and turned round to face the stage. After a few minutes, he nudged me with his left shoulder and said "Ayo, I mean what I said earlier."

"I know," I replied, with my gaze still on the performing act that had by then come on stage.

Three weeks later, he came to visit me and brought the topic up again.

"Well, the thing is, my circumstances have not changed since we started our courtship. I am still a student looking forward to graduating one day. So I'm sorry, there's not much more I can say."

He admitted that he felt a bit of a fraud after agreeing he would wait. He would back off for a while and then start to try to persuade me again.

A female friend of his, Sister Clara Kolajo, explained to me that he was a go-getter—"When he puts his mind to something, he does not back down until he's got it."

There seemed to be a lot of merit in that approach to life—determination, focus and excelling.

"I would really like to get married to him, too, just not yet."

There was that small issue of my family needing to be convinced that I had not gone completely off the rails and out of my mind; that was in addition to me fulfilling my own aspirations of completing my studies first.

Five months had passed by since my original letter to Mum, but it seemed she was still not amenable to discussions about my new status as a young woman in courtship. When she eventually wrote to me, there was no mention of Rex in her letter. It felt as though I was faced with a brick wall. She did not seem interested in finding out more about this man whose presence in her daughter's life was causing her so much pain and heartache.

"What should I do?" I asked Dr Olumide.

"Write back to Mummy and tell her Rex sends his greetings," was his reply.

Dr Olumide kept an eye out for me. He often asked me how I was getting on in my relationship and would try and give guidance on any issues I shared with him. He also advised that I continue to approach Mum carefully:

"Send her a separate picture of Rex first and then some months later send a picture of both of you together."

It was an attempt to help Mum get used to the idea of us being together.

Eventually, there was response from Mum, but as I read the letter my heart sank. Mum wrote:

"*Dear Ayo*", a deviation from her usual, "My dearest daughter", or "Dear Ayomide". The letter continued:

> "*I thank my God for his goodness and how he brought me out of my troubles onto victory . . . All my hope for you is that you will be successful in life, but I know you are keen to get married. Ayo, I never thought you would want to marry this early, all my consideration had been that it would be okay for you to start having boyfriends now, until you are twenty-four. I had always thought you will think about getting married when you are twenty-five . . . well, my God knows . . .*"

Christ help me! My mother had my life planned year by year. She was more meticulous in her planning than I could have ever imagined. It sounded to me as though I had let Mum down in life big time. It seemed finding love meant I was a disappointment to her.

Even Yetunde, too, seemed to have started getting drawn into the friction between Mum and I. My relationship with Yetunde was a loving one, although it was never without its troubles. I recognised sometimes that I could be very harsh in my verbal reprimand of my younger sister and that puts her right off me, but it was the way I knew to be. However, lately, I had noticed that there seemed to be more to her reaction to me than the occasional feeling of anger because of my strict older sister routine. She seemed to have become Mum's confidant as she was by then heading for her late teens and was able to oversee quite a few things. When Mum phoned she spoke more to Yetunde than to me, and sometimes I would not even be aware they had had previous telephone conversations in my absence. If Yetunde could do something for Mum, I was no longer let in on whatever it was. Yetunde herself became secretive. It seemed her resentment of me was growing.

One afternoon, I saw my sister in town. I had told her earlier that day that I was going to see a friend on the estate that was about a mile and a half down the road. She didn't say anything about her own itinerary for the day, let alone mention we would be heading towards the same destination. When I met her, she did not as much as flinch.

"Yetunde, where are you coming from?"

"Oh, I went to Aunty Sola's house to drop a package for her. You know, Aunty Sola, who used to work with Mum when we lived opposite the health centre."

"Yes I know. I was just surprised you didn't mention it earlier when I told you I was coming here. What were you dropping off?"

"She will be travelling to London in two days time and Mum wanted me to send some things to her."

"Oh, I see. Well, I'll see you at home," I said, and went on to my destination.

I felt snubbed but I tried to reason it off with the fact that Yetunde was growing up and needed to take more responsibility in the family. Nonetheless, the feeling was quite difficult to shake off, and accepting that I was snubbed seemed to be the only solution.

I spent a lot of time pacifying Mum and addressing her anger about my relationship with Rex. In the end I got fed up. I went to see Dr Olumide to explain to him how tired I was of Mum's letters of discouragement. He wasn't in his office, so I left him a note to tell him I called round. It was during the end-of-year holiday in August and I was back living in Aunty Dunmola's house. Dr Olumide's faculty building, like the other buildings on campus, was quiet, having been relieved of its bustling student population.

The following morning, Dr Olumide made a detour to Aunty Dunmola's house during his usual morning trip to the newsagent by the campus gate.

"Ayo, I'm in a hurry, I can't wait long. What was it you wanted to see me about, I hope everything is okay with you?"

I flipped through the pages of a notebook, as we stood on the driveway, to show him the six-page letter of ire I had drafted to tell Mum to back off.

"Ah! Ayo, you need to be careful. Don't just write letters of anger to your mother like that. A girl always needs her mother and this is not the time for you burn your bridges with her."

I was disappointed. For the first time, I doubted that Dr Olumide was right. Something deep inside me told me Mum needed a more assertive response, but I did not want to go against Dr Olumide's wisdom in case I later regretted doing so. Barely two weeks later, Mum wrote me another letter saying my friend Shewa had told her that people in Nigeria were usually put under pressure to get married quickly and I was allowing others to push me into getting married.

Shewa and I were friends from primary school when both her parents worked in the university as lecturers before their retirement. She was a very bright girl and knew more answers to the exam questions back then than I did; I had always admired her intelligence. She went to secondary school at the federal government college in Abeokuta, her home town, but came back to Ife to study economics, which was a four-year course. She graduated a year before me, after which Shewa's parents paid for her to study for a master's degree in international development at the University College London. She had travelled to London some months before Mum's letter arrived and I had taken the opportunity of Shewa's travel to England to send letters through her to Mum and my siblings. This meant she met them all over there. I couldn't, however, imagine why she would say such a thing. Even if she did, Mum was no stranger to Nigeria and its culture; I wondered who she thought was pushing me into getting married. I thought it was unbelievable that Shewa would get to London and cause trouble for me there. Still, there was not much I could do about it from Nigeria.

After months of trying to help Mum along in the acceptance of her daughter's love life, we thought it was time for Rex to write directly to her. The first communication was a Christmas card and then a birthday card and finally a letter. Still, the atmosphere over the three thousand miles of distance between us could be cut with a knife.

There was not much difference in the tone of Mum's subsequent letters; they carried as much hurt as the first. I couldn't gather the strength to keep replying them, and so I stopped. I was now straddling two realms: the first, that of the mature twenty-two year old who was fast becoming an individuated woman; the second, that of the young girl who longed for her mother's support—or at least her mother's acceptance. Each time I received a letter from Mum, my heart would skip a beat for fear of what hurtful or threatening words I might find in there. At times I was on the verge of tears from the lack of affirmation she demonstrated. I kept the letters and thought to myself that one day I would be happy and I would be able to show my mother the letters of indignation she sent me and perhaps she would read them and be ashamed of herself. But there didn't seem much that I was gaining by keeping the letters, apart from hurting myself further. Every time I saw them or remembered they were stashed away in my suitcase, a thin line of pain went through my chest. The existence of the letters proved too much for me to bear. I decided to destroy them.

One afternoon, I was alone in the house—an uncommon occurrence in my aunty's house. I took the letters out of the suitcase and page by page, I started to tear them into shreds. Somehow the shredding didn't seem to have the desired remedial effect so I took them to the kitchen, lit a burner and burnt them. Once I destroyed the letters, my pain left. From then on, each time I received a letter from Mum, I would have an annihilation ceremony. I would either tear or burn them, depending on how much hurt I felt. As I shredded the letters or watched them burn, I would make a declaration, sometimes loudly, saying, "I destroy you this letter and all the pain you were sent to cause me." I repeated my declarations until they were in shreds or they had become ashes.

Meanwhile, cracks started to appear in the relationship between me and Rex. The charming man I had fallen in love with was no longer so charming. Stupid accusations such as I was not looking cheerful enough when he visited me caused quarrels between us and he would cut me off for weeks. More fundamental spiritual beliefs, like sleeping arrangements when we visited friends, started to cause even greater friction between us. It became difficult to predict what would cause him to withdraw from me next: a well-meaning joke, a response to his joke or even a response from me during a serious conversation would start him off. He seemed always on the prowl for an excuse to show a little bit of nastiness.

He came to visit me in the hostel one day and we went for a drive. We talked about our day and the discussion drifted into various aspects of our relationship. He explained his ambition for me.

"You need to finish your studies and then study law."

"Why would I want to do that?"

"Lawyers are the ones who make the money when it comes to property."

"Well, they may do, but what if I don't want to study law?"

"Why wouldn't you want to? Ayo, I'm telling you, take it from someone who is more experienced than you; I don't want you to later regret anything. By the way, I'm not saying you should study law immediately you graduate. No, we get married first and have two children and then you can study law."

"No Rex, if I wanted to study law, I would have simply applied to do so the first time. I am not interested in studying law."

"I know you could be quite stubborn and want to do things your way but on this one issue, you really need to listen to me."

"Why don't you study law, so that you can make the money and use it to provide for your family as the head of the home?"

"You are very different from all the girls I have known," he said.

"I ought to be, don't I? Seeing that you knew those girls before you became a Christian?"

"What I'm trying to say is that there is a way a woman treats a man . . ."

I waited for him to explain what his expectations of me were but he paused there and said nothing further.

His comparison did not stop. Several weeks later during another conversation he blurted out, "You are unlike any girl I have known and I keep saying this. You really don't know how to treat a man right. Maybe it is because your parents are separated."

"Well, I won't lay claim to being an expert in relationship matters, but if you could be more specific as to what exactly you think I should be doing that I am not doing."

He couldn't point to any particular thing that made me less than the other women he had met.

The arguments were getting to me, I felt thrown back into sadness and confusion; my happiness seemed only to have lasted eight months. This is not the type of relationship I desired, I reminded myself every time I hit rock bottom. I thought deeply, I knew something was wrong somewhere but I couldn't work out what it was or how to make it right. I just kept going, not quite sure where I was heading. I questioned whether this was really the man God had in mind for me to marry but I could get no answer from God either way.

I did not have the confidence or the clarity to think the issues I faced through to a satisfactory conclusion. I felt pressured on two sides: Mum's displeasure and Rex's misdeeds. Quitting the relationship was not an option I thought I could follow through. I resigned myself to fate; I was tired of questioning his rightness or wrongness for me.

It was in the midst of my confused state of mind that Mum eventually let me in on the mysterious reason for her unpleasant attitude.

"Hmm," Mum said during a telephone conversation, "I have been praying earnestly to my God that he will destroy this relationship and scatter both of you apart!"

I was shocked. The telephone receiver in my hand had suddenly become a heavy stone and my hand went limb. What strong negativity and cursing from the mouth of my own mother!

"I do not believe this is the will of God." Mum continued, and almost in contradiction to her original assertion she said, "Well, the only thing is that it has lasted this long. It is only because it has lasted for two years now—that is the only reason I think it *might* be the will of God."

What an absurd way of establishing God's will! She had prayed for only God knows how long (two years?), that my relationship would be destroyed and because it hasn't been destroyed in those two years, she now thought it *might* be the will of God—absurd indeed.

Somehow, I knew within me and reassured myself that whether the relationship succeeded or not was not her call. I declared to myself my belief that no matter how much she cursed, it was God's purpose and plan that would stand in my life and my relationship would succeed.

When she seemed to have concluded that it was "God's will", Mum started warning me that I was not ready for marriage yet.

"You need to do a master's degree and get a job. If the man you are with loves you enough, he would wait for you to get a job."

She then put another argument forward:

"Ayo, you are not ready to get married." Mum warned me, "You have not even got enough clothes for marriage."

Apparently, I needed to look the part of a married woman. All our conversations seemed to be around why I could not get married. It did not seem to matter to her who the guy was, his character, values, which family he originated from and anything else that may impact on my future happiness with

73

him. All that mattered was that I shouldn't be moving towards getting married.

What seemed to have escaped Mum's consciousness was that the two years that had gone by since I met Rex meant, in accordance with her own timing, I should then be getting ready to marry the following year, as her stipulation had been that I would marry when I was twenty five.

I had a few friends who were also in courtship. They all seemed happy in their relationships and their families all seemed very supportive. I appeared to have been the odd one out and I couldn't even bring myself to talk to any of my friends about the difficulties I was having with Mum. I wasn't used to discussing my family problems so widely. I probably might have been able to discuss it with Tade had she been in Nigeria at the time.

Tade was my friend from university. We had met at the fellowship choir on campus, or so I thought. It turned out she had been invited to my church in town by one of her course mates. She saw me singing up on stage with the choir and said she was full of admiration for me. As it would happen, I decided to get involved in the fellowship on campus and joined the choir there; so did she and we became quite close.

She had travelled to France on a one-year exchange programme and decided to stay on to complete her bachelor of arts in French and study for a master's degree in journalism. Just before she left Nigeria (shortly after my first encounter with Rex) she came round to my room in the hostel to ask me to pray with her. Her mother had given her strict instructions, at the time she was about to leave home for the first time to come to university, that she should never court a man from tribes outside the Yoruba tribe. The trouble was, my friend had just fallen in love with a man who originated from the Hausa tribe far away in the north and did not know what to do about her mother's bar on non-Yoruba men—a bar which Tade didn't seem to know the reason for and which I therefore couldn't understand. We sat on the edge of my bed and prayed that if the man she had met was the will of God for her that He would grant her the wisdom to deal with the situation.

Tade left Nigeria just two weeks after we had prayed and wrote to me about three months later to say her mother had consented to the courtship and that her long-distance relationship was going strong. I thought about Tade's experience and it made me think she may understand my own problems and lend a listening ear, and perhaps a praying tongue. Still I doubt I would have been able to share the extent of my problems with her; there was a conservative part of me that would have curtailed any such discussions.

Tade's first letter was the only one I received from her by post. About eighteen months after she had left Nigeria, she sent me another letter through a mutual friend and complained that I had not been replying to her other letters. Clearly, they must have gone missing in the post.

I thought the best solution was for Tade to send subsequent letters to Mum in London. Mum could then forward them to me in Nigeria when there was a known Lagos-bound passenger who could hand-deliver them.

There was no one coming to Nigeria from London when the next letter from Tade arrived at Mum's place. Mum told me about it on the phone and I asked if she could open it and tell me if there was any urgent message in there, at least that way I could reply to Tade and read the letter myself at a later date. I was probably being too trusting of Mum but addressing the communication problem between me and my friend was my priority and I didn't think there was anything Tade would have written that would have caused Mum any upset. She opened it and the silence and tone of voice that followed told me something was amiss. Apart from the letter there was a photo in the envelope, I asked whose photo it was; Mum said it was Tade's photo. I decided not to probe her further but her reaction worried me.

7

GETTING MARRIED?

T he final year of my undergraduate studies came. It had been one long experience for me. Every single year there was either student rioting and the college closed for up to four months or the university lecturers would go on strike. Their most recent strike lasted six months.

It was a relief to be able to see the end in sight. I began my dissertation and got to the literature review stage, then there was more bad news—lecturers were going on strike again. It was now six years since I started the five-year course and there was a real threat of five years turning into seven years with this latest strike. There was the suggestion that it would give me time to sit down and write the best dissertation I could. I tried to believe it, but the uncertainty that always revolved around college closures was not the ideal situation to inspire focused study.

I started off doing some research from home after the closure but it became increasingly difficult and I was lost for what to do with my time. I spoke to Mum and asked if I could visit London for a few months again. Being in London the last time lecturers went on strike was almost a lifesaver.

The change of environment did me a world of good. This time Mum insisted that I had to stay in Nigeria and look after Yetunde. Even though Yetunde insisted she was fine without me, Mum was not persuaded. I stayed the whole seven months of the strike in Nigeria.

Rex kept me busy. He wanted me to visit him every day and help him with one thing or the other. We went to visit his parent's house one Sunday afternoon. They lived about a quarter of a mile away from Rex, whose apartment was right on the main road that cut through the middle of Osu. Baba Oke (as his father was called) lived with his wife of many decades on the ground floor of their three-apartment block. Even as a sixty five year old woman, Rex's mother took it upon herself, with the help of his younger sister, to cook for us.

"Mama, bring the pestle and I will pound the yam," I offered.

It was not the first time I had visited them, but it was the first time I was having dinner with them.

"You will soil your lovely skirt, go and sit down in the living room," she insisted. "Ajoke will help me, won't you?" She turned to Rex's younger sister, who was spending her two weeks annual leave with her parents.

"Yes, Ayo; in our household it is the husband who cooks, fetches water and sweeps the house. We treat our wives well," Aunty Ajoke answered as she heeded her mother and took the pestle from her while I moved awkwardly out of the way and into the living room. Aunty Ajoke was Rex's immediate younger sibling, only two years younger than he. She was the same age as Aunty Tinu, Aunty Dunmola's younger sister; therefore, as a sign of respect to her, I called her "aunty". Her answer to her mother's call was a general spiel by delegates from the groom's family during a traditional wedding ceremony, part of the comical drama that went on at such events, and which does not necessarily resemble the truth. In Nigeria, there was strict gender role separation in the home, even within the extended meaning of "*husbands*", although the smartest of girls knew how to evade such responsibilities.

Culturally, I had just broken a taboo—sitting down comfortably in the living room while my prospective mother-in-law (and sister-in-law) cooked for me to eat, notwithstanding that her son too was happy to leave her in the kitchen to cook. I decided to go back in there and hang around to hand them whatever utensil they needed. It was important that I created the right impression (with my prospective in-laws and anyone else who may happen to call by) that I had good manners and would make a good wife to their son and to the rest of their family.

Lunch was ready; Rex's mother served the stew while his sister served the pounded yam and I held the plates out for both of them one after the other.

"You go and eat, we will eat later," Mama Oke insisted.

Rex and I sat down to eat the pounded yam with okra and beef stew. I had a bite of the meat halfway through the meal; it was terribly soggy and tasted horribly bland. I was going to spit it out of my mouth but I remembered I was in potential in-laws' home. I asked Rex what on earth I had been served. He said it was the brain of a cow. Cow brain? Who eats the brain of a cow for heaven's sake? He offered to take the rest of the meat off me and I gladly accepted. Even as he ate it, I could not help shutting my eyes momentarily, I couldn't bear seeing him chew on it. His sister overheard our conversation and joined in, so did his mother. They were fascinated that I had never eaten the brain of an animal before.

We left Rex's parents and after a few runs around town we headed back to Ife. When I woke up the next morning there were rashes all over my body. My mind went back to the cow brain I had eaten the day before. I was terrified because I hardly ever reacted to food. Luckily the rash cleared after about four days. However, by the third day, I noticed my eyes felt funny. It was as if there was dust in there or some of my eyelashes had managed to get into my eyes. They didn't sting and I didn't get any gritty feeling, they just felt clouded over. I washed them many times but it did not make a difference. The first thing that came to my mind was whether it had something to do with the brain of a cow I had eaten and the rashes that I had developed afterwards. I tried to reassure myself and not let my imagination run away with me. In any case, Rex had eaten the rest of the meat and he seemed fine.

Rather than my eyes returning to normal, they were getting worse. Everything around me started to look unreal. I knew the life around me in my aunty's house was real because I remembered it existed before I started experiencing this abnormality with my eyesight. However, my eyes were telling me something different. There were times when, as if to confirm the message they were passing on to my brain, my head felt so light when I walked into a very bright room that it almost felt as though I was floating. I could only describe it as what heaven may be like if the saints there were bodiless.

Almost a month went by since my eyes started their aberrant behaviour and I was trying hard to get used to the change. Rex still kept me busy with demands that I visit him every day, for one reason or another. I tried to get out of as many of the visits as I could and I moaned the other days I visited. The daily travel on public transport was tiring and there was not much I was doing there.

As I travelled the bumpy road to Osu one morning, with my sight still cloudy and everything around me seemingly unreal, there was an unexpected thump in my chest as though I was afraid of something. I looked around me in the bus that I was travelling on, I couldn't see anything that should cause me fear; it was the same journey I had made the week before. The other people in the jagged Toyota Liteace seemed like ordinary passengers. There was no cause for panic. The day went fine but it was not the end of the thumping in my chest. Over the following weeks it became rhythmical and happened more often.

Rex invited me to his cousin's wedding thanksgiving. It was a Sunday afternoon; he picked me up from Ife after our church service and we went to Osu together. All throughout the journey, the combination of my funny sight and throbbing heart made me feel very uncomfortable. We went straight to his cousin's family home. The compound was packed with guests. There were the usual large gazebos, used at similarly big parties, which were set up by the side of the two-storey building. We saw the groom's mother on our way in through the gates of the house; she said a quick hello and rushed past. Rex's other family members were less pre-occupied; as we greeted them there were questions about when Rex himself would get married. He gave one excuse after the other to each person, sometimes making a big joke of the questions as they all laughed together. I was used to his mother, his married friends and his relatives egging him on to get married. They did so especially when someone else was getting married or there was news someone had just gotten married. I kept my poise and a decorous silence as his relatives chatted to Rex. I tried to pull myself together but I really wasn't feeling too great. Perhaps the crowded environment had a worsening effect on my pounding chest and weird vision, or maybe the symptoms were just growing of their own accord.

As soon as we could leave the celebrations and go to Rex's flat, I described what I was going through; he told me one of his brothers-in-law had experienced something similar in the past and that it was called panic attack. I felt distressed and was on the verge of crying. He suggested we go to his mother, a retired nurse, to check my blood pressure and ask for her help. I wasn't too keen on his suggestion and asked if he could take me back home.

That night at home, I couldn't sleep. It seemed the night was extra dark and my palpitating heart wouldn't stop. About midnight a dog started to bark. The dog barked endlessly. I was scared I was going to die. I had heard some superstitions in the past that when a dog barks uncontrollably, it meant someone was about to die. But I survived the night and made it to the light of the following day.

When Rex phoned that morning, I told him I would not be going to Osu anymore until I was fine. He came to see me later in the day and I shared my experience of the night before with him; he laughed.

"Glad you found that funny."

"Who told you that when a dog barks someone is going to die?"

"I can't remember but I have heard it several times before."

He stayed for most of the day and I felt reassured. I slept better that night but still could not sleep as well as I would normally have done. The next day I went to see Dr Olumide. I explained to him what I had been going through with the palpitations and my clouded eyes. It was about lunchtime when I got there.

"Ayo, are you staying for lunch?" asked the soft spoken, dark, smooth-skinned Mrs Olumide.

"No thanks. I will be getting back as soon as possible. I would just like to talk to Pastor a little."

Dr Olumide seemed to have sensed there was something wrong, and perhaps judged from the timing of my visit that I hadn't had lunch. "She will eat," he said, turning his probing stare from me to give his wife eye contact. Mrs Olumide went to complete her preparation in the kitchen while I explained my mission to her husband. I told him what I had been going through with the thumps and my funny sight. He prayed with me and I had lunch with him and his family.

After lunch he called me aside and asked if I had been sleeping with Rex. He explained that he had seen people experience some sort of nervous breakdown when they had gone against their Christian convictions and had sex before marriage. Thankfully, I could count that one out. He then suggested that I shared the problem with other pastors and church leaders at Bible study the next evening so that they could all pray with me. Pastor Stan was not at the Bible study, so I went to see him separately. He asked me exactly the same question Dr Olumide had asked and he got my guarantee.

Rex called again; he said he was going to be coming to Ife to see me. He suggested we have a time of fellowship together every day and lift the situation to God. He came as promised and we sang hymns, read the Bible and prayed. I felt blessed to have someone who would stay by me through a difficult time. At that point I thought I could not have made a better choice of a man to be with. He came everyday for almost a week.

On the fourth day, he said, "Ayo, I now understand your reluctance to come to Osu every day, it has been extremely tiring for me these past few days."

I was glad he did. I hadn't imagined he would hold my reluctance against me but I thought it was good that he got a firsthand experience of what he had been demanding from me. Later that day after prayers, he brought out a book on marriage. He said he had been reading the book and wondering whether it was time we got married. I thought, *Oh no, not now*. When I seemed to have lost myself in the recent problems and I couldn't trust myself to think straight. I promised him I would try to read it sometime.

He left the book with me and went back home. The next day he asked if I had read it. I told him I hadn't and he was visibly disappointed and angry. I wasn't sure what he expected. I reminded him I had been feeling unwell, apart from the fact that my future was somewhat in the balance with the lecturer's strike, and it was not the opportune time for me to think through and make a decision about getting married.

"I know that. That is why I have been coming all week so that you can get well enough to be able to make a decision."

Does he not see further than what he wants? To think it was only a few days ago, I thought I had made the right choice in a man.

"I thought you were coming because you wanted to be a companion in a difficult time," I said to him.

"And that too," he replied.

He opened the book and started to show me what it said. "See," he explained. "There are certain things that need to be present in order to determine whether a couple in a relationship are ready to get married." There was the financial side. He explained he had a small but stable income from a business venture with his younger brother and he also had the income from his accounting firm, albeit that was rather unpredictable. Then there was the spiritual side. We were both Christians with similar principles. We were both of age.

"The book says it all, we can get married." He tried to argue his case through.

By this point all the benefits of fellowshipping together were completely out of the window. I felt trapped. My aunty's living room where we sat seemed dark and stuffy as if the louvered windows above the sofa on which we sat did not exist. It was as if the sliding doors that opened out into the glazed front bay, opposite us, had been obscured by a dark curtain and that a black wall had been built across the clear glass door beside it. I felt a little giddy and asked if we could go out for a walk so that I could get some fresh air. He asked me if I would be able to make a decision when we came back.

"I can't promise, but I will see what I can do about it."

I had a lot of sympathy for his position. His family and friends were waiting eagerly for him to have a family of his own, and his own internal pressures were there as well, but this was definitely not the time to talk weddings. Why couldn't he wait a couple of months until I felt better? At the same time, I felt confused and wondered whether there was something wrong with me; why was I not eager to get married? What if he was right? What if it was time to get married? As we walked back to the house, I tried to psych myself up and get in the mood for a wedding; I talked about the exciting frivolities of getting married, the dress, the cake etc. Even those were not enough to take me to a place where I would make an instant decision to name a date.

We got back to the house and I explained my feelings. He then added another dimension to the discussion. He explained that it need not be a big wedding; it could be in the registry office and if we got married he would be able to apply for a visa, on account of being married to a British citizen, and go to the UK to do the Ph.D. he wanted to do.

"A small wedding will not need much preparation; we can have it when I get back from South America in a couple of months time," he said.

Rex had been offered a place on an NGO sponsored leadership training programme, and he would usually travel to Ibadan to attend the lectures. He was, however, scheduled to go to South America for an international excursion, as part of their line up.

"What about me?" I asked, shocked at his proposal of a quick registry wedding. "I would not have finished my studies by then, I can't abandon them!"

"Well you can come and join me when you finish."

This is crazy, I thought to myself, but there was no arguing with him, he was forceful in his persuasion and in the end I agreed to everything he was asking. That night again, I couldn't sleep. I was troubled and decided to tell him when he phoned in the morning that I had changed my mind. He was disappointed when I told him; he drove down to Ife, asked why I was being so fickle. I felt fickle.

"I couldn't sleep all night. I was scared again and my chest was pounding hard."

"But that has got nothing to do with being married; it is just what you've got."

"Well, maybe, but still the pounding subsided when I changed my mind."

He got into his car, revved up the engine and sped off in anger leaving a thick cloud of dust behind him. He phoned me later that night. He had been to Dr Olumide to report me to him. Dr Olumide gave him a message for me, asking that I come to see him.

I went to see Dr Olumide a few days later. He was concerned about the sudden pressurised talk of marriage and asked if I thought Rex only wanted me for my British passport. I thought about it, but as far as I was aware he had not known that I had a British passport until almost a year after I met him. It came out in conversation because I was about to travel to London and he was asking if I had my visa ready. Two days after my meeting with Dr Olumide, he sat us both down. He calmed the situation as much as he could.

"You are both still relatively young; you've got your whole lives ahead of you, why are you rushing into this? Rex, you said you are about to travel to South America, you go and pray carefully about it while you both are apart, come back in two months time and then decide whether now is the time for you to get married."

Rex went on his two months trip to South America and despite the bother he caused me before he left, I missed him very much. I missed having someone to share my thoughts and feelings with. The trauma of my "illness", for want of a better word to describe the experience, had somewhat left me always feeling lonely even in the midst of a crowd. I kept a journal for part of the two months that Rex was gone, hoping I would give it to him to read when he got back, but he had a more important matter on his mind when he returned. He asked me when we would be going to the registry.

"We have not decided we are going to the registry, have we?" I asked him.

"I thought you and your Pastor said we will go when I get back from South America."

"That was not what was said. The Pastor said go and pray about it and come back and make a decision after you have prayed."

"Is that not the same thing? What are you praying about if you have not decided to go?" he asked.

I tried to explain what praying about an issue was.

"When you pray about something, you seek God's face, you ask Him whether you should do it or not. If God gives the go ahead, then you do it. If He does not, then you refrain from doing it."

"Oh, I see, you and your Pastor pushed me to the slope and left me there to free fall," was his reply.

There was not much explanation or convincing him of Dr Olumide's intention that I could attempt. He withdrew from me for days. When I challenged him about his withdrawal he said it was all in my head. He had only been back a short while and didn't know what I was talking about. I almost believed him.

The lecturers called off their strike after six months of the university being closed. I had completely forgotten what campus life or the modules were all about. But after a very slow start I gradually settled back in and got my dissertation going again. I was determined to take my time and do a good job of it. By the time I was drawing my conclusions most other students had already engaged typists to type theirs up.

In the meantime, Mum had started to ramp up the pressure, calling for me to come and join her in the UK so that I could do a master's degree. There was pressure left, right and centre. Rex was going from relative to friend asking for a loan or grant to travel to the UK for his Ph.D., all with no joy. Every time there was a sign of help, his hopes got dashed again and again. He took the commonwealth scholarship exams, only for Nigeria to be thrown out of the commonwealth by the time the results came through. He became withdrawn and resentful. I bore his attitude with grace, and gradually his mind seemed to thaw and his behaviour improved.

He came to visit me in the hostel one Friday; luckily he was in a good mood because I desperately needed his help. I had been finding it hard getting a good typist to type my dissertation; the business centres on campus would do a better job than the typical one-woman-band typists who would use the standard typewriters, but their prices had gone through the roof and they couldn't guarantee I would get the finished work on time for submission. So I got Rex to drive me all over town to find a good typist. After about an hour of driving round with every typist turning us down because they had too much work to do already, Rex persuaded me to come and stay with him in Osu for a few days so that I could use one of his four computers to type the dissertation. I agreed, on the condition that the time I would spend there would be solely dedicated to my studies.

We got to Osu and as that weekend progressed, I noticed he had started to grow resentful and withdrawn again. I became concerned and I thought I'd try and cheer him up by cooking something special for him on the Saturday night. Perhaps it was too difficult for him seeing me there buried in my work and not giving him any attention. I went to the nearby market to buy some beans and cooking leaves for *moin moin* (Yoruba beans cake). I thought some good food in his belly should cheer him up. After all, the older and wiser women of those days always said a man's stomach was the way to his heart.

My *moin moin* didn't do the trick. He looked even more miserable as he ate it. By Sunday afternoon I was fed up of his moodiness and decided I would leave his flat and go back to my hostel as soon as possible. The next morning, I did some laundry and hung them to dry while I got myself ready to go back to campus.

I entered the bathroom to have a shower and closed the door behind me. As I stepped away from the door, I heard a voice in my head saying, *"Ayo, lock the door."* It was quite strange, as the voice sounded like mine, but I knew I couldn't have been talking to myself in that manner. The voice, even though I could hear it in my head, sounded like it was coming from someone else who was also present in the bathroom.

I argued with the voice.

"Why would I need to lock the door? Rex is the only one in the flat and he is well aware I am in here, he understands enough not to open the door."

I climbed into the bathtub and started to take a shower and then the voice came again.

"Ayo, lock the door."

My argument this time was that I couldn't step out of the bathtub because I now had soap and water all over me. I had hardly finished that thought when the door flung open.

I froze in the bath.

There was Rex with anger bursting forth from his eyes like flames of fire.

"Who do you think you are?" he barked. Let's just say the rest of the scene was not at all dignifying. Rex made me feel cheap and violated. I was so shocked that I started to laugh. Actually, it was more of tittering; but the combination of shock and laughter must have come across to him as snigger. Because as I crawled out of the bath to grab my towel, he suddenly looked confused and foolish; he sheepishly shrugged his shoulder and said:

"You can continue having your shower, I've accomplished what I intended."

It was fear that I felt at that point. *What if he raped me*, I thought to myself. I would never forgive myself for sleeping over at his house when I could have asked my mother for the money to pay the exorbitant prices business centres were charging for the privilege of a computer-typed dissertation, even if it meant I submitted the dissertation late and lost some marks because if it.

I squeezed underneath his arm that was now stretched across the bathroom door right up by the lintel and immediately went in search for the keys to his flat in case he thought of locking me in. I remembered seeing them on the windowsill in the living room, and luckily they were still there. I hid the bunch of keys under my towel, picked up my washing from the line on the back balcony and stuffed the wet washing and the keys in my bag until I had finished dressing. I was watching my bag like a hawk in case he sussed out I was about to escape and seized it.

Once I finished, I grabbed the bag and headed for the back door. He saw me as I walked out of the inner corridor that led to the bedrooms and it dawned on him that I was about to leave.

"Ayo, what are you doing? Where are you going? Ayo, come back."

My eyes were firmly fixed on my escape route. I noticed he stopped following me and I hurried my steps. As soon as my feet were out of the back door, I turned round to drop his keys back on the windowsill by the door. I scuttled down the steps from his first floor flat to the ground level exit and out into the front yard.

I was determined it was the end of the relationship, even though I had no clue how I was going to face the aftermath. He ran after me, still demanding that I came back, but by then I could sense some fear in his voice, which was now a barely repressed shout.

"Ayo! Ayo! Where are you going? Come back. Ayo, my flat is open; I haven't even locked the door. Ayo, come back!"

He was in a panic. He ran after me into a taxi to the bus station—by this time he had started weeping and begging, saying that he was sorry and would report himself to my pastors if only I would come back to talk it through. At first I remained quiet and continued to look straight ahead of me, tears steadily streaming down my cheeks like the flowing of a river. As he sat next to me in the taxi pleading his case, I turned for a moment and asked him why. He just continued begging. I looked into his eyes; I saw genuine regret for what he did, even though I still couldn't imagine why he thought it was okay for him to be violating in the first instance, nor could

I figure out his reasons for taking such a demeaning course of action.

I got off the taxi at the bus station and waited for one that was heading for Ife. He would not stop begging. I eventually decided to go back with him, and he became the perfect gentleman. He carried my bag for me, opened the door to the taxi and eventually the door to his flat when we got there.

We later sat down to have lunch and talk. Apparently, he was only being vengeful for my sin of omission, which by the way he could not specify and did not really seem to know exactly what the sin was, but according to him he did not mean to scare me, he only wanted to get his own back. By the end of the meal, he had managed to turn the blame round and I seemed to have scooped the whole lot of it because, according to him, my attitude was the cause of his behaviour.

I sat my final exams about six weeks later and finished off strongly; it was one of the best results I had throughout my course. The end was nigh! There were only a few weeks more before I defended my thesis. I had heard a rumour from one of my course mates that I was heading for a distinction with my dissertation if my defence was successful. He had overheard some conversations in the departmental office—apparently my submission was well structured and well-thought through; I just needed to demonstrate the thoroughness of my research and the validity of my conclusions during my presentation.

I defended my thesis and finished with a 2:2. By this time, Rex still had not secured the necessary funding for him to study in the UK and he continued seeking help from anyone who he thought might be good for the few million naira, all to no avail. His moodiness came back. One day, we were in the car on the way to Ibadan to introduce him to Dad. He had managed to persuade me some weeks prior, when he was of a more noble countenance, that it was time he met Dad. But as we headed out of Ife, he sat in the driver's seat with a face like a smacked bottom. He had received disappointing news from his cousin who had previously given him some hope of funding his Ph.D. It had been quite a while since he'd been feeling this miserable. I asked what he would do next.

"What am I supposed to do? There is nothing I could do."

I was wracked with guilt—I was adding to his misery by not agreeing to marry him, even if only to help him get his visa.

We got back from visiting Dad, by which time he seemed a bit more cheery and had started to think of other avenues he could explore for his funding. As we stood by the gate of Aunty Dunmola's house, waiting for someone to let us in, in the heat of the moment it occurred to me that we could have a secret registry wedding—perhaps that was the way out. It came out of my mouth before I could think it through. Rex said he had thought about it but he didn't feel he could suggest it considering my crazed principles.

"It will not work anyway." My common sense was starting to prevail. There were several reasons why it would be impossible to have a wedding without anyone else's knowledge. He went into his depressed mood for days after that, and my guilt ate away at me. I then made a decision; I was going to do whatever it takes to make him happy again. I would agree to a wedding, maybe he would start to see a way forward for himself and he would start relating to me better. I took the brave step of telling Mum my decision. I was shocked when she agreed to the suggestion; she did not resist at all.

Goodness me! How could I comprehend my mother? Trying to predict her reaction to anything was completely impossible. I had always wondered about Mum and her ways.

What made her tick? This seemed to be the million dollar question to which I needed to find an answer in order to know exactly what I should do with a mother like mine. Or, perhaps the question should be: who am I supposed to be so that I could handle the tangled relationships I found myself in?

PART II

THE WAY WE WERE

8

THE BEGINNING

"Mummy, Mummy, see, E is for Elephant!"

I ran from the living room, where I had knelt on the blue and white carpet on all fours as Olalekan guided me through the colourful book of alphabets. I went to show Mum my latest knowledge acquisition. She was outside having a chat to the neighbour and another woman—one of her colleagues, who happened to have been passing by the house.

"That is great, very good," Mum said, and turned to face her friends. I did not feel satisfied with the response; it did not feel quite enthusiastic enough. I told her I was going back to learn some more. She sent me on my way and resumed her discussion. I went back and continued working my way through the book.

That is not the earliest of my childhood memories. I seem to have a gift for remembering the odd moments and my memory once freaked Ibidun out. A lot of the memories of my childhood are as clear as watching a replay of the events. Some memories once in a while come to me like a flash of light that turns into a flicker. It sometimes glimmers as I struggle to put pieces of past events together. At other times it grows into a bright flame and the memories come rushing in.

Growing up in Ilesa, I was in every way a lastborn. I did not have any sense of suffering or not being cared for. My feelings when I was young were ones of being pampered. I was not aware of much of my relationship with my mother; I think she was quite a busy woman working as a nurse in the big hospital at the end of our road. Naturally, I spent more time with house helps and aunties, when they spent the summer holidays with us.

We lived in a house that was comprised of four apartments within a walled compound containing two buildings. At the time, the buildings seemed rather enormous. Our apartment was on the ground floor of the one that faced the road. We were renting and the owner lived in the house right at the back. The orange and fire brick red colour made the two-storey block quite distinct, particularly as all the houses on the mini estate on the opposite side of the road were white in colour. Our house was about the last house on the road before getting to the General Hospital with its manned gates. The gates turned the rather wide, partly and thinly tarred road into a cul-de-sac.

Centred steps straddling the two ground floor apartments rose gracefully from the downward sloping, concreted front yard to our front door and those of the next door neighbour. I sometimes sat on the steps and played with my friends, the landlord's daughters, Bolanle and Fola, and Titilayo, another girl who lived in the apartment right above ours. Hanging out with the other girls was my favourite pastime. Once Mum was out of the door in the morning, I would have my shower and settle down to breakfast. Having half eaten my breakfast I was always ready to go out to play with the other three girls, with the encouragement of the usually bright and sunny Nigeria days, when the sun extended a warm, tender touch towards us as its rays fell on our faces and the back of our bare necks. Its warmth gradually transitioned into intense heat as the afternoon approached and the hard concrete steps would get too hot. We would scramble to get the prime position in other spots under the shade where we could sit down without our bums feeling the burning heat of the exposed concrete steps.

"Bolanle, move. I need to sit there; I can still feel the sunrays on my arms." If it was not Fola and her sister arguing about who sat where, it would be Titilayo and I wanting to protect ourselves from direct sunlight.

If anyone wanted me back in our apartment, they either shouted my name so loud that it could be heard all over the compound or they would come looking for me in my hideouts.

"Ayo! You need to come in now, we are going out," Aunty Bolaji would shout whenever she needed to run an errand for Mum, and I would go in and get ready to go. On our way back we would walk through the primary school down the road from the house. The school was one of the state schools with some of the classroom's external walls left un-rendered.

There was dust everywhere, especially when there had been no rain for a few days. You could see the dust settling on the houses as their colours take on an element of brown. There were very few trees around the neighbouring houses and you could see tiny bushes by the way side. Other forms of vegetation were scarce except for a little forest that could be seen from the lower end of the school. The forest extended to the rear of our compound before opening up on the land beyond the house and further past the side of the hospital, spreading afar into the distance, clear of what the eyes could see.

One day—during a holiday—there was a naming ceremony happening in one of the classrooms as we went past the school. The naming ceremony party sang, "Now thank we all our God, with heart and hands and voices . . ." and so on. At first I couldn't make out the words of the song, but Aunty Bolaji helped me and I sang the few lines she taught me for days after. A few weeks later we sang the same song in our church. We didn't get to go to church often but Mum took us at every opportunity she had.

During Christmas 1977, as was Mum's usual practice, we went to Ibadan to do some Christmas shopping. Christmas in Nigeria was the time when children got special clothes; a lot of parents would save up to buy new clothes for their children. I'm not sure it would have mattered to the children if they only got new clothes at Christmas. Mum had travelled to Osogbo before our trip to Ibadan to buy us some outfits for the celebrations. Ibadan and Osogbo were bigger trade centres than Ilesa and Mum preferred to travel to either or both places for the annual festive shopping.

At Ibadan, we went sightseeing and had a great time at Leventis stores. I was full of excitement going up the escalator to get the train to Father Christmas's grotto. The train was an open top, rather low train that was only large enough to take children. One of the younger girls was crying, afraid of riding the train without her mother. It made me rather proud of my confidence as I thought to myself, *I'm not scared*. At four years old, I had found a new level of self-assurance since I started nursery school about three months earlier. At this time we lived alone with Mum. Dad was still in England trying to complete his studies. Mum had chosen to return to Nigeria with me and my siblings after she finished her own studies several years ahead of Dad.

Then one afternoon, Mum came back from work and took a letter out of the side pocket of her thick light blue uniform. The most exciting time of the day was when Mum got back home from work. It was even more exciting on this occasion as the letter was from Dad. It was already opened, but she read it again and revealed some of the content to us. Dad was fine; he asked after us. And he would soon be returning home to Nigeria.

Despite getting excited about the letters from abroad, I did not know the man who wrote them and so inevitably found the thoughts of him entering our family unit difficult.

"He is not my Dad," I claimed.

Ibidun stepped in to do the diligent older sister duty.

"Yes, he is your Dad."

Is he really coming back? I thought to myself. It seemed unreal.

"How is he going to come?" I asked Mum.

"He will fly in an aeroplane," was the answer.

"Where will he live when he comes? Where will his home be?"

"Here, of course," was Mum's reply.

As curious as I was to hear more about his impending arrival, I still could not fathom how he came to be my father, a man it seemed I had never met. I was only a baby when we had left him in England. If he stood in a line with other men, I would not have been able to identify him. Mum and Ibidun told me more about Dad in an effort to stir my imagination and help me reach the essential acceptance of this man, of whom I was a part. I argued with them. I told them my Dad was in Ife, which was only half an hour's drive away from Ilesa. But I was, in fact, referring to Granddaddy, seeing as I was not aware at the time that Granddaddy lived in Modakeke, not Ife, and that Modakeke and Ife were two separate towns.

Mum tried to explain.

"Granddaddy is my daddy; your daddy is in England, see, he has written to us. He will be coming back soon."

I was not prepared to buy their story. It did not sound true. I couldn't picture him in my mind, therefore, as far as I was concerned he simply didn't exist. I told Ibidun it was her daddy that was in England, not mine. That was my way of getting back at her for what felt to me like verbal abuse. How dare she tell me my daddy is in England? My daddy is in Ife; whoever it is that they are expecting from England is their own business, not mine.

Dad was a foreigner in my world.

I loved Granddaddy, we saw him often enough; he was good enough for me as daddy. In any case he *was* daddy, the fact that there was a "grand" prefixing that daddy made no difference to my little mind. I was always fascinated by his big house—the pale pink, three-storey building that he lived in at the time—and the vibrancy that the house exuded with my aunts and uncles usually happily bantering away. I would shout, "We are now in Ife," when we got to the junction of the house, although we would have already entered Ife several miles back.

As Dad's arrival drew near, we moved houses. I wasn't sure why we had to move, because the new three-bedroom apartment was just as big as the old one. The compound within which we now lived was a lot more compact and the buildings sat closer together. The first building had two apartments; ours was on the ground floor, and the landlord and his family lived upstairs. There was also a smaller block to the side, which formed an extension to the landlord's apartment on the first floor and was linked to it by a balcony. On the ground floor of the smaller block lived a young family of four. Their first child was a girl named Moji, who was two years younger than me while their other child, another girl, was still a baby at the time. I formed new friendships with Moji, and with Iyabo and Ranti, the landlord's youngest daughters.

The space between the smaller building and our apartment, on the ground floor, formed a courtyard where the residents sometimes congregated in the evening to relax. The smell of palm oil stew and burning firewood wafted into the courtyard when the landlord's wife cooked on an open fire downstairs in the back of the house.

The road outside was busy and dusty. Its dust would rise up like puffs of smoke when a vehicle drove by and we had to cover our mouths and noses from its fumes: that acrid smell and the harsh, gritty taste. The road led westward to one of the town's main roads, which in turn led to the hospital next to where we used to live. In the eastward direction, it led into the town centre and onwards to Osu and then Ife, both in the southwest direction.

Once we unpacked our belongings into our new home, the countdown to Dad's arrival began. It was a month, then weeks, then days. The strange thing was, as the days drew closer to his arrival, my excitement grew and I couldn't wait to meet him. I was a different child to the one who had argued that her father was in Ife. When I saw him at the airport, my excitement knew no bounds.

We arrived at the Ikeja airport, having travelled to Lagos the day before to spend the night with our cousins. Dad's flight arrived late in the evening. I must have slept in the car; I heard Mum's voice calling, "Ayo, we are now at the airport."

After we had pulled into a space in the car park, we all stepped out and went to watch some planes as they took off and landed before we headed into the terminal. I felt overwhelmed by the size of the planes and the thundering of their engines at the same time as I felt a great fascination for them. The evening breeze swept coolly across my face and felt quite refreshing. It carried a distinct smell of the various water bodies around Lagos—the lagoon, the ocean and perhaps the various rivers running into them. After about fifteen minutes outside we made our way into the terminal building. The passengers had started to come through. My neck was stretched as far as it would go, asking which one was Daddy, and Ibidun was standing on tiptoe, trying to see over the heads of the small crowd blocking her view. Mum was reassuring us that we would see him when he came through. I was so focused on the family business of the night that nothing else at the airport mattered to me. I was no longer aware who else was there with us apart from Ibidun and Mum, who were actively involved in my mission to identify Dad. Olalekan and one or two extended family members that travelled to the airport with us had disappeared from my line of sight and merged with the crowd there.

I, of course, did not recognise Dad when he came through, but Ibidun, in her own excitement, and Mum pointed him out. The picture of him standing at the airport counter waving intermittently, calmly and with poise as his travel documents were being checked, is permanently imprinted on my mind. He wore a dark suit and looked very tall and smart. He was beaming with smiles and kept wiping sweat from his forehead.

"That is daddy, that is daddy!" I cried out. Anyone seeing me would have thought Dad and I had been very close before he went on the journey he was now returning from.

"Daddy, daddy," I called out to him as Mum lifted me up to get a better view. It probably would have been difficult to believe that I had only recognised him for the first time that evening.

9

LIFE WITH DAD

The joy of Dad's arrival did not last long.

Sometime after he came back he and Mum had their first argument. It was not traumatic in any way; it felt more like a disagreement. I was not there when they started the argument and I didn't know what it was about. He seemed to have decided he was leaving again and Mum perhaps told him to take his children with him. They both called us and Dad told Ibidun and I that we were to get dressed and go with him; Olalekan seemed to have somehow made himself scarce.

We got dressed in the colourful polyester print dresses that Dad bought for us in London. Mine was orange with splurges of cream, a little bit of yellow and some black edging. Ibidun's dress was mainly purple with cream and black patterns. Dad bought me two dresses because I was the youngest and I needed to be spoilt. Ibidun got the one dress because she was older and less spoilt.

We both got ready to leave with Dad. He packed a few of our other clothes in a small bag. I had no clue where we were going. Mum asked Dad where he would go, and he said something about going to a cousin's house. Oddly enough,

Mum then locked the door refusing to let us out. We stood aside waiting with Dad. The landlord came downstairs, knocking and asking what the problem was. I was not sure how he got to know there was a problem, it did not seem as if they were making that much noise—in fact, as I remembered, it was a quiet argument.

"The madam of the house has locked us in," Dad shouted to the man outside, who eventually left when he realised his intervention was pointless since no one would open the door for him. After a while, Mum called me back and said I could stay. Ibidun was left with Dad at the door; later she was allowed to stay and eventually Dad got to stay, too.

Dad was required to go on an NYSC placement as he was a university graduate, notwithstanding that he did not study in Nigeria. He was posted to Akure about fifty miles from Ilesa to teach in a secondary school there. He would stay in Akure all week and come home only at the weekends. After their one off argument, things seemed fine between my parents; Mum seemed contented and happy as Dad continued dividing his time between Akure and Ilesa. I was quite a happy child and enjoyed being part of my family. I especially liked it when extended family members visited us. Our house would become extra lively as various kinship discussions went on, although one particular visit gave me and my older sister cause for concern. There didn't seem to be enough of Mum to go round—and having to share her with a cousin didn't meet with mine or Ibidun's approval.

The visitor was Bola. She had travelled from Lagos to spend part of her summer holidays with us. Her dad was Mum's younger brother and she had visited us in the past with her mother and siblings. This time she was holidaying with us alone. She had a rather quiet and gentle manner, as

I recall. I didn't have much interaction with her as she was probably closer to Ibidun who was only two years older than her. However, when Mum asked Bola to plait her hair, I didn't consider it acceptable, and neither did Ibidun. Bola was very good at plaiting hair but Ibidun and I got jealous that somebody else was working on our mother's hair. We insisted we wanted to do the plaits ourselves. Mum had to part her hair into three sections, Bola was to have the bigger part and Ibidun and I, who knew very little about plaits, would have the smaller ones. I argued with the split but Mum convinced me to take it.

In our spare time together, Mum and my siblings played board games and I would sometimes join in. Our favourite game was Ludo and we sometimes played the *ayo*, a southwestern Nigerian board game, played with particular seeds that look like small marble balls, which Granddaddy had given us. When we played Ludo, Mum would ask Ibidun and Olalekan to allow me to win so that I didn't get upset when they beat me at the game. I was pleased to win but did not like the idea of them "allowing" me to win. I wanted to win on merit because Olalekan and Ibidun would constantly remind me that I'd won only because they allowed me to. But winning wasn't always that straightforward; throwing six on the die so that I could move my tokens out of their start position was challenging enough.

"You only have one go," Ibidun would remind me. "Pass the die clockwise," she would insist.

By the time I managed to throw a six on the die and get one of my tokens out, most of their own tokens would have made their journeys half way through the track on the board towards home straight. Then I had to battle hard so that their remaining tokens do not catch up with mine and knock them back to the starting point.

"It is because you chose the colour blue," Ibidun would tease. "Blue never wins."

"Okay, can we start again and I will choose the colour red this time?"

"Oh no, we can't do that, we need to finish this game and then you can choose another colour; you can even try yellow or green."

She seemed to derive particular satisfaction in me losing the game, and then Mum would step in.

"You know she is your younger sister, she is only little. Give her a chance to win."

Ibidun sometimes flatly refused Mum's request.

"No, Mummy, it's a competition and I shouldn't allow her to win."

"Don't worry, Mummy, I can win by myself," I would say.

Mum then devised an alternative way for me to win the game. She directed my moves. Her attempts did not go down well with me as it was still undermining my innate capability to win off my own back.

"Ah! If you make that move, she will move this one and knock you out."

I swiftly saw the wisdom in what Mum was telling me.

When I wasn't too caught up with winning on merit, I got confused and wasn't sure what Mum was telling me to do.

"Move aside. Let me play it for you," Mum would say and she would try to push me to the side very gently.

My smaller hand would go up very quickly to block her larger one, "No, Mummy, I don't want you to play it for me; maybe you can just tell me what to do."

Playing it for me always seemed that one step too far. I found it difficult claiming the victory after the game; those siblings of mine simply tore down any sense of achievement I got.

"No, Mummy! You can't play it for her; she's got to play it by herself," Ibidun would protest.

"Who says? Okay, I am in the game as well, me and her are a team."

One way or the other, Mum would make sure I did not leave the games with my tail between my legs.

Months went by after Dad's arrival. Then one Saturday, an ordinary day it seemed, I had breakfast and set about my mostly playful day, starting with getting my doll ready for its own inconsistent schedule by styling its hair. I heard Mum shout out to me from the bathroom, while she took a shower.

"Ayo! Bring me my towel from the bedroom. It's on the bed."

I ran from the living room into Mum's room and took the towel to her. As I peaked through the bathroom door, she thanked me for my help, and took the towel from me.

"I'm pregnant," she said.

I felt embarrassed. I did not know what to do or say. I fiddled and rambled randomly. What I was saying didn't make sense to me and I doubt it made any sense to Mum. It was a gabbled mumbo jumbo. Mum had enough of it and told me to go.

I left her and started to wonder about her revelation to me.

"How does a baby come about?" I asked Mum later in the day. She had a very good explanation; it was something about an angel bringing the baby when we were all asleep. It made sense to me. When I went to bed that night, I laid there in the dark and turned towards the window, I couldn't see through the pulled curtains but I knew what was out there—the stars twinkling in the sky and the moon sending its blue light down on the streets. I saw in my mind's eye an angel in all its glory, as I had seen it in pictures, reflecting its own light as well as the light of the moon and carrying a fragile precious baby, warmly snuggled inside its folded wings. I felt very privileged that an angel would visit just to give me a little brother or sister; I was engulfed in the awesomeness of it all.

My younger sister was born and I became grown up overnight; I was six going on sixteen. She was named Yetunde and was given the same *oriki* as me. *Oriki* is a praise name, one of the many names babies usually got christened with by the Yorubas. The names usually have strong meanings; mine meant one who delights in having a father. I initially resisted having the same name as my younger sister, but my aunt, on Dad's side, who gave all *orikis* was determined it was what she wanted to do. I eventually accepted and even loved the idea.

Yetunde was mine, my own baby sister. It was God himself who sent his angel to bring her and no one was going to take her from me.

"Mummy, I want to carry her on my back," I said about two weeks after Mum came back from the hospital.

"She is still very small," Mum explained. "Maybe you can carry her in a few weeks time when her neck is more stable."

I couldn't understand Mum's reasoning because my sister was a big, chubby baby.

"Mummy, she is bigger than Moji's younger sister when she was a baby, even the neighbours were saying so. She is big enough for me to carry her."

Eventually Mum obliged. She secured Yetunde on my back, with her wrapper and a woven sash. I rocked her as she slept. My back ached from the baby's weight but I wouldn't let go; the pain was a small price to pay for the pleasure of carrying my younger sister. She slept peacefully. She was adorable! Her skin was soft and feeling her body rest on mine was pleasing.

I displayed my caring older sister act as I sat in the courtyard in the middle of the day; I sat there, like a watchman guarding a house, and I proudly showed off my nurturing skills by adjusting the tightness of the wrapper when anyone passed by. They would look at me with a little puzzle and assurance that the suspicion they held within them was right. They would ask:

"Is that baby not too big for you to carry?"

"No," came my quick answer.

"Does your back not ache?" They would ask further.

"No, my back is fine, Yetunde too is fine," I would reply sharply.

All Mum could do was keep an eye on me to ensure we were okay and that we weren't going to fall over.

Months after Yetunde was born, we moved to Ife. Ife was more of an elite town by virtue of being home to one of the country's most prestigious universities and the big teaching hospital. Otherwise, it was quite similar to Ilesa that we were leaving behind. Things started to go awry at home as Dad settled in and showed us his true colours with rage and violence.

Late one evening we were home alone with Dad; Mum was working night shift. Getting my little sister to sleep without her mother was a challenging task. Yetunde was so attached to Mum that Olalekan always had to take her for a walk before Mum could leave the house to go to work. She grew wise to their deception. On her return from their walks, she would look around in search of Mum before letting out a scream after realising what had happened. Sometimes I felt her pain and wished the rest of us could be enough for her, but no one else would do for my younger sister.

That evening, I got busy with my imaginative homework. I was using an old clock to tell the time and drawing the face of the clock for each answer, while Dad and Olalekan tackled trying to settle Yetunde into bed. She cried unceasingly as Dad held her up on his shoulder and patted her back while rocking her gently to soothe her. Olalekan made some more Farex baby food for her, in case she was hungry, but nothing seemed to be working. I think she eventually got tired and started to doze off. Dad placed her in her carrycot and asked Olalekan to rock the cot until she was sound asleep. Ten minutes later, Dad decided to take Yetunde into the room and lay her on his bed where she would sleep until the morning. As Dad emerged from settling Yetunde down, fascinated by my sheer ingenuity or simply looking for trouble, Ibidun decided she wanted to be part of the fun and teach me how to complete my homework correctly.

"It is not that way, it is like this," she snapped as she grabbed the clock away from me. My instinctive reaction was to yell.

"Give me my clock back, give me my clock back," I shrilled and demanded she left me in peace.

It was the shout that got to Dad. In his frustration and anger that I was going to wake Yetunde up again, without saying a word, he went straight back into the bedroom, got his NYSC belt with its bogus buckle. He gave me a lash of the belt not caring where it landed. I knew what I had done wrong without having to be told—Dad always required us to be quiet when Yetunde slept, anytime he was in charge.

The first stroke of the belt landed on my head and the sharp edge of the round metal buckle slashed my upper forehead. I grabbed my head with both hands in an effort to soothe the pain. When I brought my hands down they were stained with blood. My head was bleeding and Dad did not seem to have noticed. I screamed as I tried to run for my life but there was nowhere to run to; he was in the way and I was backed up against the living room wall. With each scream came an additional beating until Olalekan was successful in alerting Dad to the fact that I was injured and bleeding. The beating ceased and I was able to control my screams. Olalekan wiped the blood from my face. I changed from clothes that had been stained with the blood into my nightdress and went to sleep.

I was still sleeping when Mum came back from work the next morning. She had apparently seen the bloodstains on the floor as she came in, asked what happened and Olalekan had filled her in. I woke up quite sombre and hazily heard Mum call me. I went to her; she was in the bathroom bathing Yetunde.

"Ah, Ayomide," she said in a croaky voice. She was full of pity, self-pity as well as pity for me. She checked the cut.

"It is deep," Mum said. Her voice sounded even sadder than before. "Go and get ready for a shower, I will finish with your sister and take you to the hospital. We will go to the teaching hospital . . . I think they will need to stitch this."

Luckily when we got to the hospital the doctor checked it and decided it was not worth putting me through the agony of stitching and that it should heal all by itself.

The situation grew worse as Dad became angrier, withdrawn, and even more violent. There were arguments about Dad not contributing enough money for the family upkeep. At that age, I knew that whenever I needed or wanted something, I asked Mum for it, although my friends in school would say that many times they would ask their daddy for it. I didn't really understand how the family finances worked and I didn't get too inquisitive about it but their argument had started to open my eyes to my parent's joint responsibility for the family.

One day their argument got really bad, and he hit Mum. I screamed and wept as Mum took to her heels. I'd never seen anyone hit my mother before; it was one of the most horrifying events of my life at the time.

Mum went to Dad's older cousin, to get his help. He came with his wife and got Dad to agree to contribute more towards the family upkeep. It seemed they had to come a second time for the promise to be fulfilled. Eventually, Mum decided to open a licensed bar in order to supplement her income and reduce the reliance on Dad.

As December of that year approached, Mum started to press Dad to get staff accommodation from the secondary school he worked with; that way the burden of paying the rent would be firmly his and she could save some money as part of the capital outlay she needed for her business.

The following year, shortly after my eighth birthday, we moved into a semi-detached bungalow on the grounds of Ife Comprehensive High School where Dad worked as a Senior Tutor. The school was built on several hectares of land and the onsite staff quarters, composed of only three houses, sat on the northeast corner of the school.

As our car rolled in behind the removal van on the earthy ground in front of our new home, on a Friday evening, in the middle of the rainy season, an Asian man emerged from the adjoining bungalow, got into his car and drove past us. He nodded in acknowledgement of our presence as he went past.

"That is the neighbour," Dad said. "His name is Sengupta."

"He could have at least said hello properly," Mum complained.

"He always keeps to himself," Dad explained.

"Well, I suppose he's in a strange culture," Mum reasoned.

The Senguptas were an Indian family of four. The father taught physics in the school and the wife was a stay-at-home mum who looked after their one-year-old son. Their firstborn, a girl named Anisha, was four years younger than me and attended my school.

The third house on the grounds, which looked more like a mansion, was about seventy meters away from the semidetached bungalows; it was home to the school's vice principal, his wife and their servant.

Shortly after we moved, Mum woke up one Saturday and said she had received the name for her proposed bar in her dream the previous night. She would call the bar God's Blessings. All she now needed was to find the space and the finance to stock it.

By September, two months after the move, Olalekan prepared to leave home for university. He had been offered a place at the University of Lagos to study electrical engineering. It felt strange to be saying goodbye to him. I was in school the day he left. On my return, I looked in his bedroom and saw his bed empty. The crease-free, dazzling white bed sheet was no longer on the mattress. It was comforting to know that he was gone for his own good and that he would be returning after some months, but I knew I would miss him.

We adjusted to life without Olalekan as Mum continued to look after our physical needs, ensuring we were properly clothed and fed. She also looked out for our spiritual well-being. I often heard Mum praying for us. She knew thevalue of prayer and would pray all manners of prayer and in whatever way it was prescribed. When I had nightmares and screamed out of my sleep, Mum would be there in a shot. She would read the Psalms and bless the house.

Even though Mum prayed a lot, we didn't attend church very often and when we did, it was usually a branch of the Apostolic Church, the same denomination Granddad belonged to. Dad came from an Anglican background but he did not like attending church, so we couldn't attend with him. I enjoyed our visits to church, however irregular they were, and I found a passion in the children's Sunday school but my involvement was limited because of our inconsistent attendance.

Olalekan soon came home for his first holiday. It was nice to have him back with us again. On the Sundays that he was around, when Mum and the rest of the family didn't attend church, he would sometimes volunteer to take me there and pick me up again. I usually waited patiently while he got ready, in glad anticipation of the great time ahead. Once he was ready, we would trot along the road all the way to church.

Around Christmas time, there was a children's annual celebration in the church and I sang with the children's choir. It was such a joyous thing to do; we sang at the top of our voices, more or less shouting the songs out, and we danced vigorously. Some of the children got to sing solo parts or do a reading. We all yelled out to be picked for a special part when the teachers asked who would be able to take a lead role. I joined the other children in seeking the attention of the teacher by shouting "Me! Me! Me!" I was determined not to be left out, but in the end I never got a special part. However, singing with the choir in itself was pretty rewarding. I threw myself into the songs and did not have to worry about getting a special part right. Some of the children who did get to sing a solo or do a reading were nervous on the day of the performance, and I was glad not to have been in their shoes as I would probably have been just as nervous as they were.

Dad kept himself busy with work. He spent most of the days and evenings in his office and when he was at home he was usually in his bedroom. Time spent with Dad was limited to the car journeys with him when he picked me and my siblings up from school. This sacrifice that Dad made for us was not without its own set of challenges—Dad forgot to pick me up from school one day. It was getting dark; everyone had gone home. The night security guard arrived to resume work at around six-thirty in the evening. He asked what I was still doing in school when it had closed at one-thirty in the afternoon.

"I think Dad must have forgotten to pick me up. It has never happened before."

I was not particularly scared but I did not want to spend the night there. I decided to make my own way home. Home was a good few miles away, maybe about four. The closest way out of the university, where my school was located, was very deserted. The road, Road 7, winded around the forest and over the river. The thought of walking through all that was scary, but I thought I had to do it. I needed to brace myself and put my fears behind me; otherwise it may be an endless wait for Dad. Hunger had vanished; all I wanted was to be in the comfort of my own home.

I set out on my journey, not quite sure what I was doing. Somehow I knew if I took it one step at a time, I was sure to get to where I needed to go. I was about to cross the river when a man saw me as he drove past. He stopped a few yards away and reversed his car to meet me.

"Where are you going?" he asked.

"Home," I answered.

"And where is home?"

"Ife Comprehensive High School," I said.

"Ok, just get in the car, I'll give you a lift."

I heard him mumble as he wondered to himself aloud how much of the long distance I could walk. He kindly dropped me off a few hundred yards from home. As I was walking the last leg home, Mum's voice rang out from a taxi. She had taken it to school to look for me after she had returned from work and realised I hadn't been picked up. She got there to be told by the security guard that I had found my own way.

On his return, Dad was furious.

"Why did you leave the school premises?" he shouted.

"It was late . . . and everyone had gone home . . . it started to get dark . . . and . . . I was not sure you were coming," the words stumbled out of my mouth.

He argued with Mum that I could have stayed with the security guard and that it would have been perfectly safe if I had done so. Thankfully I was spared the trouble of having to argue my own case. Having a mother who stepped into the breach was a gift of immeasurable value. It was eventually decided that I could make my own way home from school if Dad forgot to pick me up again—which he did once or twice more.

Having demonstrated my ability to look after myself and find my way home from school, Dad thought he'd increase my level of responsibility; he assigned me the task of buying him newspapers from the newsagent whenever he wanted to keep up with the editors' take on various national events.

One bright Saturday morning, probably about three months after I proved myself dependable, the sun was out; Dad had gone out first thing and returned as the world was waking up from a lazy lie in. I heard him go straight into his room and he shut the door behind him. About fifteen minutes later, he popped his head out of the door and called out to me.

"Ayo! Get me the *Daily Times* from the newsagent, will you?"

I left the house and had a jolly bright morning walk to the kiosk on the main road about half a mile away, hopping part of the way. It was extremely busy. The newsagent might as well have been running a drive-thru; several cars were honking, the drivers eager to be served. Others on foot picked up their paper and thrust the money at him through the opening in front of his kiosk. Some of the people shouted at him demanding their change. I peeked through the side door of the kiosk and my squeaky voice managed to rise above the chaos.

"I want to buy the *Daily Times*."

The man looked down in my direction.

"We've run out of the *Daily Times*," he said.

I turned round and walked back home innocently disappointed at the wasted journey, unaware of what was waiting ahead. For some strange reasons, Dad did not believe me when I told him there were no *Daily Times* left. He had the idea that I was lying because I was too lazy to walk to the newsagent's. How he came to that conclusion was beyond me, when he had been cooped up in his room all morning.

He made me go back again and then again and warned me the last time not to come back without the paper. I went back to the newsagent for the last time and it was one time too many. He looked quite worried and angry at my persistence. He seemed fed up of giving me the same answer. He gave me a searching look as if trying to discern whether I was a child possessed with witchcraft and sent by the coven to frustrate his day.

"Is there something else to this, you girl, huh?" he asked, implying was there more to my search for newspaper than meet the eye. When such a question is asked, it usually refers to some dark, evil intention.

"Don't let me see you back here," he warned, wagging his index finger at me.

I was now stuck; a position that seemed congruent only to that of the historic Israelites when they were caught between the host of Pharaoh and the Red sea. It was then that Mum decided to step in—unknown to me she had started to walk behind me with Yetunde. They met me as I was coming back looking lost and sad. I gave her an update on my ordeal and she followed me to the newsagent. She explained the situation to him, asked if he could come home with me to explain to Dad that he had actually run out of the paper. Thankfully, by then it was past midday and the man had completed his sales. He obliged and saved the day. I don't know what would have happened if he had not agreed to come with us. To my surprise, Dad was no longer the angry man I was not able to appeal to about an hour before. When he saw the newsagent, he was all smiles and said it was absolutely no problem, I was only a lazy child, that's all! But Dad was not the only one guilty of dishing out over the top punishment, Mum was too.

10

ONE SHAMEFUL ACT

B y the December of 1981, Mum had opened her bar and it was running full steam.

It was located on the ground floor of granddad's house, on the east end of Modakeke along with other retail units he let out to other businesses. The area was a well commercialised part of town. There were shops all around the vicinity with many of the buildings combining retail and residential uses like granddad had done. Further up from granddad's house, and a few yards from the main road, were purpose-built rows of shops that effectively consolidated retail use in the area.

The bar itself was basic but highly functional. There was a long, narrow, blue Formica-finished table surrounded by quite a lot of chairs, on which customers sat. There was also enough space outside to put a few chairs for the special customers who fancied fresh air. Mum's friends were entertained outside when they came to see the bar. Half of the space, to the left of the table, was used for the off-licence and bulk sale of drinks. It also housed the gigantically tall fridge from which drinks were served.

We had a house help named Fatima, who ran the bar in the day time when there was not much for her to do at home. My sisters and I would usually return to the bar from school and we would all go back home after it closed at night. It was an arrangement that Mum put in place to make family life easier. Olalekan would follow similar routine when he was home in Ife.

When he was not working out of town on one of his construction contracts, Granddad would sometimes come downstairs to sit down and relax in the bar, reading his favourite newspaper with his prescription glasses and a magnifying glass. Once in a while he would request that his lunch be served to him there. It was always good to have Granddad's presence with us; there was a recognisable aura of calm and order that he carried with him.

Unfortunately, on one particular day, neither Granddad's presence nor that of any other real adult, was there to save me from an error of the same order of magnitude as a giant. Mum's enterprising skills seemed to have rubbed off on Ibidun, who had started to show some eagerness towards a small money making venture: she sold whistling pop and other sweets to her classmates in secondary school and decided to sell some in Mum's licensed bar.

On the day in question, she had taken her wares to the bar and laid them out on a tray by the entrance. It was during Easter break. Mum had dropped us off in the morning after breakfast and went out to her suppliers to order new stock. The bar was usually quiet until the evening, apart from people using the off-licence and those buying in crates. Olalekan was home from university and had got a lift from Mum to go to the library on Ife campus.

Fatima suddenly had the "enlightened" idea that if someone hawked Ibidun's sweets in the surrounding streets they might sell faster. Both of them seemed to have concluded that I was the one for the job. They called out to me as I was outside, playing with Tosin my cousin. I ran in and they asked me if I would help my sister by selling her sweets on the streets around the area. Bizarrely, I was over the moon at the idea of hawking sweets in the streets and couldn't wait to do it! They placed the tray filled with sweets on my head and told me which streets to go to.

"Don't go up the main road," I was warned. I could see the fear in my sister's eyes as she spoke. The road directly outside the bar was a busy road named Ilowa Road. It was near its junction with the town's main intercity road. The intercity road was an arterial route that cuts through town from east to west. It led in the northeastern direction to Ilesa and to Ibadan in the southwest direction. Its junction with Ilowa Road is a main transport node for buses and coaches travelling out of town and the in-town interchanges. There was never a quiet moment there, with taxi drivers honking on every corner, some of them driving recklessly as pedestrians struggle to get their own share of the highway. Passengers shouted their destination to the taxis and bus conductors too shouted their own destination to potential passengers.

"Go to the quiet residential streets, starting with this one opposite us. We will take you across the road and when you get back, just stay on the other side and we will help you across again," Fatima explained.

With their instructions fully understood, I set off. By the time I returned from my expedition, Olalekan was back and was furious. He flipped the tray from my head to the ground with a promise that he was going to report me to Mum. Tosin was a few steps to his side, chuckling almost uncontrollably. I was thoroughly embarrassed. My attempt at sisterly love and adventure was not working out well.

Naturally I was scared stiff, not daring to imagine what was going to happen when Mum found out. Even though at that point I couldn't remember being personally beaten by Mum in the past, I had seen her mete out punishment to Olalekan when he was a lot younger and it was not at all funny. Corporal punishment was not illegal in Nigeria. You were beaten everywhere: if you misbehaved in school, the teachers would bring their canes out and give you a right flogging. And at home, the older ones would say spare the rod and spoil the child! Even the neighbours were given permission by your parents to smack and, if necessary, to flog you if you were found fooling around. The fear of punishment was a great tool for the adults when it came to discipline, therefore it was important to them that they mete out their own form of justice every now and then.

Fatima then had another "brilliant" idea, based on a superstition. She claimed that if we each plucked out some of our eyelashes and managed to get them on Olalekan's head, it would make him forget what had happened and he would not be able report to Mum. I was not quite sure what the science or psychology of this idea was, or the probability of it being true, but desperate to avoid Mum's wrath we tried it. Someone needed to take the task on—it was not going to be me this time. At fourteen years old, Ibidun was the tallest of the three of us, taller even than Fatima who was three years older; therefore the job of placing the lashes on Olalekan's head fell to her. She climbed on a high chair near the entrance to the bar so that she could drop them on Olalekan's head as he entered. She did not manage it. He looked up and scolded her for climbing the chair.

Mum came back at around 5pm that afternoon and true to his word, Olalekan reported the incident to her. She went completely mad at the thought of her own daughter peddling anything on the streets. I think she found it so shameful that she had to rub the shame into me as she took me to task with what seemed every ounce of energy within her. I was promised the full recompense for my action when we got home.

Thankfully, on getting home we were greeted by a power cut. Mum had to focus on trying to put some fuel in the lantern and finding some candlesticks in the darkness that had engulfed the house. After that, it was having to make supper in the dimly lit kitchen that she had to grapple with. The extra burden that the power failure placed on Mum meant she couldn't take on an additional task of beating me, so the lack of electricity got me out of an impending lash of the belt. I cried myself to sleep that night. The shame that I felt was enough punishment even though I was lucky enough to have escaped some serious thrashing.

I woke up the next morning and didn't want to get out of bed; I did not have the confidence to face the world. I pulled my cover cloth over my head, buried my face in the palms of my hand. I wished that the ground would open up and swallow me so I could disappear, forget about it all and not have to face anyone after the ridicule of the previous day. That seemed to be the only way I could escape any further shame. It didn't happen. Instead of a gaping hole appearing in the earth to gobble me, Mum dragged me out of bed.

I noticed, though, that Ibidun was spared any severe reprimand and I bore the brunt of it all.

"It's not fair." I cried silently to myself in the bathroom. Ideally, Ibidun should have taken responsibility for me, being five years older, or at least she should have acknowledged her part in the whole shenanigan. Even Fatima, the brains behind the idea, managed to wriggle out of any responsibility for it. As a nine year old child, I think something in me recognised the injustice of it all and I hated it. The other thing I saw was that Mum realised that I felt very ashamed and seemed to have been satisfied that I "got the message". She gladly told me if I had done nothing shameful, I would not be in the situation in which I found myself. I had no choice but to meet the world, that morning, shamefacedly.

11

LIFE WITHOUT DAD, AGAIN

Mum and Dad separated about four months before my tenth birthday, on account of Dad's extreme violence.

Our house, along with all the other buildings within the school, was not connected to the main water line; we never got water from the tap. A tanker from Water Works would sometimes deliver water into a storage tank that sat outside the house next to the front wall of Mum's bedroom, and that served as our source. During this particular period we were for some reasons extremely short of water. For weeks we had to go to one of the fishing lakes hidden on the school grounds to get water, and did our laundry there.

Mum arranged for water to be delivered into the storage tank but her request was not scheduled in immediately. It was several weeks before the tanker came. When it came, Mum was out getting supplies for the bar and Dad was arriving from an outing. Mr Kolade, the school's vice principal, suddenly appeared at the top of the lane, hurrying down towards our house. He was calling out to the men in the tanker and waving his the hands up in the air for them to stop. My sisters and I were watching him with astonishment. As he moved nearer, he saw Dad.

"Ah, Mr Adeniola, I didn't realise you are here..." he said. He had a very short conversation with Dad and they both sent the tanker away.

When Mum returned home, Ibidun and I couldn't wait to tell her what had happened. Mum immediately went to the Kolades' house to express her upset over the tanker being turned back. She moaned in agony over her plight.

"How am I supposed to cope?" we heard her ask the couple as we lurked around their house eager to hear what she had to say to them.

The following morning, I had just had a wash with not more than a few cups of water and was in the bedroom getting into my school uniform when I heard loud shouting and pounding in the living area. I came out to see Dad picking up and throwing the furniture around the room, including the three-seater sofa. I stood by the dining table that was by the back wall of the living room, speechlessly watching Dad on that bizarre morning. Somehow, I gathered that it was about the water situation from the gibberish he spoke as he wildly turned the house over. He marched right across the room towards Mum, who was standing by the door leading into the bedrooms and bathroom, a few feet away from the front door on the adjacent side. She was trying to talk Dad back to calmness. Hearing Mum's voice must have incensed Dad, he got hold of her and pinned her right against the wall next to the door. I was terrified. It looked to me like Mum was in serious danger. My brain immediately stepped up to a higher level of performance than usual, telling me we needed help. I ran round behind Dad and out of the house like the wind; I needed to search for a solution to the terror at hand and I needed to do it quickly.

I ran as fast as I could towards the Kolades' house, weeping in fear of what horror might be developing behind me. As I ran, anger brewed within me against the Kolades because I believed their intervention the previous day was at the root of whatever argument that started the fight. I was shouting at the top of my voice for the Kolades to come out and resolve the problem they had caused, calling them troublemakers. They came out, both of them trying to get into their respective house coat or shirt as they ran along behind me, back to our house. Mum had slipped away from Dad's grip; she had run out of the house and he was following her in what seemed a determined effort to beat her into submission or probably finish her off once and for all. Thankfully, as soon as Dad saw the Kolades, he withdrew into the house and Mum was saved. That was the last straw; his past violence that I had witnessed had not gone this far. They went their separate ways. We went with Mum.

Olalekan was away in university when the fight occurred. He came back to hear how terrified we all were. It would not be an understatement to say there was a general feeling of revulsion towards Dad by every member of our family, me included.

After my parent's separation, the atmosphere at home changed. It was pleasant not to have the fear that revolved around being with Dad, to not have a need to tread carefully in order to avoid his fury. There was a sense of freedom; we were a family unit again, in contrast to the way Dad isolated himself from the rest of us. We dusted ourselves down and picked our lives back up again. Our new home was a three-bedroom apartment on the top floor of a three-storey building inside Modakeke. We were not very far from Granddad's house. It took about thirty-five minutes to walk from home to Mum's bar.

Its height and aspect gave our I-shaped apartment a very bright and airy feel. The sun shone into the south facing front balcony, through the French double doors and into the living room. The gentle midday and evening wind took the same route, bringing a cooling effect into the tranquil home environment.

We attended the Apostolic Church for our new area. Our attendance became more frequent and I joined the choir, this time the main church choir. I enjoyed the singing practice and the singing and dancing on Sundays. During the procession to give our offering at the altar, the choir would do a slow side-to-side swing and sometimes we would dance backwards a little bit, wriggling our shoulders. That was until one Sunday, when one of the elders warned the choir that the tradition of the Church was not in dancing but in clapping, and if we held the procession to offering up with our dancing again, he would ring the hand bell to stop us.

What a downer!

We eventually moved into the accommodation provided by Mum's employer, opposite the health centre, where we lived until Mum started to prepare to travel to Saudi Arabia. As we settled into our new life, away from Dad, attitudes at home gradually changed. Olalekan and Ibidun brawled more frequently anytime he was home on holidays. They had not been the best of friends for some years, but their clashes before the separation were limited to once in a while. Things, however, seemed a lot worse now. It seemed every discussion they had led to a fight, no matter how the discussion started or what it was about. Olalekan's return home from university, that in the past had always been an event to look forward to, started to become a double-edged sword—the joys of having my older brother back home and the wary expectation of fights between him and Ibidun.

I came back from school one day and Ibidun had locked our older brother in the bathroom. I was trying to figure out what was going on when Olalekan called me from behind the locked door and asked me to check the dining table for the key and open the door. Ibidun was fierce in her reaction to my attempted interference and I drew back, much to Olalekan's annoyance. She released him soon enough when Mum came back from work.

Ibidun had become the terror in the house. It was almost as if she was trying to step into Dad's shoes to make the home a miserable place to be, or perhaps the absence of Dad's forceful approach to discipline was her cue to do as she pleased—talk about taking liberty for licence. By the time Olalekan grew out of fighting her, I was her next target.

Ibidun and I went to the same secondary school; I was in my first year when she was in her final year. One afternoon we were all crowded round the dining table watching Mum as she tried in vain to get her broken torch working again. It was probably our tussle to get the best view of Mum's repair skills that sparked an argument between me and Ibidun. She told me that none of the seniors in school liked me; they all thought I was as proud as a peacock. I was baffled. I believed her, but I thought the seniors were wrong in their judgement. I scouted round the dining room for some support. I couldn't remember Mum ever telling me I was a proud person; I expected she was going to intervene and correct my errant older sister but she didn't. Instead, the look on Mum's face told me she seemed to be in agreement with the suggestion. I, however, noticed Yetunde's countenance. She did not seem to believe what Ibidun was saying. I received such comfort from the young girl's expression that day, but it really wasn't enough! I needed my mother to believe in me.

I got to school the next day and started watching out for all the senior girls that passed by, wondering what they were thinking, whether they were looking at me with abhorrence. Most of them appeared preoccupied; not many of them seemed to care or notice that I was there. I wasn't quite sure whether it was a sign of indifference because they had given up on me or whether they really had other things on their mind. I forgot about it over the following days and weeks as there was enough to distract my thoughts.

Sometimes I wondered why I had to be lumbered with this nasty older sister. Other people had sisters who looked out for them, but mine was always causing trouble in the house. Mum's way of dealing with the situation didn't help, either. She condoned Ibidun's behaviour and expected the rest of us to excuse it as well. She believed that was the way to getting peace at home. A part of me told me Mum was scared of Ibidun's ferocious manner but Mum put the approach she adopted down to the need to be careful with Ibidun because she suffered from epilepsy; she put Ibidun on a pedestal.

I never liked it because it felt unfair and did not resolve the problem. Her erratic behaviour worsened with the result that I was getting punished for things that were not my fault. If I responded to her taunting in any way, I was blamed for the lack of peace in the house. But Ibidun was difficult to ignore; she hated being ignored. She would provoke me until I broke my silence. Sometimes I fought it out with her physically and she would lose the fight.

One of the fights ended shortly before Mum came back from work one afternoon. Yetunde filled her in on the events of the day and I could see how frustrated and angry Mum was on hearing the news. She complained she was fed up of coming back home to fights and arguments. I felt bad that I had caused Mum such grief. I wrote her a letter of apology and left it on her pillow. I could not bring myself to face Mum and apologise to her; I wasn't sure why.

Hours later, Mum went into her room; I waited for her to say something about my letter, but she didn't say a word. I knew she had seen and read the letter; as long as I didn't get any reprimands because of it, I knew what I had written was okay.

Two days later, Ibidun had not stopped goading me. I was angry and frustrated that I was trying my best not to start another fight, yet she was not allowing for peace. I went into Mum's room to report her, quite loudly in my agitated state. Mum threw my attempt at being a good child right in my face.

"Ayomide, I need peace of mind, give me peace of mind."

Mum picked up my letter from her bedside table, waved it at me and asked, "What is the point of your silly letter of apology if only two days after writing it, you go about shouting the odds around the house?"

She threw the letter at me, told me to take it away from her and get out of her sight. I was broken; I vowed never to apologise to anyone again. It was not just me that Ibidun hurt, many times it would be Mum or Yetunde and I would stand up for them. Mum did not really mind then. She still did not like us fighting but at least I did not get blamed for it.

It was about this time that Mum started to reveal a different side to her. She became an extremely nagging and unappeasable woman. It was almost as if she hated me. She only needed to know I was involved one way or the other with Yetunde's crying and she would be there in a flash beating me with whatever she could lay her hands on: a broom, a belt or some stick.

One afternoon, Yetunde returned from school; I had prepared her lunch and was trying to encourage her to eat. Mrs Akeem, our newlywed neighbour popped into our apartment to have a chat a with me and we sat in my bedroom having a chinwag. Yetunde emptied the contents of her school bag and lunchbox on the floor, in the doorway to my bedroom, I had an eye on my sister as I listened to Mrs Akeem.

"Yetunde, are you not going to eat?" I asked

"Leave me alone," she snapped.

"Yetunde, clear that up," I demanded, and insisted that she have some lunch, as she definitely must be hungry. It was my attempt at being the good caregiver who recognises that a child needed to eat after a long day in school.

"I said leave me alone, it's none of your business."

I picked up one of her books and insisted she tidied up the floor before getting it back. Angry, she hit me in the stomach with her lunchbox. She was going to keep hitting me in the stomach, so I decided to hold her still to restrain her. Restraining her made her feel powerless and she started to cry

Unfortunately for me, it was at that precise moment that Mum walked by my bedroom window as she made her way through the side of our apartment to the back door on her way back from work. Mum must have heard Yetunde crying right from when she approached the house and then saw me holding Yetunde as she kicked and screamed. By the time Mum emerged in my bedroom, it was with a broom from the kitchen. Whack, whack, whack, the broom landed all over me, it's fibres leaving delicately embossed marks on my skin. Mrs Akeem felt angry on my behalf. She tried to make an argument for me but Mum had a stronger argument, which was that I should have known better. Known better about what? This was not quite clear. The woman walked out of our home clearly disappointed at what was happening. That day after Mum's beating, I wondered if there would be any justice for me in my family, at least as far as my mother was concerned.

12

FAITH CORNERSTONE

It was in February 1984 that one of Mum's colleague at work introduced her to Foursquare Gospel Church and we started to attend regularly after our first visit. It was different to the Apostolic Church. The building was not as grand; it was a temporary structure of timber frame and walls, and was painted yellow and blue, the church's corporate colours. The church was constructed on the foundation of a building that the owner had not been able to complete. It had a corrugated iron roof and no ceiling; the bare roof radiated heat from the sun into the church and usually made it an uncomfortably hot environment in which to take in the message that was being preached. It was clearly a newly planted church that was making the very best of the resources available to it.

We would normally go late as we were not too good at timekeeping during the weekends. The weekdays were usually so busy and tiring with work and school that trying to keep to time at the weekend was a challenge.

Six months after we started attending the services, an event was organised by the church. They titled it "The Weekend Seminar", but it was far from a traditional seminar. We were told that the evangelist who had been invited to preach had a ministry in the impartation of the gift of the Holy Spirit, with the evidence of speaking in tongues. I had never heard of this before. I knew people in church spoke in a strange language but I didn't know how it came about. I had thought once or twice that it would be nice if I could speak in that language too—perhaps I could pray for longer than a minute or two. People who spoke the language seemed to be able to rattle on in prayer, although it was difficult to understand what they were praying.

Apparently, people fell down under the influence of the anointing when they were being prayed for. It all sounded quite fascinating; I was intrigued to know what the spirit felt like and how it made people fall.

"Sister, have you witnessed that before?" asked Aunty Bisi, a staff nurse whom Mum worked with in the health centre. Most people who knew Mum from work called her "Sister", from her job title.

"What?" Mum replied.

"People falling under the anointing," repeated Aunty Bisi.

"No," Mum said with a marvelled look.

"Ah, people fall under the influence of the workings of the Holy Ghost, it is awesome."

"Huh uh, I've never seen it before."

"Don't worry, Sister; you will see it during the weekend seminar."

The weekend of the event came and we spent the whole day on Saturday and Sunday in church. Mum packed our lunch so we could stay all day, as it would have been exhausting going back home after each session and rushing back to church for the next one. On Friday and Saturday, the preacher preached about deliverance. He explained that repentance and being saved was not enough and that deliverance from the old ways and any evil or idolatry practices had to accompany being saved. He also mentioned that there was the need to formally accept Jesus as one's Lord and personal saviour.

I couldn't remember formally accepting Jesus; I thought being in church and generally being a good person was all that was required. He called out for all who wanted to accept Jesus, be saved and go to Heaven. He was going to pray for deliverance at the same time. As there was one single line for getting saved and getting delivered, I went forward, thanking God nobody need know the shameful truth that I was only now coming out to formally accept Jesus, after all my years of being in church. On the Sunday evening, he asked those who wanted the gift of the Holy Spirit to come out for prayers. I went for that too and I was baptised in the Holy Spirit.

My fresh salvation and baptism in the Holy Spirit re-energised me. I got involved in the church, attending Sunday school, which was a series of teachings for people who wanted to become registered members of the Church, as opposed to Sunday school for children. I also joined the choir and that kept my spirit up.

A challenge to my newly-found salvation came. It arrived in the form of Pastor Luke. A middle-aged man at the time, he was a tall and slim albino who walked with an awkward bounce. He was the pastor of one of the churches we had attended in my early childhood and had recently started his own denomination, the Evangelical Church of Nigeria. He was making contact with several of his old flock to increase the membership of his fledgling congregation. He got in touch with Mum and continued to visit us on a regular basis.

Each time Pastor Luke visited, he pestered me and teased me about how young I was, almost like it was unheard of to be young.

"Look at you, Ayus, Ayus. You, this young girl . . . I just can't believe how young she is."

I would recoil and fiddle with my fingers as I looked to the ground in embarrassment, sometimes wishing I was a lot older and that I looked big and mature.

If he had pulled my leg only once or twice, it may not have been so bad. But he did it repeatedly; no matter how many times he saw me in a week or in a month, he hassled and harassed me all the time. There were dozens of other children around, some of them about ten years younger than me, but they never seemed to get teased by Pastor Luke. It seemed fine to him that they were young, it was me being young he did not seem to be able to come to terms with. There came a Sunday afternoon that we had not gone to our own church, as we had been invited to a special event at another venue. Pastor Luke was at the event and offered to give us a lift back home. Ibidun, myself, some of my friends and some other children he knew all crammed into his car. Mum and Yetunde were going to visit Granddad after the event and were making alternative arrangements for their travel there. I got in the back seat with my sister and some of the other children, while Layo, my friend from school and her younger cousin Esther got in the front seat. Pastor Luke insisted that Esther sit in the back of the car and that I sit in the front passenger seat with Layo. Layo then decided she would sit in the back and leave Esther in front. Esther moved in and I sat by the door. It became a bit embarrassing when Pastor Luke insisted that I should swap places with Esther so that I sat nearer him next to the gear box. As he drove, he teased me, called me "Ayus Ayus" in his usual manner (as did a number of other adults). Then, he started to take one hand off the steering wheel to pull me. He pulled my ear, pulled my cheek, pulled the collar of my dress and pulled my scarf until it almost fell off my head. He pulled whatever he found to pull on my body.

At the start of the trip, I had thought nothing of him asking me to sit in front, other than that he was being friendly and creating some humour. However, I thought it was a bit unnecessary and inconsiderate of him to insist on it and single me out for "special treatment". As the journey progressed, I felt picked on. It was discomforting but I just sat there and said nothing.

The next day, back in school, I saw Layo, who was sexually more clued-up than I. Layo was mortified. She said Pastor Luke's harassment in the car, the day before, was sexual. Layo's feelings gradually turned into rage; she wouldn't keep quiet about the incident, explaining the sexuality of it.

"That pastor yesterday, he's *ashawo* (a whore). Hun! He was stylishly rubbing your body pretending as if he was playing with you. He's *ashawo*. And he calls himself a pastor. Next Sunday he will go back to church and be singing whoa, whoa, whoa, whoa . . . like yesterday. He can't even sing *ashawo*! *ashawo*!"

I felt thoroughly embarrassed. I remained silent because I didn't know what to say. I just hoped she would let it go. Layo's attention was later turned away from me. After that, anytime I saw Pastor Luke, I tried to keep a physical distance between us but he still was able to tease me about being young.

As his harassment continued, I started to feel quite out of place because I was young. I felt shy and ashamed of being young and had a lot of self doubt; I wasn't sure I was saved despite the fact that I had gone to the altar in church and accepted Jesus' salvation. At times I wondered whether the shame I had felt about the fact that I did not give my life to Christ earlier meant my salvation was not complete. I thought that perhaps if I rededicated my life to Jesus, or went out to the altar again when a call for salvation that was not combined with a call for deliverance was made—and everybody witnessed what a fraud I had been for remaining in church all those years and not giving my life to Christ—then my salvation would be complete and true. I had a feeling of God's looming judgement upon my life and did not feel I was definitely going to heaven when "eloquent" men and women of God spoke about rapture.

Yemisi, a girl my age, sat a few places away from me at Sunday school one morning. She talked boldly about her assurance of heaven and panic gripped me.

I don't think I'm going to heaven, I thought. *How does she know she would go to heaven? Well, she is a lot more spiritual than I am, isn't she? She's a better person than I am.*

I knew I would not be saved by my own effort, so there was no need for me to try and earn the salvation. In moments when I didn't doubt my salvation, I felt the need to be close to God and do His will by reading the Bible and learning more about Him and the instructions He had given. I also continued with the church choir because I enjoyed it so much and I considered it was my service to God.

Being in the choir meant I left home early, leaving everybody else behind, but Mum always insisted that I took Yetunde with me on Sundays. Yetunde, however, was usually not keen on getting to church early; she would rather go when everybody else was going. I ended up going late for the meetings because I had to wait for her.

One Sunday morning, Yetunde picked up her books and sat down to do her homework while I nagged her to get ready. She insisted she had to finish the homework before she went for a bath.

"Mummy, can you hear that? She's not even interested in going to church early. Why didn't she do her homework yesterday?"

No one appeared to have heard me, or, more precisely, I was ignored.

"I am going to get ready and go. I am definitely leaving her behind."

I headed for my room to get my things and leave. I noticed Mum followed me but I had not realised I was her intended target. Flip, flop, flip, flop, flip . . . I heard Mum's footsteps dogging mine as I went through the dining area. She was still behind me as I rounded the corner by the dark corridor leading to her bedroom. I entered my room and went straight for my Bible and notebook which were carefully placed on my bed, in readiness for the journey to church. I detected Mum's presence by the door and I looked round. I caught sight of her bending down to pick up a slipper which had lay on the floor by my dressing table but I still hadn't quite figured out what was about to happen. I picked up my Bible and as I turned round to go back out, there was a loud slap on my face; the slipper had landed on it. Mum was beating me because I said I was not going wait for Yetunde.

At that point I had had enough. I was going on thirteen so I had a fair deal of strength in me. I held Mum's two hands very strongly to prevent her beating me anymore and also to show her she did not have as much power over me as she thought she had. My slightly taller frame towered above Mum's shorter height as we looked each other in the eye. There was something to be said for me taking after Dad's stature—I could intimidate anyone shorter than me who wanted to take advantage of my good nature. Mum was frightened and shouted out to Ibidun and Olalekan. She thought I was going to beat her back. As she was shouting out in fear to both my older siblings, she was also shouting at me and trembling.

"Ayomide, do you want to beat me? Eh, you are going to beat me! Are you going to beat me?"

I merely held her hands and said nothing in response. Ibidun called Olalekan who was for some reason not within earshot. When he came, he started beating me and Mum joined in; both of them beating me to the ground. I felt humiliated, not necessarily by the beating but because in the process my dress lifted and wrapped tightly around my upper body showing my underwear. I struggled to get off the floor and away from their blows.

The anger of the whole morning turned into aggression against Yetunde as I held her hand on the way to church. I became discouraged after that and gave up on the idea of going to church early. Mum tried to force me to get my passion back, but it was not her call this time. I got myself involved in helping her on Sunday mornings to do whatever it was that kept her from going to church early. Once I found something she needed doing and I got stuck into it, she forgot all about the need to attend church promptly.

Mum later got involved in the church; she even became the president of the women's fellowship for quite a number of years and there was peace. At least I did not have to fight to get to church early; she now had a vested interest in getting there on time. Although, by then, my own fervour had greatly diminished. Some of my passion returned when Ibidun too joined the choir. She started the Sunday school classes after me but managed to progress faster to gain full church membership long after I had lost my zeal.

13

IT WAS MONEY AND IT WAS
GOD TO THE RESCUE

Mum closed the bar in Granddad's house for two reasons. Trying to keep it going was putting her under too much stress. Fatima, our housemaid who manned the bar whenever Mum was on duty in the health centre, had left and Mum was not having much luck replacing her. But more importantly, the concept of having a bar that sold alcohol was against our newfound faith.

The lack of a second income strained Mum's finances. At the end of the month, she would lie on her bed and plan how she would spend her salary—her only source of income. She divided it several ways. There was Olalekan's living allowance in Lagos, there was food for the house, there were school uniforms etc. As we lived in the health centre rented accommodation, the rent was deducted at source.

We would perch on the bed and budget with Mum. We reminded her about what was needed and what we may be able to do without. After we had sorted the budget out, I would go with her to the market to do the food shopping for the week or the next few days. Ibidun had heard the neighbour talking about the savings her family made by buying food in bulk; she came up with the idea that Mum should try and buy in bulk too. This did not go down well with Mum, she was angry partly because of the way it had been expressed by Ibidun. Mum must have felt Ibidun was calling her prudence into question. I knew Ibidun did not mean it that way; Mum simply got the wrong end of the stick. Ibidun's tone of voice was aggressive even when she did not mean to be aggressive. I supported her in trying to convince Mum that it was possible to shop in bulk, even on her limited resources.

Before we left the house to go shopping, Mum would kneel down and ask God to give her good bargains. She also haggled hard in the market and we usually came back home with a bounty. The money most times went further than expected and Mum didn't forget to thank God on our return.

Even the non-bulk shopping was rather plenty and the shopping bags got too heavy for me to carry. At such times when one faces a challenge, the brain is never too far behind in coming up with a solution. On one Thursday evening, we had finished our shopping and we were walking to the market entrance to hail a taxi. I had about three heavy plastic carrier bags, containing several kilograms of rice, beans, yam flour etc on each hand and Mum had similar amount to carry too.

"This is really heavy," Mum admitted.

"I think next time I should bring a sack and we can pack them together so that I can carry the sack on my head," I suggested to Mum.

She looked a little horror-struck.

"No, I don't want you doing that."

"But it's better than my arm almost dropping off under the weight of the food."

Mum shrugged with resignation.

The next time we went to the market, I took a sack along as I had said. Once we finished shopping, I carefully packed a lot of the shopping into the sack and balanced it on my head. It was not the most fashionable thing to do, especially for a teenager, but helping Mum out was my priority. Some of the girls at school ridiculed the idea of carrying shopping on their head. They were concerned about their public image; needless to say, certain boys were part of the consideration. I couldn't care less about a prospective boyfriend seeing me on the road with shopping on my head. Thankfully I was not alone; there were one or two other girls who had the same view. Balancing the shopping on my head distributed the load more evenly throughout the body, there was no strain on my arms and shoulders, and I only needed to watch out for my neck muscles. I knew I had to be strong for Mum; she had more than enough to worry about in making her salary stretch to its furthest.

It had been agreed that Dad would continue to contribute towards the family upkeep, but he didn't always keep his promise. Mum assigned me the task of going to him to collect our monthly allowance, as Dad called it, but it was difficult to get him to part with his money and many times it turned into a wasted journey. He sometimes would be out of town and would not have called to cancel. At times I would not meet Dad in a good mood and somehow I had to come up with tact and diplomacy to get the money out of him in peace, without recrimination and, most importantly, without being subjected to his anger.

Sometimes he would miss a month or two and Mum wasn't too careful in dealing with the situation, she would give me strong messages for him. Naturally, I tried to be as subtle as possible for my teenage wisdom, but there was no pulling the wool over Dad's eyes. He got the messages loud and clear and would give me extra strong replies for Mum, after having an angry outburst.

On one occasion that Mum had given me a message for Dad, I was to tell him the money he was giving us was far too little. I did broach the subject as best as I could but Dad shouted as if I was my mother and he was giving her the answer she deserved.

"I will not be duped by a woman. You can tell your mother, to * * * * with her. No one will defraud me of my money. The gods will . . ." Dad went on. He used to curse and swear by all the gods he knew whenever he was angry—the god of thunder, the god of lightning and that of iron.

"She can budget, go to the market and buy food in bulk."

I might have been tempted to believe Mum did not have enough wisdom to spend his money judiciously had I not been familiar with market prices and the art of budgeting. As he went on, one of his neighbours came in to visit him, asked what the matter was and Dad recapped the message from Mum that had been delivered to him. The man understood his anger and tried to pacify him. It was all going well until the neighbour told him I was too young to be receiving such angry outbursts from him on behalf of my mother.

"Ehn, you see, this kind of thing needs to wait. So that when you see her mother, then you can trash it out with her. She is too young for this, hun, she is too young."

Dad's fury was rekindled.

"She is old enough, she is a very intelligent and smart girl," he retorted.

"Oh, I see," the man said, "there is no problem with it then."

I thought, *Great, the man who is supposed to help him see sense has given up. Now what am I supposed to do? Should he not at least put in some more effort?* But I realised it really was not the man's business; he had done the best he could to show neighbourly love and concern. He probably would not put his own child under such a strain—that was, if he practised what he preached. It was up to Dad to decide how he wanted to care for his own children. I couldn't wait to get out of the place.

"Mum, I really don't like going to Dad for money. He is always angry."

Mum offered to cover me with prayers the next time.

"I think the transport cost is a waste if he does not give us any money."

No matter how many times I tried to make my case, Mum insisted I had to go. And so, a few months later, Mum and I were on a bus travelling to Ibadan for our bulk shopping when she told me we were going to stop by at Dad's place of work so I could ask him for some money. She said we could buy those things we had left off the shopping list with the extra money we would get from Dad.

Oh dear. *Why doesn't she realise we are better off making do with what we've got and if Dad happens to give more, it would be a bonus? Why go looking for trouble?*

Mum had resumed her long lost practice of shopping in bulk which she had apparently been used to in the days when my aunties and uncles visited us frequently in Ilesa, long before Ibidun heard about bulk shopping. The bigger markets in Ibadan had cheaper and good quality food; hence we made the bimonthly seventy five kilometres journey there for the bulk purchase. We would usually go on a weekday when Mum was off duty, and sometimes I took the day off school to be able to help her if we were unable to schedule the travel for a holiday period. I enjoyed the bus rides, although they could prove uncomfortable at times. More than the manufacturer-intended number of passengers were usually squeezed into the seats and the roads were bumpy in places, despite it being one of the better intercity roads in the area. We usually got the direct bus that would bypass the towns and villages along the A122, between Ife and Ibadan, in order to expedite our journey.

At the end of this particular trip, the bus we were travelling in pulled into the bus station and, instead of heading to the market, we got off and asked for directions to the polytechnic where Dad taught. It was that job that took him to Ibadan after the family break-up. I was delighted for him when he got it and was extremely proud that he was doing well in his work. It meant he had to live in Ibadan most of the time and would only travel to Ife some weekends and college holidays.

As we walked towards the building that housed his department, I was filled with trepidation. Luckily, Dad was not there. We met his two colleagues who shared a large office with him. The room was a bit unorganised; there were several desks, most of which were raggedly stacked with books and papers. The desks didn't seem to have been placed with any particular setting in mind and the chairs around them were at odd angles to each other.

"Aw, your Dad had just left. Did he know you were coming?" asked one of the two men.

"No, not really," I replied.

Mum nudged me to ask the man for a pen and paper so we could leave a message for Dad. I had been hoping we would slip away and when next I saw Dad I would pretend we were only asking after his welfare.

"Please can I have a pen and paper, I will leave him a note."

"Sure. I think there is a pen somewhere here," replied the seemingly kind and gentle man.

He rummaged through the heap of paper and stationery on one of the tables and spoke as he searched.

"I think he must have gone back to Ife. If he knew you were coming he probably would have left a message." He was rather anxious on our behalf. "Oh, I found a pen, here you are . . . and paper."

Mum insisted I had to let Dad know some basic facts about our so-called allowance and the first was that he had been paying it in arrears rather than giving us the money to spend for the coming month; the second being that he had missed the last two payments and he needed to pay up. I thought, *Oh no, those are real strong messages to give Dad; it will not go down well at all. If I wrote that, I was bound to face a mighty wave of anger.* I was getting nervous.

I started to write:

> *"Dear Daddy, how have you been? Hope all is well. Mummy and I came to Ibadan to . . ."*

"Tell him he is giving you the money in arrears, write it there; write it. Put it in there," Mum whispered.

I continued with the note:

> *". . . do some shopping and we thought we might be able to catch you to perhaps get some money to add to the amount we have."*

"Put the message in there; tell him he has missed the payment for the last two months," Mum muttered rather forcefully.

I gave in:

> *"Dad, you have been giving us the money in arrears and you have not given us any money for the past two months."*

149

I thought to myself, *That's it, I'm dead, I'm as good as gone, dead meat.* As we walked back to the bus stop, I thought there was no way I wanted to face that man or ever see him again after this, all hell will break loose. Meanwhile Mum was strengthening her position with words.

"He needs to know that the money he is giving is nothing, it does not buy you food; it buys nothing. He needs to increase it and know that he has been paying in arrears and missing payments. What does he expect you to eat and wear? Walk around naked? Or open your mouth to thin air? He needs to know."

Yeah, Mum, next time do me a favour and be the one to tell him. Not that I had the guts to have said it out loud.

Three weeks later, I went to Dad's house in Ife as previously arranged. He brought out a piece of paper. I recognised it, only it was slightly dirtier and more wrinkled than it was when I had written a note on it three weeks prior. By this time, everything inside me was shaking with fear. He calmly gave me the paper asked me to read it and tell him who the note was for.

Oh dear.

"Me and Mummy thought it would be good to have some extra money for shopping."

He told me to take my note and get out of his house. I asked him when I could come back for some money; he said he would let me know when he was ready. I went back to give Mum the bad news, the look on her face told me she felt more of a victim then than before.

Mum's quest to engage Dad seemed not to have a limit. Even though Dad had admitted openly that he was not capable of looking after his children, during the summer holiday following the note incident, Mum insisted that I ask him if Yetunde and I could come and spend the holidays with him.

I was extremely dubious of this and asked what she would do if he said it was fine.

I knew for certain my mother would not let Yetunde out of her sight. She could let me go, though. If Dad said it was fine and Yetunde did not go, Dad would have felt Mum and I made a fool of him and I would have been the one left there to receive his anger. I hadn't realised Mum was a hundred percent sure Dad would not agree to such a thing. When I got to Dad's, I did as I was told, and he declined. He said we were better off with Mum because he was not able to cook for us and look after us properly.

I admired the honesty and the humility that Dad displayed in being able to admit his weakness. It was not what I would have expected of Dad; it would have been less poignant if he fobbed me off with one excuse or the other. But Dad was right; I had witnessed his home management skills when I was a lot younger. Shortly after Yetunde was born, Aunty Omolara, one of Mum's younger sisters, was getting married in Ife and I was one of the bridesmaids. Mum and I, with my siblings and Aunty Deola, our housemaid at the time, travelled a few days ahead in preparation for the wedding, leaving Dad behind to join us the day the ceremonies started. On arrival at Ife, Dad boasted about his cooking and his housekeeping skills. He was particularly making a point to Aunty Deola (who was many years older than even Olalekan, the oldest of us, hence we all called her aunty), encouraging her to learn from the example he had set, which we would all see when we got back to Ilesa. On getting back home, we saw the leftovers from his cooking and could not figure out what the strange grey asparagus coloured thing in the pot was. He made such a mess of everything; from the cooking to the cleaning up. He seemed to have started with the usual ingredients including some vegetable leaves and ended up with something quite inedible. His attempt at cleaning the house was definitely not one to emulate. It was catastrophic. He had left some of the rubbish in the saucepan; but I suppose if he was committed enough he would have learnt over time.

When I got home from Dad's, I gave Mum the feedback and realised all she wanted was an admission from Dad, albeit quite unnecessarily, in my view, that she was doing a good job of looking after us.

My feelings towards Dad changed somewhat after his honest assessment of his ability to look after us. He was no longer just the Dad who didn't deliver when his family needed him to pull his weight. There now seemed to be plausible reasons why he sometimes could not fulfil his obligations towards us, although I was still finding much of his actions difficult to understand, especially the level of financial contribution he made towards our upkeep. I felt let down each time he reneged on his promises. The most painful and embarrassing of all was when my school fees went unpaid.

State school education had been free for all until the government, in my third year in secondary school, decided we were going to start paying fees. It was a relatively small amount, and Mum decided it was going to be Dad's responsibility to pay it. Unsurprisingly, the fees went unpaid several times and I would usually be threatened with exclusion from exams or from school altogether. I looked to Mum to bail me out each time I reached a seeming dead end with Dad but Mum never budged. What bothered me was that she took on the responsibility for my siblings whenever they needed their school or examination fees paying. I had to devise my own way of getting Dad to pay, which was to start asking for the school fees the term before; even then he would not pay it if he did not want to.

I felt sorry for Dad because he was working hard and was earning a significant amount of money (as far as I was concerned) and all he could afford to part with was this tiny fragment of it because there was always one thing or another that he had to pay for. He always had to fix his car, spend a lot of money on his car, and spend even more money on his car—it was always about the car.

He rented a room in Ife and had a very old left hand drive Peugeot 504 car that he shipped into the country from England. He was not living it up or eating in luxury. I worried for him because I could not imagine how his money disappeared. I prayed fervently for him that God would remove the devourer, as I saw it, from his life. Sometimes I got angry wondering if he was only being miserly. I had enough and told Mum I was not going to get any more money from him. I didn't care if it meant we starved, in any case the allowance he gave us was only enough to cover the cost of my monthly travel to school.

Olalekan was not there to help Mum out this time; she had to accept that I was not going. She kicked up a fuss about it but the most she could do was tell me she was not going to give me money for travel to school. She made good on her promise of punishment. I walked part of the way in the afternoon and spent some of my savings on the rest of the journey. Three days later, Mum came into my room and she threw the money at me. I felt worthless as the money landed on the floor next to my dressing table. I bent down to pick it up, almost crying at the way she treated me, but at the same time I could not help smiling at my victory.

My refusal to keep going to Dad for money did not last long; I was old and wise enough to know that we were in a financially difficult situation at home and I couldn't expect Mum to pay all the school fees, provide food and shelter for us and continue to fund my travel to school day in, day out. I soon resumed my monthly visits to Dad.

Life was unrelentingly difficult at home; I didn't want to be there, it was not just the financial difficulty but also Ibidun's nastiness and Mum's bitter nagging. It was difficult knowing what to do to be right with Mum. She carried the weight of the family on her shoulders; she did all the cooking and complained about doing it. I taught myself to cook because I longed to ease my mother's pain and I was basically sick of her complaining but still refusing to teach us to cook.

Mum was mostly at work in the daytime which meant we got to cook lunch. One day we would cook and she would find a reason to tell us off for cooking. The next day we would decide it was better not to cook; she came back and scolded us for not cooking. It was a catch twenty-two. The worst came when Ibidun messed the cooking up and I got blamed for allowing her to mess it up. It apparently was my responsibility to supervise her and ensure it all went well. I was made responsible for my sister who was five years older than me, but without the authority or the guidance to effectively correct her when she did it wrong. When I tried, I told her off like Mum would tell me off and it would degenerate into an argument. I was growing into a rather irritable young girl. I didn't really know how to handle the tricky situations I was faced with and turned to petulance.

There was a man who lived alone in one of the flats, in a block two doors away to the right hand side of our building. He worked in the health centre as a senior engineer and would usually come to our compound to fetch some water and chat to his friend, Mr Taiwo, one of the senior health centre executives who lived on the ground floor next to us. We never really knew the engineer's name; we simply called him the engineer—not to his face though. There was never a need to call out to him or refer to him in his presence.

They came to our home one evening and I was irritated by the presence of this engineer in our apartment. Earlier that day, I had gone to see Dad. As I was walking to the taxi rank, I saw the engineer and his friends going in the same direction. One of his friends walked up to me, leaving the others behind. He started flirting and tried to chat me up; I ignored him. He seemed pretty determined to engage with me and kept pressing for a response. Eventually, he seemed to have realised he was getting nowhere, instead I was only getting annoyed by his lewd come-ons. He left me and went back to join his friends, including the engineer.

The engineer must have been in his late thirties at the time; he and his friends would have been between fifteen and twenty years older than I was, apart from the fact that I was only fourteen and therefore underage. When the engineer came into our apartment that evening, I had just finished baking a cake.

"Is that cake I smell?" said Mr Taiwo. He was a jovial man who liked to tease; he would gently rock his short stout figure as he cracked his jokes and cackled.

"I cannot just smell it; I can see it as well." He pointed to the cake on the dining table in the living room. He turned to his companion and said, "We do have great timing, don't we? Imagine how we have been specially directed to Sister's flat this evening."

The engineer, who was only a tiny bit taller than Mr Taiwo, nodded in acceptance and told how he had developed itchy feet in his flat and decided to pay Mr Taiwo a visit, not realising it was all going to end up by a dining table with a delicious cake on top.

"Sister, we cannot come in and suffer the smell of something this sweet without the comfort of tasting it," Mr Taiwo insisted.

I'm not sure there were many people who would have come into our apartment and insisted on being served in the same manner. Mum asked me to get side plates and dish the cake up for them.

"Ayo, are you the chef?" Mr Taiwo asked.

"She was the one who baked it," Mum replied.

The engineer then decided to pull my leg.

"Ah ah, I saw her earlier going to the market. She must have been going shopping for the cake ingredient."

At that, I fumed. It now seemed clear that the engineer had been aware his friend had been up to no good and he had allowed it to happen, which to me meant he probably would have done the same if he felt able to.

"No, I wasn't going shopping," I growled at him as I left the room to get the plates. I was disgusted at the thought of serving him the cake. When I handed him his plate, I almost shoved it into his hand.

After they left, Mum and Olalekan berated me for my attitude towards "the gentleman".

"Ah, Olalekan, I didn't know that you saw it too. She behaved *appallingly*," Mum said.

I hinted at what had happened with his friend earlier. Olalekan seemed to have gotten the message and refrained from further reprimand, but Mum would not let up. To my surprise, Mum seemed to then insinuate it was my fault the engineer's friend behaved the way he did.

"Oh, I see," Mum said. "Maybe this man too has been making similar advances towards you? Hun? Has he? Let us know, because it will explain why you were behaving like that, wouldn't it? Just let us know if they have been making advances."

She was sarcastic, as though it would have been my fault if he did! I somehow knew the way the engineer's friend behaved was his responsibility, but I became a bit confused as to how it was my fault that he behaved the way he did. What should I have done, smiled and welcomed him and he would automatically behave with morality towards me?

Even petulance did not help much in answering those questions and it was at that stage of my life that I started to know what sadness was; I felt constantly sad. I always knew we could be happy despite struggling financially, but Mum expressed too much bitterness and Ibidun was always looking for trouble. Even though I engaged in fights with her, I never threw the first punch. Ibidun always seemed to forget she lost the last fight and would punch me as a last attempt to get me to comply with whatever she wanted, which basically, as far as I could see, was for her and her troublesome ways to be worshiped. A lot of the time she did not even seem to know what she wanted from us.

I found a lot of comfort in singing with the church choir. We sang songs of the sweet by and by and songs of heaven, the place where there will be no more sorrow, no more pain and no more death. The songs had very strong meanings for me and I would sing them crying and looking forward to the happy days in heaven.

My freedom was rapidly approaching—the end of secondary school. There was less than two years to go. *I would be out of this environment. I will leave Ibidun to battle it out with her mother*, I said to myself. I wondered what would happen to Yetunde when I left, whether she was going to be suffering unjust beatings at the hand of her older sister. I thought it was unlikely; Mum would take adequate measures to protect her.

Anyway, all that was still two years away. I must study hard to ensure I got into university; otherwise there would be no freedom.

Two years' preparation time soon dwindled into months and it was time for me to take the school's internal examination for the last time. I was threatened with exclusion from my final secondary school exams for not paying the required fees. It seemed the school's unusual parting gift to us was to ask us to pay to sit this ultimate end of term examination. If only they knew what trouble I went through to get my fees paid. This time Mum too was worried; she borrowed the money to pay it until we got it back from Dad.

It was instances like this that softened my heart towards Mum. If Dad had been more supportive, life would have been a lot easier to live. Mum needed support from the man who chose to have a family with her, but he was not prepared to take on that responsibility. Mum's much-needed aid came from strangers, passersby on the road that was our family life. But surely it's got to get better someday, I thought. Perhaps all these struggles would cease when we are all grown up and are successful, but Dad seemed to have had that covered as well.

He had started to feel isolated from the rest of us. It seemed the tough authoritarian figure I had grown to fear had his own insecurities too, and that sense of vulnerability went beyond his perceived lack of child minding skills. On what was perhaps my last visit to him for a couple of years, he gave me a warning and sent the same warning to Mum.

"Whether you like it or not, you cannot do away with me," Dad said. "You may abandon me now but there is coming a time in your life when people will ask for your father—when the time comes for you to get married, your proposed spouse's families are going to ask for me. They will want to know who your father is. You tell your mother that for me. There is no way she can take my right away from me. I will take my place."

I hadn't actually thought of it that way. Dad's threat was a blow to my hope for future happiness and it made any marriage prospect a potentially unpleasant one. As I walked the craggy road from his house to the main road to catch a taxi home, my consciousness switched from the scenes around me—the people that usually littered the front and sides of the various houses doing their Saturday morning chores, and the lack of trees along the road that deprived it of natural greenery and serenity. I was buried in my worries. I imagined what the future might be like, me ready to get married, looking forward to a peaceful family life, Dad prepared to assert his authority, either by hook or crook, as head of the family; and Mum, well, probably wanting a reward for her years of hard work. Is a life of peace too much to ask for? I desired neither riches nor fame, not even power. All I ever wanted out of life was to be happy and contented. I wondered why my family wouldn't allow me this. I thought that perhaps if Jesus's second coming would happen before I was old enough to get married, it would save me the trouble of my wedding being turned into a football by my father. Those thoughts, coupled with the rate at which the various preachers around kept shouting about the imminence of the second coming, boosted my expectation for it. I imagined it was bound to happen before I grew up. God would definitely save me from the jaws of my family, bent on killing any form of happiness I could have. Yet as it turned out, it was not Dad's threat that I had to worry about the most.

PART III

TOMORROW'S HOPE

14

PASSAGE TO LONDON

"Ayo, I need you to send me a copy of your birth certificate."

It was Mum; she had called to let me know that she was getting my plane ticket to travel to London. Mum never missed a bargain. She had seen a deal for young people who are under twenty-six years old and she wanted to take advantage of it. She needed my birth certificate to prove my age. Mum was not only keen to get an under twenty-six deal, she was anxious to get me out of Nigeria as soon as possible. I could hear the desperation in her voice. It was the same mother that I was unable to convince of the benefit of me visiting England about a year before, when lecturers at my university had gone on strike. Her intention was clear enough to me; Mum was eager to get me away from Rex. I knew she still thought if only she could create a distance between us, the relationship would blow over like puppy love. It seemed Mum was still not ready to accept the "will of God"—or she had forgotten she now thought it might be God's will.

As Mum concluded her preparations for me to fly out of Nigeria, I sat beside Aunty Dunmola one afternoon as she spoke to Mum on the phone. Aunty Dunmola responded to Mum, "How can you say it is not the will of God, how do you know it is not the will of God?" I did not ask Aunty Dunmola further about it; I knew what was being discussed.

It hurt that Mum didn't have listening ears, that she was bent on doing what she wanted to do, and that what I wanted out if it was not a consideration for her. It wasn't that I didn't see any benefit in travelling to England; I actually wished to study for a master's degree and settle into a good career, but as it was, Mum was pushing me without recourse to how it may work best for me. I explained my feelings to Dr Olumide. He was sympathetic and encouraged me not to throw the baby out with the bath water.

"In any case it is a chance for you and Mummy to talk face to face about whatever her concerns are," he assured me.

I took up Mum's offer of a ticket to London and she made sure it was a one-way ticket. She booked my flight for the night of September 15, 1997. It turned out to be a one-way to years of pain and misery. I could not have imagined I would face so much agony from being with my own family.

My departure date was drawing near. We were in Ibadan visiting Rex's brother and his family one evening. Rex's sister-in-law had prepared supper and she had asked us to serve ourselves. As I ate the rice and fried plantain I served on my plate, my mind drifted to my impending future in the UK. I felt a strong urge to pray earnestly.

Tricky.

Earnest prayers have a tendency to come out loudly. The urge couldn't be resisted, I prayed with my mouth full of food, I said very fervently in my heart, "Father, in the name of Jesus, I pray that you go ahead of me and prepare London for me. Prepare London to receive me, my God . . ."

A couple of weeks later, Rex showed me a letter from the University College London. He had been offered a place to study for a Ph.D. The letter claimed the offer had already been deferred once, and they would not be willing to defer it again.

"I would have written back to them but there is no proof that I could give them to show I will be able to take up their offer in the near future," he explained. "Clara Kolajo said they will take any request for another deferral seriously if it was in person."

I took the letter from him and put it in my handbag.

"You need to go there as soon as you get to London."

"Yes, I will, of course."

"Actually if you could go there the day you arrive or the next day."

"I may not be able to make it the day I get to London, but I will go there the next day."

I travelled to Lagos two days before my flight. Rex came down from Osu earlier on the day to pick me up and take me there. Yetunde came along with us. She wanted to see me off at the airport and stay in Lagos for a while after my departure. We stayed with my uncle, Mum's older cousin, as we usually did whenever we were in Lagos.

On the day of the flight, Daddy Ajayi, as we called my uncle, took me, Rex and Yetunde to the airport in the afternoon to check my luggage in. In those days, we used to make two trips to the airport whenever we were boarding a late afternoon or night flight. The first would be several hours before take-off, to check our luggage in. We would then go back for the actual flight. That way we didn't have to loiter in between check-in and boarding—we would just go straight through customs and immigration and onto the gate.

I felt pangs of fear as we queued for check-in that afternoon. *This is it*, I thought to myself. *I am not coming back this time. It is not a holiday, it is final.* As we moved along the line, Rex asked Daddy Ajayi's permission to drive me to the airport later when I went to catch my flight, and Daddy Ajayi agreed.

We got back home and I rushed back out to my aunt's salon on Ibadan Road to have my hair done. There were a number of customers waiting so I ended up leaving the salon late. I was cutting it fine. We got back to my uncle's house. Yetunde helped me with the stylish, triangular, green and gold vanity case that I had packed as my hand luggage and I feverishly looked around our bedroom to make sure I was not leaving anything behind. One final look around and we both hurried downstairs and got in Rex's car to go to the airport.

On the way to the airport, Rex suddenly slowed the car down. I looked at him.

"What's the matter?" I asked.

"I think we've got a flat tyre."

"You are joking." I couldn't believe it!

"Ayo, don't worry, we will get there on time."

He got out of the car and replaced it with the spare in the boot. Yetunde sat quietly in the back seat. I could feel her movement as she occasionally stretched her neck to see through the dim lighting of the street how Rex was getting on. Each time I felt her movement, I also turned round or opened the door of the front passenger seat to catch a glimpse of Rex as he replaced the back far side tyre. I was trying to be as calm as possible, hoping all would be well and I would not miss my flight. Rex finished and we got back on the road.

"Let's just hope that will be fine," he said. "There is a second spare tyre in the boot but it has a puncture, too, although it only leaks air very slowly."

At that, I started to pray for a miracle. We travelled another two miles and he slowed down again.

"Oh my God, not another flat tyre."

"It is."

At this point, it looked pretty likely that I was going to miss my flight. Rex got out of the car again and checked the tyre out. It was the one he had replaced a few minutes before. He said it looked like it was a fresh puncture. Luckily, he reckoned the second spare tyre, which was leaking air slowly, could take us all the way to the airport and get him somewhere afterwards where he could repair one of them. He changed the tyre and we got going again. I was praying desperately to God that the car would not malfunction in any way all throughout the rest of the evening.

We finally got to the airport, just on time. We stood in the departure hall, savouring the final moments together, for what we thought was going to be many months. I glimpsed Yetunde as she stood to the side. I knew I was going to miss her, despite our differences and Mum's recent influence on our relationship. My fondness of her had grown stronger in the years that we had both lived with Aunty Dunmola and that affection for her held strong in my heart that night.

Rex asked me to come back for a final goodbye once I cleared immigration control. I really wasn't sure it was allowed, but I had learnt not to argue too much with him so I agreed to go back. I headed for the security area; as I offered my passport to the immigration officer I noticed a ground staff by the corner. Immediately my passport was checked she asked:

"Air France?"

I said yes.

"We have been waiting for you. Can you please make your way straight down the corridor?"

167

I could hardly ask the lady to wait a few minutes while I went back to say a final goodbye to my fiancé. I did as she had directed and as I navigated the corridor round to the departure gate, there were ground staff at almost every corner repeating the same thing.

"Air France? Can you please quickly make your way to the departure gate?"

After what seemed an age long encounter with Air France ground staff, I eventually made it to the gate. I got to my seat and tried to settle myself down. I noticed another passenger who seemed rather short of breath as he scurried onto the plane. No sooner had he sat down than the plane started to reverse out of its parking position.

Phew! That was lucky! Any later and I would have missed my flight.

I walked out of the baggage reclaim area in Heathrow Terminal 4. Mum and Ibidun were by the entrance waving frantically; their faces lit up with smiles immediately as they realised I had spotted them. I too was overjoyed, but someone was missing. Olalekan was not there. I had expected he would pick me up in his car and I felt a slight disappointment that I would have to haul my luggage through the airport onto the underground train, no minor undertaking. My disappointment soon faded as I chatted with Mum and Ibidun.

It had been almost three years since my previous visit to London and I hadn't been on the Piccadilly underground line before. About fifteen minutes into the journey, the train exited the underground tunnel and travelled on surface track for a few miles. I looked out of the window of the crowded carriage as Mum and Ibidun sat opposite me, clutching my heavily packed suitcase with one hand each. My hand luggage sat securely on my lap with my handbag placed precariously on top. At various points along the way, I saw the back of a range of terraced Victorian houses, some of them quite similar to the terrace in Tooting where I had spent three winter months living in Olalekan's house during my last visit. The familiar environment seemed to be sending me a message of reassurance—I was now in London and all would be well. Even though I couldn't be certain of what lay ahead of me, my fear seemed to have been swept away.

We went straight to Ibidun's flat where Mum was also living. Nothing much had changed since I was last there except that the carpet was no longer as crisply new as it had been and there were a few other signs to indicate the onset of wear and tear on the other pieces of furniture. She had moved into the flat just before I arrived in London for holiday three years prior; at the time, the novelty and smell of brand new furniture and fittings had increased the snugness of the relatively large apartment. We sat in the living room with my cases dumped all over and I filled them in on what had been happening back home in Nigeria. There was plenty of news, what with the renewed tribal war between the Modakekes and the Ifes, which I did try not to discuss in too much detail.

"I have some application forms for a master's degree for you," Mum said.

She handed me the application form for South Bank University and some money for a week's travel card. I wasn't too keen. I wanted to study at one of the leading universities. In any case, I was not ready to study immediately. Getting a job was my priority.

I remembered Tade's letter.

"Mum, where's my friend's letter?"

Mum looked under the pile of paper on a desk behind me and handed me the envelope. The reason for Mum's reaction on the phone was now clear; the picture that was enclosed in the letter was a classy picture of Tade and her fiancé! Maybe this was what Mum was referring to when she claimed I was being pressured into marriage—peer pressure. I put the picture back into its envelope, dropped it in my bag and continued the natter with Mum and Ibidun. Olalekan came by in the evening to pick me up and that was the start of life in his house, at the least for the next year.

I woke up the next day and headed for the University College London to ask for Rex's admission offer to be deferred. *It may be wise for me to apply for a course and then defer the admission*, I thought to myself as I walked through the busy Tooting High Street opposite the market.

My mind wandered a little to my surroundings (probably for the last time for many years to come). I couldn't sense the familiar London smell that I had been accustomed to on my previous visit. It was a bit worrying. Could it be because my senses had been disturbed by the attack I had suffered recently? It had been over a year since it had happened, but my sight was still not as clear as it used to be; perhaps my sense of smell had gone with it too. The last time I was on holiday, London had a peculiar smell to me. It was a combination of sweet, woody smell with a hint of putrefaction. In Nigeria, I had been used to the dry dusty smell of Harmattan and in the rainy season, the fresh rain and grassy scent that was at times infiltrated by a burnt smell.

As I arrived at the entrance to Tooting Broadway tube station, I directed my thought back to my mission for the day. If I made an application and deferred it, that would at least allay some of Mum's fears. It would also give me some comfort that I was gradually working towards my own goal. I got off the tube at Euston Square and found my way to the Bartlett Faculty of Built Environment, aided by Olalekan's London A-Z maps. The university looked very different to what we had in Nigeria; it had various clusters of buildings which were integrated with the city rather than having a defined geographical boundary for an exclusive campus. I found the exact room I needed in order to speak to someone about Rex's admission deferral; a tall, blonde, short-haired lady dealt with my enquiries. As she finished the necessary procedure for the deferral, I asked her about their master's programmes; I collected the prospectus and the application form and headed back home.

At home, I looked through the prospectus—the prerequisite for the various courses and the application procedure. The school required a short essay that was related to the course. As I had nothing else to do, I started on the essay. I focused on it and the rest of the application form for the remaining days of that week and saved some of the money Mum gave me for travelling around.

Mum gave me some more money the following week so I could buy whatever essential things that I needed, including new travel cards. The first thing I did was buy an international phone card to call Rex. I told him about my journey to UCL, and that his admission was securely deferred. He gave me his opinion on some of their master's courses. I had thought a course with international relevance would be good for me, so I chose an MSc in sustainable development. He thought my choice of course was fine.

All was going well until he asked, "Why did you not come back to say goodbye after you cleared customs and immigration?"

I knew that depressed tone he spoke with. I could picture the facial expression that would have accompanied it—that of a deprived, sad but angry child.

"I was about the last to get on the plane; it was practically waiting for me," I explained.

"Actually, Yetunde and I thought as much because not long after you went in we saw the Air France plane in the sky."

There went Rex again with his typical behaviour. I wasn't sure why on God's earth he thought it was right for him to have brought the subject up when he already had his answer, probably another reason for me to have felt that I never got it right with him.

15

ON THE OTHER SIDE
OF LONDON

I started to settle down into my new environment with earnest job hunting. One evening, I arrived from my daily visits to the various jobcentres in the city and put my head through Olalekan's bedroom door to say hello to him.

"Here, take this," he said as he passed me a small gospel tract. He had been handed the leaflet by a group of Christians who were evangelising by the tube station entrance. It was rubber stamped at the back with the name Bethel Community Church and the address of a nearby school where the church met. He thought I might be interested in trying it out. I had been moaning about Olalekan's church, the Pentecostal Church of God (PCG), which I had been attending with him. There was a lovely atmosphere in the church, but from my rough estimate, about eighty five percent of the attendees were between thirty-five and eighty years old, with the larger part of that statistics tending more towards the upper limit of the age range. The other fifteen percent appeared to be mainly children. Olalekan was in no doubt that I found it difficult fitting into his church setting.

The Sunday after Olalekan handed me the tract, I started attending the Bethel Community Church. It was part of a larger group of churches with their headquarters (usually referred to as the main church) in Drayton, West London. On my first Sunday there, I walked into the school hall where they met and I was greeted, at the entrance, with big smiles and light hugs by a lively, elderly West Indian couple who were the church's stewards. I appreciated their warm welcome but I was a bit apprehensive at first, wondering whether the membership would be similar to PCG. I was used to their stewardship role being played by the church youths back in Nigeria but I needn't have worried. I soon realised the church, though very small, had a diverse congregation.

Inside the large hall, there were not more than forty people sitting closely towards the front with three young, Asian men on various musical instruments. One was playing the piano and another one was on the guitar; the third guy was playing the drums. There was a young English man, who I judged would be in his early-to-mid twenties, on the microphone in the front and leading the praise worship. I tiptoed through the middle aisle to the last row of seats that was occupied and sat behind a very young Indian couple. The wife looked round, our eyes met, and she beamed with a broad smile, revealing her almost perfectly sculpted white teeth. As the service went on, I could see a middle-aged English couple sitting next to each other on the front row; they jumped up and down when they danced. I later came to understand that they were the pastors of the church when the man took hold of the microphone and preached immediately after the praise worship, citing various examples of how the Bible applied to us in this century with references to his wife and son—the young man who led the worship.

At the end of the Service, the congregation mooched around and gradually moved towards the back of the hall where there was a table laid with cakes and drinks. I spotted quite a number of black faces and a petite, light skinned black lady approached me. I reckoned she was not much older than I was. She offered me coffee and a piece of cake.

"Hi, I'm Tayo."

"Oh, you're Nigerian," I said, almost showing my relief that there was someone there I could relate to culturally.

"Yes, so is Funmi, Yinka, Sumbo . . ." She listed about six other Nigerians and pointed in various directions, as if trying to identify them, before she stopped. I tried to follow her pointed finger with my eyes but it moved too quickly for me to spot who it was she had pointed to.

"My name is Ayo, I am Nigerian too, as my name suggests, and it's my first time in the church."

"I guessed as much because I've never seen you before. Well, Ayo, we will be having a special women's meeting in February, is that something you will like to attend?"

"That's next year isn't it? I'm sure it will be a good meeting to attend; perhaps we can talk more about it nearer the time?" I wasn't sure if Tayo had run out of things to talk about or she really was giving me four months' notice of the meeting, perhaps a mixture of the two. She was the only person I had the time to speak to before I headed back home for lunch with Olalekan, but over the following weeks I met the other Nigerians in the church and got to know Pastors Jack and Leila better. Gareth, their son who led the praise worship, was their only child and they had been pastoring the church since he was ten years old. It was nice to experience such a close multicultural community and get to know more about the

175

history of the church, but more importantly, for me, was the ability to make new friends.

As the weeks rolled by I decided to confront Mum about her attitude towards my relationship. She came to visit me and Olalekan one evening and I thought I would see her off to the tube station and chat to her on the way; I ended up following her all the way home as there was not enough time on the journey to the tube station to conclude our talk. Mum did not have any concrete reasoning for her behaviour. She claimed she heard that my love for Rex was unrequited and she did not want anyone to ridicule her children. How Mum came to hear that was unclear. She was initially smug, which made me wonder whether she had any idea what impact her actions had on me or even their potential to hurt deeply.

"Is that enough justification for the pain you put me through?"

I repeated the contents of some of her letters to her as I tried to reconcile her explanation with her actions. By this time we were already in Ibidun's flat—the journey there had appeared to have been shorter than normal. It would usually take a total of about half an hour on both the Northern Line and Victoria Line to get to Vauxhall where they lived. But this time it seemed it took only a quarter of an hour. As Mum settled herself rather uncomfortably into one of the two armchairs in the living room, I remained standing still, demanding a satisfactory answer. She then claimed she was upset because she thought I had been to Rex's family with Aunty Dunmola and had a traditional wedding done, because it was also called engagement. Mum was full of surprises. I had not seen that one coming. At that point, Ibidun joined in the conversation. She was forthright about the fact that she and Mum knew exactly what I was referring to and they were well aware I was talking about a courtship.

Since she had gone to live in London, Ibidun had become a completely transformed person. She was no longer the "problem child" who made everybody else's life a misery. She was now a mature, responsible woman. Her letters and the various gifts she used to send to me and Yetunde in Nigeria had been the first indication of the change, and now in London I was experiencing that different personality first-hand. I couldn't tell what had happened to her that had brought about her reformation, and to be honest I didn't care what it was; it was simply good to experience my older sister in a different way than we had done when she was in Nigeria. She was the bearer of truth that night. Her testimony would have resolved the problem a great deal, had Mum not been bent on seeing that she was discredited. Mum turned on Ibidun and called her the trouble mastermind. I didn't want Ibidun taking the flak for me, but at the same time I wanted her to do whatever she believed was right for her to do, so I left both of them to argue it out.

I thought I would see what Shewa had to say about her own explanation for my desire to get married one day. Shewa insisted she never told my mother I was being pressured into getting married. She had her own perfectly plausible description of what happened when she met Mum.

While all these confrontations were going on, unbeknownst to the people around me, my relationship with Rex was reaching a major crisis point. My subsequent telephone conversation with him didn't go as well as the first. He was not happy that I had obtained an application form for a master's degree as soon as I arrived in London. It was a bit difficult to understand at first, seeing he had sounded very affirming when I had first talked to him about it. He, however, claimed he was angry because I had agreed with him that I was not going to study until I was well settled in a job and had invited him to London. That way he could work for a while, save up and then start his Ph.D. My explanation of wanting to defer the admission, like he had done with his own Ph.D. admission offer, fell completely on deaf ears. He wrote me a strongly worded letter, and in my frustration I replied in the same tone. Things deteriorated fast and the relationship tethered on the brink of collapse. To be honest, by that point I just wanted the relationship to end. The fierceness of Rex's letter had filled me with dread and I wondered to myself why I did not end the relationship during one of those times, in Nigeria, when he had been abusive one way or the other. As timid as I was, even with the latest quarrel, I still couldn't bring myself to end it with him, until one day when he called me and asked that I called him back the next evening.

Rex told me that since I had decided to pursue my own agenda in London, that perhaps it was time for us to go our separate ways. I agreed. He sounded quite surprised as he paused a little and then asked me to confirm my agreement. I think he suggested the break up as a threat, thinking I was too emotionally invested in him to allow it to end. My saying yes must have confounded him.

He clearly had some scheming in mind because after speaking to him he then told me he had brought a close cousin of mine, Dolapo, who worked in the only bank in Osu, to his house and that she had been listening to the discussion from his own end. He handed my cousin the phone. I was going to gloss over my relationship problems and chat to her normally, not wanting to open up sordid details of my dirty linen to her. I was shocked when she told me she had read the correspondence between me and Rex!

This is it, I thought. *There is no coming back from this.*

"What will you do now, Ayo?" Dolapo, asked. "You have been in this relationship for so long, what are you going to do next?"

"Don't worry about me, Dolapo. I will be fine. God will take care of me." I tried to be the responsible older cousin who would not burden her younger one with her own problems. The next thing I knew, Rex spoke up. Apparently he had been on the other receiver in his bedroom and Dolapo had been using the one in his living room. Rex claimed that I was cocky in saying that God would look after me and that I had implied God would not look after him. All the while, the fact that I was the one paying for the telephone call had completely escaped me. I was so dazed by the revelations that were coming through. By the end of the call, I had no doubt in my mind that I wouldn't like to marry Rex.

Unfortunately, he seemed not to be able to make up his mind as to whether he wanted the relationship to end or not, continuing to ask me to confirm to him that I did not want the relationship anymore. He even told me to put it in writing, which I was happy to do.

"But that is what we have both just agreed to, that we need to go our separate ways," I reminded him.

"No, I did not agree that with you. You are the one who is trying to break this relationship up. And it is your family who have turned you against me but you just don't want to admit it. Why when you got to England did you change your mind, just like that?"

I was starting to suspect that the reason he invited my cousin over was so that she got the impression that I was the one who ended the relationship. I wondered why he was desperate to pin the blame on me. If I had been as bad a prospective wife as he usually made out, why couldn't he just say, "Ayo, you are not the woman for me, goodbye," and stick by his decision? He seemed very much a coward to me. He continued his argument until the credit on my international calling card was spent. I dropped the receiver and slumped on the sofa in Olalekan's living room. *Can my life get anymore upsetting?* I thought. *Can it get any more difficult?*

I didn't think it was appropriate for me to involve my family. All I could do was to keep living life as best as possible. I faced my job-hunting with a new determination and made new plans for my future. Rather than working to invite Rex over, I would work to save money for my master's degree. Even on that front, I wasn't having much success; application after application got turned down. I couldn't depend on Mum's generosity forever; I needed to do something. Shewa introduced me to her supervisor at C&A, the fashion retailer's Oxford Circus branch, where she worked on Saturdays and during college holidays.

"I'm sure they can give you a job. They need people for the Christmas period."

Alison, Shewa's supervisor in the young adult section on the ground floor, directed me to the third floor of the five-storey store. I was to meet Mr Brown, who would take my name and give me an application form. The shop had only started trading for the day about fifteen minutes before I arrived and was devoid of customers. I walked up the escalator and checked the floors out as I passed by; pondering what life would be like working on one of them. The sales assistants were all dressed in navy blue skirts and trousers with cream-coloured shirts. The female assistants had green waistcoats and the male ones had navy blue waistcoats to match the colour of their trousers; they looked busy tidying rails and restocking them.

"Hi, can I see Mr Brown, please?" I asked the puckish girl on the deserted third floor. She was the only person there and I seemed to have startled her with my presence. She turned round with a judder from trying on one of the shoes from the sales rack. The sales floor had an eclectic mix of women's wear. The shoes were tucked in one corner at the end of the floor, but they still managed to grab my attention on approach as I stepped off the escalator. Nearer by were winter sports collections—ski jackets, gloves, hats, and there were appealing accessories like scarves and jewellery on my right hand side.

"Who wants him?" There was a look of contempt on the girl's face as she seemed to judge from my appearance that I did not pose a threat to her risky conduct.

"Ayo Adeniola," I said, unsure if my reply carried an undertone of self-importance. Perhaps I should have explained my mission rather than stating my name.

Mr Brown came out. I wondered why he was not out there playing basketball and making big money as his slender frame towered above me. He must have been about six feet tall and that may have been a conservative estimate. He seemed approachable enough and I felt quite relaxed in his presence. He explained to me that they were only offering short-term contracts for the Christmas period and that they would review each contract at the end of that period. His offer fitted in with my aspirations. I thought, rather presumptuously, that I should find a job in surveying by the end of those three months, as long as I continued to put adequate effort into my job search.

I soon started work on the second floor of the store. I worked shift duty, morning duty mainly, and would leave home in the morning to start work at ten and finish at four-thirty in the afternoon. I tried in vain to get more hours of work.

"They tend to give the overtime to permanent staff," Shewa explained to me.

My first salary was handed to me in an envelope; if I remember correctly, the total amount after tax was about two hundred and eighty pounds. A relatively small amount of money for three weeks' work, compared to the cost of living. It was not enough to lodge in someone else's house for a month. I would need to pay at least two hundred pounds to be able to rent a room; that would be before I bought my monthly travel card, which at the time was about thirty-six pounds, and contributed towards electricity and gas bills . . . and then buy food to eat and clothes befitting the English weather to wear. How much would I have left to save for my college fees? It was depressing but I was thankful to God for the gift of a relative who would put me up for nothing, other than whatever I could afford to contribute towards the upkeep of the house.

16

HURTS . . . AND MORE HURT

While I got to grips with my new life in London, Rex was busy doing the rounds with extended family members and the church members that he knew, telling them about our relationship breakup and his own heartbreak. He told his family members as well as mine.

He called me one evening and asked me to call him back. He explained that his sister, who was older than him by about six years and lived in New York, was in Nigeria for holiday and that she would like to speak to me. I went out to the newsagent by the tube station and bought a calling card. When I spoke to his sister, she sounded as much of a bully as her younger brother. The woman had never met me before and she seemed to be so upset by her brother's heartbreak that she almost didn't give me a chance to speak. As she talked to me on the phone that evening, I was somewhat overwhelmed by the fury that came through in her voice.

"What is all this that I hear? What is happening here? Hun? Ayo. Please resolve this because in our family, we hold you in such high regard and we would be glad to have you as a member of our family. In fact we have been so much looking forward to it . . ."

When I was eventually able to respond, I said to her:

"Aunty, I appreciate your concern but Rex and I need to resolve this on our own. I wouldn't like even my mother to get involved."

I could feel my voice shaking by reason of my fear of her intimidating approach as well as the upset that I felt at being treated in such a manner.

"Okay, if you say so, I will keep out and I will look forward to you resolving it, because we think much more of you than all this."

Could I feel any more bullied into marrying a man I had started to fear? "No," was the answer I gave myself. I then determined that not Rex nor any member of his family would intimidate me. By the time I finished speaking to his sister, the five pounds credit on the card that I was using had run out. I went out to buy another one for ten pounds and called Rex back.

"What is that with your sister? Why was she talking like that as if it was my fault that we broke up? Was that what you told her?"

"I didn't tell her anything," was his reply. "She was only speaking out of her own concern for us. Ayo, let's put all these behind us and get our relationship on track again."

I felt patronised.

"So you mean we should just sweep everything that has happened under the carpet and pretend none of it ever happened? Rex, you cannot build a house on a faulty foundation. If you do that the house will collapse. You need to repair your bad foundation before you continue building the rest of the house."

He sounded rather smug that evening and the whole conversation left even me confused as to the status of the relationship that I had previously believed was over.

My extended family and church members that Rex went to see took a different approach. They didn't speak to me personally, but they alerted Mum to the fact that there were problems between the two of us. I didn't understand how the communication dynamics worked between Mum and the friends and family in Nigeria, but it seemed every time Mum spoke to someone, she became desperate for my comfort and backup. It appeared to me that people back in Nigeria blamed Mum for the relationship ending and it was not difficult to see why they would have done so.

Mum became anxious. She was eager for me to rescue her reputation, which appeared to be in tatters. Seeing Mum in such distress wasn't pleasing, even though I was tempted to think she had brought it on herself. I went to Ibidun's flat to listen to Mum and to help her reach a place of peace over the whole situation. It took two hours for my mother to make a point. She kept beating about the bush and I was constantly trying to bring her back to the topic at hand.

Eventually, I realised Mum was the one making matters worse for herself. She had received one message to phone Aunty Dunmola who had informed her something was going wrong in my relationship. I figured out Aunty Dunmola might have insinuated Mum was to blame for Rex and I breaking up. I could only speculate on what may or may not have happened, as Mum was never clear on what was said and what she was worried about. Aunty Dunmola also seemed to have passed on a request from Pastor Stan for Mum to call him. It seemed to me that Mum then took it upon herself to call not only Pastor Stan, who had requested the telephone conversation, but every other person that Rex had been to as well.

"How did you know what Sister Kemi said, did you call her?" I asked Mum, trying to understand the situation better. By the time Mum had finished giving me her answer, I had almost forgotten what my question was and I certainly didn't get an effective answer to the question I asked. I still was none the wiser as to how the views expressed by Sister Kemi from church in Nigeria were conveyed to Mum.

I was bored and started to twiddle my fingers as I sat next to Mum on the edge of her bed; we had left the living room in order to have some privacy to talk. The fact that we had left Ibidun on her own in the living room without as much as a polite excuse to her also bothered me and increased my unease; there had been no subtleness in Mum's demand when she insisted we went into the bedroom to talk.

"Shut the door," she had ordered, after we entered.

Overall, in all her talking, what seemed clear was that Mum was desperate to stop what appeared to be rumour mongering. She was also eager to set the record straight (whatever the record was). But it appeared to me that the more she tried to convince people of her innocence, the more they were convinced of her guilt. This caused her even more frustration and the only person she seemed to believe could save her from it all was me. That belief, however, posed a rather unsolvable problem.

Mum had asked me to phone Pastor Stan, at his request, and I had done so. He asked for an explanation, but the more I tried to explain to him what had led to the relationship hitting the rocks, the less he believed me. I was the one spending money on international calls trying to clarify the situation with him. I did not see any point in wasting any more money calling people who had made up their minds one way.

Apart from that, Mum didn't seem to care how all her various discussions with people in Nigeria might affect me—the subject of everyone else's conversation. My heart was broken; it was as if my life was falling apart and all that my mother cared about was her reputation. Not once did she ask me how I felt or offered me any kind of comfort. Calling other people who were not prepared to be objective would only make matters worse and hurt my already broken heart more.

There was always news of someone else that Rex had gone to talk to—my uncle in Ife, my uncle in Lagos, another member of my church. The list just seemed endless.

"What? Why is he going about with all these tales?" I almost shouted at Mum when she called to give me the latest news.

My biggest fear was that he might eventually land his trouble at Granddad's door.

"Why is he going about? Where will he end up, at my grandfather's house?" I said to his brother's wife, whose husband was not at home at the time of my call.

"Please, I do not want him going to Granddad. The man is old and he does not need this. Rex is old enough to sort his own relationship out, why does he need to go to all these people, why can't he be a man and face his own issues?"

News came—Rex had been to Granddad.

It felt as if the worst had happened. Rex had preyed on my fear. I never thought he would be so spiteful. Mum told me one of my aunties had encouraged him to ask Granddad for help. As I heard, Aunty Sade had told him it was the only other solution she could think of. How about asking Rex how he thought he might have contributed to the problems? Perhaps if he tried to make right his own wrongs there would be a few less wrongs to deal with?

Notwithstanding what I might be feeling or how I was coping, all Mum wanted to do was talk about what she was experiencing and how she could get out of it. It would have been fine if talking resolved some of her issues. But talking about it was always a repeat of the last time—me listening for one to two hours as Mum skirted around points she was uncomfortable addressing. I thought I'd put her mind at rest and give her my perspective.

"Mum, I think you need to know that I don't blame you for the breakup. You didn't even know it happened. If Rex and I had approached our issues maturely enough, we would have resolved them."

No matter how often I tried to reassure Mum, my words just didn't seem to scratch the surface of the sticky situation she seemed to believe she was in, which I really couldn't comprehend. One afternoon, on my day off, I had gone grocery shopping and was filling the shelves when Mum phoned.

"I'm calling a family meeting on Sunday, so I need you to be there," she said.

"What is the meeting about?" I asked her.

"Just be there and you will know what it is about!"

"It would help us to prepare for the meeting if we know what you want to discuss."

"Do I not have a right to call my own children for a meeting? What are all these questions about? Let me tell you one thing, you have changed. You need to know you have changed!"

I thought, *Good heavens! Who has she been talking to? Someone must have told her what they thought of me and she's now repeating what was said.*

"Have you spoken to anyone in Nigeria lately?"

"What has that got to do with anything? You just come to the meeting and if you don't want to, don't come."

She hung up the phone and left me wondering what was wrong with asking her what she wanted to talk about. A couple of hours later, Olalekan was back from work. I came out of my room as soon as I heard the front door opening and waited on the landing as he climbed up the stairs.

"Hiya, how was your day?"

"Err, fine, thanks." I think he sussed out something was up. I relayed Mum's message.

"What does she want to discuss?" he replied.

"I don't know."

"Did you not ask her what it is about?"

"I did, but she wouldn't say."

That evening, I unburdened on Olalekan a little. I explained how Mum's attitude was getting me down. He went into his room and brought out a copy of a daily devotional.

"Here, you need to read that."

He advised that I needed to get peace within me and not let things happening outside of me affect my inner peace. What pearls of wisdom from my older brother's lips!

When we got to the meeting at Ibidun's flat, Mum explained that she would make some food for us to eat after the meeting; I knew that would be some late-night supper. Mum then kicked the meeting off with some long-winded introduction about what a family should be like.

"Uh, when Olalekan gets married, his wife should be friends with all of you, same with you, Ibidun, your husband should be . . ."

Olalekan himself was rather angry and agitated. He got impatient with Mum as she carried on and took over the meeting. He told Mum in such a firm way that I'd never seen of him before that she needed to show us some more respect.

"Mum, why couldn't you say what this was about? It is not that we have ever had a family meeting before."

Mum insisted she was always very respectful towards all of us. Ibidun was keen to talk about Rex and me, but I decided

I didn't want them dragging my affairs into a meeting. She persisted.

"My own concern was that we had to hear from outside sources that something was going wrong and that is not right."

I thought of giving her a somewhat sarcastic but angry reply that when the inside source wrote them letters saying something was going right, what good did they do with the information? And what did she think qualified them to hear from that same inside source that something was going wrong? I thought it would be good to take her back to my letter of a few years earlier that they never responded to, but I had a second thought and managed to temporarily stir her away from the subject. Apparently the discussion about my failed relationship with Rex was the reason Mum called the meeting in the first place, but Mum's goal was now lost as she darted around the topic.

It didn't take long for Ibidun to return to the subject of Rex. She continued on a rather offensive path.

"What I don't get is this—why did you introduce him to your family when you didn't know what you were doing?"

In other words, I disrespected myself and my family by introducing to them a man who I end up not marrying. My head was whirling at this point. I needed to shut this woman up. She doesn't even know what she is talking about!

"Whoa, whoa, whoa, hold it there! Don't you ever, ever, say that to me again!"

If I had said anymore than that, I would have hurt her.

Olalekan eventually wrapped the meeting up and we left carrying our late supper with us. The meeting, clearly, didn't help anyone, least of all Mum. Days later, she was still in a fix. I did not understand the depths of how she continued to be caught up with the problems between me and Rex. Then, two weeks after the meeting, as I spoke to Rex on the telephone—a call I had made at his request—he had one of his aggressive outbursts.

"I know you and your mother are not capable of inviting me to London for April next year."

I wondered where the April date sprang from as I had not discussed any particular timing with him. Then it dawned on me that Mum must have been making telephone calls to Rex without my knowledge. She had probably promised him that she was going to sort it all out and he would be invited to England to start the Ph.D. he wanted to do, maybe in an attempt to prevent him involving more people than he already had. It occurred to me that it must have been during her conversation with him that Rex told her I had changed and that this change was the cause of the problems we were having. I went to see Mum a day later and confronted her with my suspicion; she could not deny it. She said her telephone call to Rex happened just the once.

"Mum, even if it was half a time, it is not right for you to be phoning my fiancé, or in this case my (mostly) ex-fiancé, without my knowledge and permission."

She looked unbothered about my stance. Mum always believed she knew better. I got tired of her requests to "talk" and I started to refuse them. Each time she called me to come and talk about "it" and I refused, she would start a new round of trouble. My not rescuing her sparked new level of hostility from my mother towards me. Mum would call Olalekan to make some random false accusations about me. The way she tried to play on my intelligence hurt just as much as the accusations.

"Ayo, please come round and plait my hair for me tomorrow after church," Mum requested one Saturday evening.

When I got there her hair was already plaited.

"What happened, Mum?"

I asked her why she did not phone to let me know I was no longer needed. I could have got on with my preparation for work.

She replied with a grin that she did not need her hair doing, she only wanted to talk.

"What about, why couldn't you simply ask to talk?"

"I knew you would not come if I did. I wanted to talk to you about all this that is happening."

I was angry at being made a fool of and being dragged away from more productive things I could have been doing. But, despite my anger, it was clear to me that Mum was still troubled, so I decided to sit down and listen to what she had to say. She went on beating about the bush as usual. I had had enough, so I left.

I went to work the next day and on my return, as I walked through the front door, I heard Olalekan talking on the phone. He was upstairs and I could hear his footsteps on the carpeted floor as he walked past my room down to the landing.

"I think she's the one coming in now," I heard him say.

He told me it was Mum on the phone and that she wanted to speak to me. Had I a hunch what was going to happen afterwards, I would have found every possible excuse not to take the call—perhaps a quick dash to the toilet, or a rush back out of the house before he could call me back, whatever! I took the phone from Olalekan and Mum asked me where the key to the apartment in Nigeria was. I couldn't remember; it had been about four months since I left and this was the first time she'd asked me anything about the apartment. I knew the key would be with either Aunty Dunmola or Yetunde. I knew for certain I had not brought it with me to England. I explained this to Mum. She descended into self-pity and a rant about how I never cared about her or her properties. She asked to speak to Olalekan. After speaking to Mum, Olalekan called out to me and asked what had happened to the key. I explained.

"Why didn't you just tell her that?"

"I did."

He spoke to Mum some more and then he let his verbal outrage fly. The fact that his mother was upset appeared to have been more important than what was right. He went on about how Mum had worked so hard and me, an ungrateful child, had been treating her with contempt and causing her grief, not caring about the things she had worked so hard for. His words pierced my spirit like several sharp knives. They flew off his tongue and travelled in hot pursuit over the staircase to cut the deepest part of me. Olalekan told me how stupid, how foolish I was, how I cared about no one else but myself, how in my foolishness I had landed myself in a mess and caused problems for everyone else in the family. I couldn't take it all lying down. I stood up to him and fought in my defence but found myself weeping. It did not deter me, I had to reply.

"Who was there looking after the apartment and the building project in Nigeria? Where were you when Mum needed a new place to live and I was walking all around Omole Estate, in the scorching sun, helping her look for somewhere else for us to live? Where were you then, eh, where were you?"

I had sacrificed so much for this woman and the whole family; why then should I be subjected to such abuse? I wondered why he took leave of all level of reasoning just because his mother was upset.

I became a pariah as far as my family was concerned. Mum marched a brigade of hate and disgust against me; I couldn't understand why Olalekan (and Yetunde too) allowed her to use them against me. I had to accept it was their choice as much as it was Mum's desire.

My head, not just my soul, was downcast. I had no one to turn to. I did not know how life was going to pan out for me. The career I came to London to establish seemed out of reach. In difficult times, relationships should be a comfort, but I had none. I knew I had to be strong for myself, resist all temptation to descend into self-pity, focus and work hard to make life better, but despite my best effort life was just one long black tunnel. Each day was the same. I woke up with sadness in my heart. The freshness of a new day brought short-lived hope. I managed to drag myself out of bed each time and go to my customer services job, which had turned from a temporary job to a permanent one with all the hours I could toil.

Even at work, I couldn't get away from the burden of my despair. A depth of misery followed me everywhere. My reprise was each minute I was engaged in active customer service; at least for that moment, I was bearing someone else's burden, yokes which were extremely easy to bear compared to mine.

It was in the midst of this despondency that I received a letter from Dr Olumide at the end of January 1998. It was such a comfort to know he still cared enough to write to me. He wrote:

> *"I heard the stories about your fall out with Rex. Ayo, it pains my heart that you have to go through such pain as this. You are almost like a daughter to me and I care about you very much."*

Tears rapidly filled my eyes and the letter I was reading received the drops. I wanted to reply to Dr Olumide's letter but I was short of words. I was so stupefied by my own life experience that I couldn't find the words to express myself. I picked up my pen and writing pad . . . *how do I start?* I thought to myself. *Tell him everything—Rex's unreasonable behaviour? Take the opportunity to defend myself? Or just tell him about the constant rain in England?* I thought the incessant rain might be a safer topic. I was tired, weary from the battle with Rex, I couldn't stomach another round of fight with him; he'd been cruel and my heart couldn't take any more cruelty. In any case, who would believe me, the people back in Nigeria had chosen what they wanted to believe; would my defence make any difference?

I started the letter; I wrote what I could remember of the weather pattern, I couldn't even do that well enough. I couldn't remember what the weather that week had been because I had been living each day absent-mindedly. I read the few paragraphs I wrote and they sounded patronising towards someone who had expressed his fondness of me with such heaviness of heart. I tore up the letter and decided to take up his offer to listen to me if I needed to talk. He had told me in his letter that their home phone was out of service and if I wanted to speak to him I should call Sister Kemi and Brother Darius' house and leave a message for him to be there at a particular time and he would be there to take my call.

I spoke to Dr Olumide and apparently the story Rex had told them was that I had turned round, on getting to London, and said I was no longer interested in him. Hearing Dr Olumide's voice, his affirming words, brought some comfort to me, even if it didn't end my troubles; the crises of my life still continued to weigh heavily on my mind. I walked the roads of Tooting Broadway on autopilot. My gratitude to God many times was not getting knocked down by a vehicle. There was too much going on—coping was becoming increasingly challenging.

One day in the thick of it all, I walked out of the house in the morning, having forgotten to put my trousers on. It was a dry, chilly and windy winter morning with temperatures nearing zero.

I had put my tights on and all of my other items of clothing, including my knee-length coat. I stepped out of the house and made my way up the road towards the station. As I shut the door behind me, it occurred to me that my legs felt cold. Not being able to think of anything that might be out of place, I continued walking. I had barely walked twenty yards when I felt a strong cold breeze brush up my legs underneath my coat. I looked down, realised what was missing and rushed back into the house.

Shewa remembered the story for months after I told her. She couldn't stop laughing. I hadn't found it so funny myself but her hysterical laughter was contagious. I caught the bug. It was the one good thing that came out of it, as I had forgotten how to laugh by then.

It must have been about two weeks after I walked out of the house half-dressed when Olalekan and I went to visit Mum one Sunday evening, as we usually did. Ibidun ushered us in and I could hear Mum on the telephone having a rather loud conversation. *A topic close to her heart,* I thought, as we took turns for light embraces with Ibidun.

As I walked through into the living room, I smelt the lingering aroma of cooked food and it brought to my attention how much the years of cooking in the kitchen had taken its toll on the flat, which didn't have the indulgence of the all-year-round cross ventilation that homes back in Nigeria had. Its windows were kept firmly shut during the winter months. The smell stained the air like smoke on a wall. *That would be Mum's handiwork*, I thought. Mum, like many of her Nigerian contemporaries, was a staunch believer in cooking and eating at home, none of that nonsense about eating out, as she called it.

"You cook good and healthy food for yourself and your family," she said. "You could buy the odd KFC but at least most of the food you eat should be home cooked." Mum definitely did make her views known when she considered she needed to.

Mum beckoned us to sit down and she continued her conversation. I sat on an armchair next to the study table and the chair on which she sat; Olalekan sank into the sofa right opposite me and Ibidun perched on the arm of the sofa next to him. We all seemed to be giving Mum some space to conclude her telephone conversation. I could tell she was talking to Yetunde and the topic of their conversation soon became clear:

"It is Rex doing that . . . huh uh, yes," I heard Mum say.

I was surprised to realise their conversation was about me. Perhaps she would tell Yetunde I was there and include me in the discussion. I waited a while but Mum continued.

"Is that Yetunde you are talking to?" I asked Mum.

She nodded and continued her discussion, quite loudly. I couldn't take it anymore, I had to say something.

"Mum, if Yetunde wants to talk about me, she is free to talk to me, please don't talk about me in my presence as if I am not here. Bring the receiver and I'll talk to her."

Mum quickly took the receiver away from her ear and held it far out on the other side.

"I don't think Yetunde wants to talk to you."

"Well, if she does not want to talk to me then don't talk about me in my presence."

"Yetunde, Yetunde, do you want to talk to her? She said she wants to talk to you . . . Yetunde said she doesn't want to talk to you."

"I am not interested in talking to her either, but you need to find something else to talk about."

I am not sure there is anything quite as disrespectful of the other person as talking about them in their presence as though they were dead to the world. Mum eventually wrapped her conversation up and turned her attention to us her guests.

I knew I was a pretty strong person; it is one of the traits I inherited from Mum. I knew life was grim at that point in time. I also knew I was experiencing an unusual level of difficulty (even by the standards of what we had been through in my childhood). But I really did hope things would start to get better at some point. I hoped that Mum would tire of her hurtful ways and desist from them. Was I mistaken? Yes, it turned out I was wrong in my optimistic view of life with my family. In fact, it seemed Mum was only just getting started in her difficult disposition towards me.

17

Hence, I depart

I woke up one morning; the clock on the bedside table next to me indicated a quarter to seven. I had worked late the night before and slept late. Getting up to go to work wasn't quite what I would have preferred to do but I was due to start work at ten.

I could hear the phone ringing, and wondered who on earth phoned someone else's house before seven in the morning on a work day. There was a knock on my bedroom door; it was Olalekan. He held the phone out to me.

"It's Mum for you," he said.

Mum calling me first thing in the morning did not sound good.

"Hello Mum."

"Hello Ayo, your Aunty Tinu travelled to Ibadan to tell your Aunty Margaret what has been happening between you and Rex."

"What did Aunty Margaret say?"

"She phoned me to ask about it and I told her it was being resolved."

"Well, that's the end of it, isn't it?"

"No, not really, you need to come and we need to discuss this because I don't know about all this tale bearing."

"Mum, we can discuss it until we are blue in the face; it will not stop Aunty Tinu from telling whomever she thinks needs to know. If you don't want Aunty Tinu talking about it, tell her you don't want her discussing it with anyone anymore."

"You are always too full of yourself behaving as if you know best, before long everybody will hear there is a problem. I can't be phoning Tinu."

"What is it with you Mum, why are you always stirring trouble, calling me at the crack of dawn?"

Mum broke down in tears. My heart broke; I still couldn't bear Mum crying.

"My God will save me from you, all these years I have suffered and you treat me like this, just because you are desperate to get married . . ."

Mum's tone of voice turned from self-pity to indignation.

". . . honest, Ayo, you go on into that marriage, you go ahead . . . !"

"Mother, why does it always have to come down to whether I get married or not, why is it always that with you?"

I felt like trouncing Mum's negative attitude into complete obliteration.

"You know what, Mother? I will get married, yes, I will be married and God will be my joy and protector in that marriage."

"Ah, my God knows I never told you not to get married." There was a fresh outburst of weeping and I backed down.

"Okay, if you can't talk to Aunty Tinu, I will talk to her; I'll come straight to your house from work, phone her in front of you and tell her to mind her own business."

Mum seemed satisfied. She was calm. I ended the conversation and went downstairs to get ready for work. It seemed everyone had conspired against me. They all seemed determined to ensure peace of mind eluded me. I wondered why Aunty Tinu couldn't mind her own business and leave me to mine.

Towards the end of summer, Olalekan moved from his Victorian terraced house in Tooting to South Norwood in search of convenient off-street parking, which seemed to have become scarce in the Tooting area. Knowing he was moving, I started to think about my own need for accommodation. It seemed a perfect time to part ways with him and find my own home where I would be in control of my life, but Mum would not hear of it. She begged and badgered me into moving to Norwood with Olalekan.

"We need to stick together as a family, be united, eh. If you move out, that is not unity."

To tell the truth, I was still struggling to find a better paying job and worried how I could afford a decent place and also save for college on my modest wage. I eventually agreed to move home with Olalekan.

His new home was another terraced building, which had recently been refurbished with brand new, state of the art appliances and the parking spaces that he wanted: right in front of the house was a driveway for two cars. The change of location, however, did not have any positive effect on our relationship; hardly any friendliness now existed between us.

Whilst growing up, I had always blamed others each time I had a falling out with him because, back then, when he had beaten me, it was in defence of either Ibidun or Mum. But I couldn't blame Mum for his attitude any longer. He was responsible for his actions, notwithstanding what Mum might have said to win his sympathy. I knew deep within me that I had to move out of his house and start to cut the apron strings.

My wages had increased slightly but the fear of my financial survival was still there, and in particular, my need to save for my master's degree. God, however, spoke clearly to me that living with him was like confining myself within a shoe box.

It was another Sunday evening in early November, two months after I moved with Olalekan into his new home, when I made that final decision to move out. He had come back from visiting Mum and had lashed out because Mum had told him I was making negative comparisons between her and another woman.

Earlier that evening, before Olalekan's visit to Mum, she had called and asked me to come to see her so that we could talk to Dr Olumide together. I was in my room, styling my hair in preparation for work the next day when Olalekan handed me the phone. I propped it up with my shoulder.

"Ayo, please, I need you to come and plait my hair this evening," she said.

I wasn't falling for that trick this time! I told her I couldn't come that weekend and if she didn't mind I would come during the next weekend. Deep down inside, I knew something was fishy about the request, even though I couldn't tell what it was. As it would happen, Mum let slip that she had spoken to Dr Olumide two days before. She suddenly realised her error and she stopped abruptly mid sentence—Mum knew I had caught her out. She then owned up to the fact that she really wanted me to come so we could phone Dr Olumide and speak to him together. I declined still. Mum went quiet. I could feel the coldness of her silence and within that silence I could sense her disappointment and disapproval of my stance.

Olalekan prepared for his weekly Sunday visit and asked if I wanted to come along. I excused myself and he left. I was preparing to retire to bed when he came back. I said goodnight and was about to go upstairs.

"Yes, come here. What is this about you comparing Mum to Mrs Obatunde?"

I was a bit confused.

"What? I haven't seen Mum for two weeks."

"Yes, she said it was the last time you were there."

"Well, I didn't."

My claim of innocence did nothing to save me from another round of verbal abuse from my older brother. He yelled at me and called me an ingrate. It was being labelled a thankless wretch that got to me this time. Weeping was not far off, tears rapidly filled my eyes. He had brought some food from Mum. Mum would cook soups, fried rice and meat stew for us. She would pack enough to last us for a week in plastic containers. The truth was, Olalekan threw most of the food away when he did not fancy eating or when he was too busy to eat at home. Because of this, I would try and encourage Mum not to cook as much food, that we could cook for ourselves when we needed to, but that turned me into the number one enemy.

When he called me an ingrate, Olalekan marched from the dining room, where we had been standing, through the wide archway into the kitchen. He pointed to the food, which he had unloaded onto the work surface, and described how I would bring my stupid big mouth and eat out of the food that mother had laboured to cook.

"You have the audacity to compare her to another woman after she had worked so hard to provide for you."

He continued with his usual tirade of how much of a foolish person I was and how I had got myself into a mess and got everyone else into trouble. I was never clear who "everyone" was and how that "everyone" had got into trouble on account of my foolishness. I could only imagine that the mess he was referring to that I got myself in was my relationship with Rex and how Rex was going from person to person trying to sell his story to them for sympathy and the embarrassment of it all.

The irony was, it was Olalekan that had compared Mum to the woman in question. It seemed Mum had run out of things to accuse me of, so she grabbed someone else's offence and labelled it mine.

A couple of weeks before her accusation, I had bought some outfits for Mum. I wasn't too sure what her size was and mistakenly bought them a size too big. When I took the outfits to her, Olalekan and Ibidun were there. Mum tried them on and was extremely grateful for the gift. I was proud of Mum for her gratitude and when I realised the clothes were too big, I offered to exchange them for smaller sizes, but as they were in the sale, Mum might have to take something different if the shop had run out of those particular styles or the required size.

"No, don't worry. I like it; you don't have to change it. I am going to study days this week, I can wear them to college."

I couldn't bear to think of Mum wearing the outfits within her home, much less wearing them to study days. I tried to encourage her to let me change them. Ibidun too joined me in trying to convince Mum. When Olalekan stepped in, he used this particular woman, who was a family friend, as benchmark for a fashionable look. He asked Mum what she would think if she saw *Mama Bola* wearing an outfit like that.

The expression on Mum's face showed she was taken aback by the comparison and she felt hurt by it, but she tried to hide her feelings and insisted the outfits were fine. No one likes to see their Mother humiliated, we only deal with it differently; Ibidun made a point of saying she was not interested in comparing her mother to someone else, that she only wanted what was good for her, which I emphatically and loudly agreed to. So, two weeks later, it came as a surprise that I was the one being accused of comparing Mum to the woman in question.

That night of the altercation, I made up my mind to leave Olalekan's house. As I got in his car the next morning, getting a lift from him to the train station, I knew it was my perfect opportunity to break the ties.

"I just want to say thank you for putting me up this past one year. I am very grateful. However, it is time for me to move on, so I will be looking for somewhere else to live."

"Well, good luck to you."

His good luck sounded more sarcastic than wishful.

All throughout that day at work, my mind wandered many times to Mum's accusation. I felt hurt because I knew how comparison could be damaging and I came close to tears at various points during the day. Mum did a lot of comparison when we were growing up—every other child seemed to have been smarter in one area of life or the other than me. I, it seemed, was not smart enough in every aspect of my life.

I was meeting Julie, from church, at Clapham Junction after work. We were going to prepare for a job interview together. I was still so upset by the whole argument that I met Julie in tears. She was kind; she comforted me like a child.

I felt compelled to accept responsibility to make things better for Mum. More importantly, I wanted to ensure I was not in any way implicated in damaging someone else's self-esteem in this way. It is not that I had never been guilty of making hurtful comparisons of other people; I remembered comparing Yetunde to her peers when we were growing up. It was my quest for her to be the perfect little sister that I had desired her to be, but I realised the folly of it soon enough.

I called Mum from a phone box while Julie looked on. I apologised to Mum that she felt I had compared her to Mrs Obatunde. I, however, knew that I needed to make the truth clear, so I told Mum that she should know I never compared her, never have done and never will compare her to anyone else, because I knew the damage that comparison can cause. Mum sounded smug on the phone, satisfied she had made me apologetic. Yet I had achieved my purpose; I needed to kill the comparison thing because it had done so much harm to me. I was never enough for the man I had broken from, who had spent a lot of time comparing me to other women, including his former girlfriends. I was not going to let comparison in my life in any way anymore.

I got back from work later that evening and prayed that God would open the door and provide me with a home. A week after that, I found a nice home. I walked through the front door of the Edwardian terrace house on a long street near Tooting train station; it was a world of difference to Olalekan's squeaky clean and up to date house. As Ibukun, the young lady who owned the house took me round, I knew I was going to move in there. It was a spacious three-bedroom house, generally tidy, albeit with dated fixtures and decoration but it was good enough for me. God has a unique sense of humour and He throws it into all aspects of His intervention in life. I went for a church meeting immediately after my viewing. There was a guest speaker at the meeting, Penny, the wife of one of the leaders from the main church in Drayton. She decided she would pray for each person in attendance and when she got to me, she paused and asked me where I was living. I told her I lived in South Norwood.

"No . . . no . . . no," Penny said with a bit of agitation. She explained she meant who I was living with. "Is it a man?" she asked, with a suspicious look on her face.

God had apparently shown her I was living with a man and she seemed to have thought it might be a boyfriend! I explained the situation and she confirmed to me what God was already saying—that I needed to move out. That was that resolved, no going back! I was out of Olalekan's house in a week.

Mum, seeing that I was determined to cut the apron strings, didn't seem too receptive to the idea. Although she did not express any opposition to it, I noticed she distanced herself from me. Without asking for Mum's help, she told me she and Ibidun would have offered to help me pack but she did not want Olalekan to feel offended. She did not want him to think they were in support of me moving out of his house. I felt hurt by her excuse. Would it be too much for Olalekan to bear if my mother offered to help me when I needed help? In any case we did not even know he felt bad about me moving out. He probably felt relief that he would have his house to himself again!

18

A CHANCE FOR PEACE

Olalekan helped me move my things to my new home. I was going to be sharing it with a guy named Jide and with Ibukun. Sharing a house seemed to be the norm for singles in England, especially when you are of limited financial means. In any case I didn't want to live in a flat all on my own; I always wanted people around me. There was a very friendly atmosphere in Ibukun's house and this made all the difference to me. Jide looked pleased to be having a new housemate; he welcomed me with a broad smile and a cheerful look and I knew right from then that I was going to be happy living there.

The first night I slept in my new home, I woke up the following morning feeling free. I lay still on my bed and turned my head to the left and then to the right. I noticed there was peace and quiet around me, but the greater peace that I felt was inside of me—all my fears had disappeared. I did not have to worry about anything I might have done to get on Olalekan or Mum's wrong side. It was just me and a peaceful existence on my comfy bed, in my cosy bedroom.

Once I settled in, Olalekan dropped by to visit on his way home from work one evening. I gave him a tour of the house. He did a little inspection of my room and asked where a stain that had been on the wall had gone. He had seen it the day I moved in. Typically, you could always trust him to notice every speck of imperfection.

"I've got some baguettes in the car, do you want some?" he asked.

It seemed extraordinary enough that he dropped by for a visit. The offer of a baguette blew my mind. I seemed to be receiving a new level of respect from my brother. It had got to the stage while I lived with him that I would see Olalekan on the tube or in a shop on the way home and he would pretend he did not know me. If I greeted him in my excitement he would react as if a stranger had said hello. Now, he's visited and even made me an offer of a baguette. *How nice*, I thought.

"I can bring you the small TV in my room; you could do with one in your bedroom," Olalekan offered.

All my Christmases seemed to have come together on this one evening. Life seemed to have started to work so much better with me and my brother keeping a little distance between us. But those happy moments weren't for long; with my mother involved, life was always going to be a seesaw—up one minute, down the next.

The following Sunday, only a few days after Olalekan's visit, I woke up to another peaceful morning and as I savoured the quietness in my spirit, the phone rang. I looked at the time, it was eight o'clock.

"Hello Ayo."

It was Mum. She was phoning me this time to tell me Yetunde had gone to Osu to visit Dolapo, our cousin who worked in the only bank in the town. Rex visited the same bank, saw Yetunde there and invited her back to his parents' house. He wanted Yetunde to say hello to them.

Just when I thought I finally had peace!

"Why would Yetunde want to do such a thing? Was it to spite me? You know what, Mum, when things were good between Rex and I, Yetunde used to make a conscious effort to avoid Rex's mother when she visited Aunty Dunmola's house with her son. Why now that we have parted in such an acrimonious way, would she consider it was appropriate for her to visit them?"

"That is not even what I care about," Mum replied. "She said they served her some food and I don't want anybody poisoning my daughter."

Oh no!

"Well then, Mother, you need to tell your daughter not to accept food from strangers and tell her not to accept invitations from Rex or his family."

All the fears and worries that had left me in the past few weeks rushed back. I remembered the cow brain I had eaten in Rex's parent's house and everything that happened to me afterwards, some of which I was still battling with even then, a good three years later. I remembered how Olalekan had told me repeatedly that I was to blame for all the distress Rex's actions were causing the family. If anything happened to Yetunde, whether it was my fault or not, I would get blamed.

I went to Ibidun's flat later in the day so that I could have a witness when I spoke to Yetunde on the phone. I knew if Ibidun witnessed what would happen, her changed self would want to do the right thing and speak the truth. When I got there, both Ibidun and Mum had just finished lunch and were tidying up. I waited until Ibidun was seated in the living room before I picked up the phone to call Yetunde. Mum too came in from the kitchen and sat on the armchair opposite me. As the phone was ringing at the other end of the line, I was trying my best to be composed and attempt a civil resolution.

Mum suddenly stood up from her chair, she paced a little and finally stood in the middle of the room.

Yetunde picked the phone.

"Hello Yetunde."

"What is the problem?" she answered.

"Yetunde, it's me, Ayo."

"Yes, what's your problem?"

I paused for a second or two.

"Okay, my problem is, Mum said Rex invited you to his parent's house and you went to say hello to them."

"I didn't go to his house; it was Dolapo I went to see. He was the one who asked me to come to his house."

"Well, Yetunde, if you decide you have to strike a familiarity with him, there is nothing I can do about that. However, know this—whatever comes out of your friendship with him will be your sole responsibility, not mine."

She kept repeating, "It was Dolapo I went to see. He was the one who asked me to come to his house . . ."

She was the rudest I had ever known her to be. Even my own sister now resented me so much that she couldn't stand hearing my voice. Mum was angry. She accused me of bullying Yetunde. Mum's voice was breaking as she spoke. It was as if she was about to cry because she felt hurt for Yetunde.

Why can't my mother have similar motherly feelings for me? I wondered to myself. I wanted Mum to understand why I felt betrayed by my younger sister, but she looked angry and belligerent. I turned to my older sister for comfort.

"Do you understand what I am trying to say?" I asked with self-pity in my voice. "If she had been a very friendly person towards them at the time when we had a good relationship, it would have been a different story, but she was not!"

Ibidun looked at me with what seemed like empathy and I continued my argument to her, feeding off her evident compassion for me. I glanced at Mum, who by then had gone to sit on the sofa, to see if she was now on my side. Outlandishly Mum began to curse me! Apparently she had thought I had cursed her first.

Anger rose within me. I looked at Mum and what I saw was ugliness.

My head felt light. I couldn't feel the rest of my body. I was completely devoid of my natural senses. The brute in me arose, ready to waste its prey. I was set to tear Mum's "ugly" face into pieces, my claws in formation of that of a predator.

I couldn't see my mother in the woman that was sitting in front of me.

No! She is not my mother!

"You are ugly and I feel like tearing your face apart!" I shouted at Mum as I trembled with rage.

I couldn't hear any reply from her but, in the distance, from my seeming out-of-body experience, I saw Mum pull away as I lunged towards her. She receded further into the sofa as if trying to escape. At that moment, something snapped inside me and I came back to my senses and retreated. But with every scrap of energy I could muster, I disowned her to her face.

"You are not my mother," I told her and walked out of the flat.

When I got home the realisation of my actions hit me. I wondered how I had become so angry and where the anger had come from. I became afraid of myself, the feelings of wildness that rose up in me and the violent anger I had felt, whether I acted on it or not. I fell on my knees and asked God for help.

Help came, barely two hours later, in the form of Pastor Matthew Ashimolowo who was preaching on Premier Radio about family life. I picked up the phone straightaway and called his church office. I got an answering machine. The next day I phoned again and insisted I wanted to speak to Pastor Matthew. The lady at the other end of the line, in a kind and empathetic tone, explained to me that Pastor Matthew's diary was usually full for more than six months in advance. She gently persuaded me to make an appointment to see one of the other pastors. I reluctantly accepted the next appointment she had, which was about two weeks later.

Christmas was fast approaching and I was starting to fear it was going to be a lonely time because of the strained relationship with my family. I had a feeling it would not be a good idea to spend Christmas with them. A couple of weeks later and Christmas cards started to flow in from work colleagues. The sheer number of cards I received ignited the hope of a bright Christmas within me. It felt as though I had never been given personal Christmas cards before.

Olalekan called to give me a message from Tade, my friend from university in Ife who now lived in France. She wanted me to call her back. Tade was planning to come to London and would like to stay with me. She would be getting married in March the following year, so she wanted to do some shopping for her wedding. Tade managed to get a visa and flew in with her friend Sola. They arrived on a Thursday, two days before Christmas. I picked her up from Sola's brother's house, where I met him, his wife, Sister Lydia, and their two children, Charlotte and Samson. Sister Lydia invited Tade and I to spend Christmas with them. The significance of the invitation wasn't readily apparent to me.

On Christmas morning Tade and I coordinated our outfits—red trouser suits. Tade had suggested the outfit coordination when I mentioned to her that I had a similar colour suit to the one she was wearing. Sister Lydia and her husband, Brother Dapo, picked us up from home and we went with them to church. After the service we all retired to their house for a lovely Christmas turkey and jollof rice lunch, after which we sat on the carpet in the living room and watched T.D. Jakes video, "Woman Thou art Loosed" and Juanita Bynum's video, "No More Sheets". I sat between Tade and Sister Lydia and wept as Bishop Jakes pronounced freedom on every abused, oppressed and troubled woman.

Not that I could say I understood what it meant to be abused or oppressed; I did not see myself or my situation in those terms. Nonetheless, something inside me was stirred and tears rolled down my cheeks. Tade held me and placed my head on her shoulder. She stroked my back gently until I got my composure back. By the time Juanita Bynum's video came on, I was perky again.

After a delightful Christmas day, Sister Lydia called a taxi for us. By then I was tired and had started to feel quite ill. It was the first day off I had in weeks and the stress of work and a seasonal viral attack had started to take its toll.

Back home, I jumped in the shower, hoping it would help me feel better. Then came a continuous loud banging on the bathroom door. It was Olalekan.

"Hey, you are coming with me to Norwood."

"What?"

"You are coming with me to Norwood."

"Why?"

"Does there have to be a reason?"

I got out of the shower; he went downstairs into the living room while I got dressed. I had bought all of them Christmas presents, which I had left half wrapped. Olalekan left a present for me with Tade, who then helped me complete the wrapping of their presents and packed them in a bag. Tade and

I scrambled into the back of Olalekan's Mitsubishi Shogun where Mum sat plumped in the corner behind the driver's seat, the aggrieved matriarch.

At Olalekan's house there was plenty of roasted chicken, soups, stews and rice. Their aromas blended and filled the air in the house; it was a feast. The food was clearly cooked and brought in by Mum. Olalekan apologised to Tade that he did not have turkey on the menu. Tade, being her accepting self, dismissed his apology and told him we'd had more than enough turkey for the day anyway.

There was a rather suppressed look of shock on Mum's face.

"What? You had turkey? Where did you have turkey?" I interrupted.

"Some friends invited us for Christmas and they cooked turkey, not a big deal really, but we can't eat much."

After dinner, there was silence. Ibidun and Mum sat on one sofa; Tade and I sat on another while Olalekan dashed up and down seemingly sorting his house out. I gave him his present and I got a hug in return. I gave Ibidun her present and got a big smile and a thank you. I then turned to Mum, Mum precious Mum. I stood up and offered Mum her present, neatly boxed. She gave me a disdainful look as she straightened up in her seat to "give it to me".

I thought, *Here . . . we . . . go . . .*

"I don't need your present, in fact, I don't want your present, so take your present away from me," she said, squeezing her lips sideways.

I withdrew the box and went to sit down. Tade, acting the grown up friend, turned to Mum.

"Mummy, I know that sometimes, as children, we misbehave but I am asking you to forgive Ayo for whatever she might have done."

216

"Thank you, my dear child, you ask your friend what she has done and let her tell you exactly what it is," Mum replied and gesticulated in my direction with her hand.

Tade turned towards me, motioning to me to beg Mum for forgiveness.

"Eh eh eh, Tade, don't you dare, you stay out of this," I said sternly. "She doesn't want the present. I've got the receipt; I will take it back and get a refund."

My firmness with Tade frightened Mum. She looked a lot more measured in her attitude. I could not really understand Tade, what did I need to be forgiven for? For being caring enough to buy Mum a present? For not being able to convince people in Nigeria that she was not at fault and everything Rex said was not true? That she said I compared her to another woman when I never did? For cursing my relationship and praying earnestly, according to her, that God would destroy it? *Please, Tade, give me a break*, I thought. To all intents and purposes, that was the end of my closeness to Tade. She became withdrawn from me. She did not speak to me much for the rest of her two weeks stay. She was like a stranger sharing my home.

Tade left London about four days after New Year's Day. It then became customary for her anytime we spoke on the phone, to tell me what a stubborn and aloof person I was, living life on my own away from my family. Each time she said it, it hurt. I had become emotionally attached to her because of the love that she showed me as I wept in Sister Lydia's house. It was to me an expression of love never before received, almost like a motherly love. I thought it meant Tade understood my feelings, my hurt, and would try and see my point of view. She was not alone; when some of my other friends got to know of my fragmented relationship with Mum they said the same thing in different ways.

I tried my best to put the past behind me and press on with life but the pain of my mother's betrayal was heavy in my heart; it felt like a dagger had been pushed into my back, through my heart, and straight out of my chest. It got to a stage where I started to feel a physical pain in my chest. The pain became severe, at which point I knew I had to let go of my hurt. Otherwise I was in danger of harming myself with its side effects. I was not sure how emotional pain connected with physical pain, but the headaches and chest pains I got whenever the reality of my situation dawned on me told me something was not right.

Life couldn't continue that way. I phoned Mum up and told her how much pain I felt as a result of all that she had done. To my surprise Mum was blasé about it all; it hurt more to have told her than not to have done so. In the end I slammed the phone down as I was boiling with rage. I guess I expected her to care for me, care about what I was going through and how I was feeling, it never occurred to me that she might actually not be able to.

She must have been shocked by me slamming the phone down on her, as she came round to my house. Mum was rambling again. I ignored her, it was the only thing I could do. She was not in a place where she was prepared to reason and be honest with herself, much less me. Mum asked what exactly she had done to hurt me, because she could not fathom how she could have ever hurt me. She seemed to be taking it as one big joke. I ignored her until she picked up her bag and left.

The only way I felt peace was to stay away from Mum. I refrained from visiting her often. Nonetheless, I still cared about her; I cared very much about all the members of my family despite the bitterness that was tearing us all apart, and for that reason I couldn't stay away from them for too long.

About two months after my phone call to Mum, I phoned her one Saturday afternoon to see if she was at home and I decided to pop in to see how she was. Mum was pleasantly surprised to see me but it didn't stop her nagging me. She complained about my attitude, saying I was destroying the family unity and it was my cockiness she could not stand.

"I really don't know where you got that arrogance from. Even your father, he may be all things, but he was never arrogant."

That was a new one—we couldn't hear enough from her about Dad's arrogance when we were growing up.

"That is exactly what your brother said too. I know there is no one that you respect, not even your brother. No one who could talk to you and you would listen. He sat here and told me he couldn't speak to you because you are too proud to listen to anyone."

By that point I had grown out of caring about what she or Olalekan thought of me. I knew she was talking out of resentment of the fact that I hadn't rescued her from the rumours that circulated in Nigeria. I was not sure why she was so bothered anyway, because when I spoke to Pastor Stan and read the letter that Sister Kemi from church in Nigeria had written to me, it was clear that they thought I got to London, grew wings as the new western girl and decided to dump a good man for whatever London had to offer.

After that conversation with Mum, or, more appropriately, after she made it known to me how she was feeling, I noticed the distance between Olalekan and myself grew. His infrequent phone calls had stopped altogether, apart from phoning me up one day to tell me to go to Mum and apologise to her for whatever I had done that was causing the rift between us. I was always the one who needed to apologise, never mind that I was the wronged one.

19

RENEWAL

I focused on getting my life back. I put more hours into work and started to save for my master's degree. As life started to get back on track and the days got brighter with the summer sun, things fell apart yet again. This time not with my family but with my church; the Pastor was not happy with me. He considered that I was not showing enough commitment to church activities because I chose to work on some Sundays for extra money. He told me I was putting money before God and if I thought I could do that and expect God to answer my prayers for a better job, I was deceiving myself.

That was all I needed! Why couldn't peace come and stay? Why did it have to show up for what seemed a split second and then disappear to make way for more aggravation? I stepped down from the worship team. The only connection with the church that I had left were my friends, and they eventually pulled away too. Troubles come in threes, they say; I wondered what the third one would be. Actually, that was the third one—there was first Mum, who dragged other members of the family with her, then there was Rex and now Pastor Jack.

Could it be that if I got through this one, that would be the end of my troubles?

I felt stripped of all my relationships except two. There was Jide, my housemate, and one female friend, Busola, whom I had met when she and her husband accompanied their pastor on a preaching assignment in my church. Over the months following our meeting, Busola and I had become very close. She lived in Balham, just two stops away from Tooting Broadway, and had a young family with two girls aged five and three. Her husband was one of the leaders of the church they attended in Balham. Despite her busy family life Busola always made the time for a chat and whenever she went shopping during the sales period she would buy me a top, skirt or a pair of trousers. She was like a sister to me. We had a lot in common—our heights, at about five foot five inches, our sense of style, and our dress size, but more importantly, our penchant for long telephone conversations. She was the only one I felt able to talk to about the hurt I felt as a result of what Pastor Jack said.

Jide was like the brother I never had. He was a kind person and looked out for others; he definitely looked out for me. Despite these two close friendships, I started to feel very lonely and I cried to God. I asked why all this was happening to me, why my family was falling apart. In response, God gave me a word in Hebrews 10:9 that, "He taketh away the first that he may establish the second" (KJV). The word did not keep me from feeling lonely; I told God I wanted more friends close by, but I felt God say to me that I had all the friends I needed. I thought He must be joking, God, two friends? Again He reminded me of His earlier word that they were all I needed.

I soon started my master's degree and my focus shifted to understanding my modules and passing them. I had eventually decided to continue with an MSc in estate management, but returning to university after such an eventful two years took its toll on me. I struggled to assimilate what I was being taught; eventually, I managed to get myself readjusted to the rigours of learning.

I went to visit Mum the weekend after I started attending lectures and told her I had returned to university to study for a master's. Mum brought out her chequebook, saying she would like to give me some money as her contribution towards my studies. I didn't feel like taking it. I remembered how Mum had always said she was penniless because of her children. I was now grown up and did not want to be blamed for any continued financial struggle she may face. She insisted on writing the cheque and handed it over to me. I did not present Mum's cheque at my bank for months until she persisted in asking me to cash it.

Twice or more I received phone calls from Olalekan to see how I was doing. It seemed things were changing for the better until I noticed his calls were few and far between. They usually came after I had seen Mum and she had been particularly pleased with me for one reason or another. When I challenged him, he denied he was calling as a reward for what, it seemed, he had perceived as my good behaviour towards Mum, but somehow I did not believe him. It had been too much of a coincidence.

Meanwhile, it was not all fine and dandy with him and Mum. The following year, it was Mum's sixtieth birthday. I ordered her a big 6-0 cake and took it round to her. She had organised a thanksgiving service and a reception for the Sunday following her actual birthday. On the morning of the thanksgiving service, Mum got herself worked up and rang me, saying Olalekan was letting her down. She complained that he did not care very much for her; he only tries to fulfil "all righteousness" by tossing pieces of kindness her way.

"His love is not deep from his heart," she told me.

Having learnt how my mother plays one child against the other, I asked her if she'd spoken to Olalekan about it.

"You may want to take it up with him if you feel this strongly," I explained to her.

Mum went quiet. It was clearly not what she wanted to hear.

One year speedily rolled by. I completed my master's and felt adequately equipped to start my professional life as a surveyor. For the first time, I had the confidence that I could genuinely contribute towards my employer's business at an executive level and I was looking forward to doing my best to get to the top of my career ladder. Five academic years of studying estate management in Ife and one year of further rigorous study at Southbank University (yes, I did go to Southbank in the end, more for its affordability than anything else—but it turned out to be an excellent choice.) I came to understand that estate management was more than just looking after the completed building and that as a surveyor, I had the ability to influence the shape of the skyline long before the builders moved in with their JCBs and cranes. I could think carefully about the investment being created in order to take a more long-term view. Development appraisals had become my favourite subject and I had developed a keen interest in investment analysis.

After another round of unsuccessful job applications to various firms in London, I started to apply to other employers outside the capital. At first I was very disappointed that I did not secure an offer in London until it occurred to me one day that I hadn't got any real ties with London. Apart from the fact that I was born there, there were no meaningful family relationships in the city that I could say were stopping me from moving out.

I was finally offered a job in Bath, a hundred and ten miles west of London. I prayed about the job offer and I felt an incredible peace and assurance that accepting it was the right thing to do. I would be working as a development surveyor and I felt blessed that I was able to secure a job that would help me make the most of my skills and education. My contract was signed by the middle of December and I agreed with my employer that I should start work in January after all the Christmas and New Year festivities.

I saw Sister Lydia about two weeks before Christmas day and got another invitation to spend Christmas with her and her family. A week later, Mum phoned me to say she would like us to spend Christmas together as a family. The thought of spending another Christmas day in my brother's house filled me with dread. It had been two years since Tade was around for Christmas, and I had spent the previous one with other friends. My only comfort was that I would soon be moving out of London and would be spared any more Christmases with my family.

I told Mum I already had another invitation and would not be able to make it; Sister Lydia's offer was a more appealing option. Mum started a pity party. She went on about how God was her only support; how she had no one else and just wanted her children around her. I agreed to visit her when I came back from visiting Sister Lydia. To ensure I came she said she would ask Olalekan to pick me up early in the evening. My anxiety level rose. I wondered how I was going to survive that one evening with "the family".

Sister Lydia arranged for her pastor to pick me up first thing on Christmas morning on their way to church. The pastor and his family were also spending the day at Sister Lydia's. They lived in Colliers Wood and I lived in Tooting; the church was in Stockwell. They journeyed northwards from

Colliers Wood to Tooting and then, with me, to church. Just before they arrived to pick me up, Olalekan arrived. He said he came to take me to his house at Mum's request. This was during a time when we had drifted apart and he had picked up his aggression again. He became even more annoyed when I told him it could not be as I had agreed with Mum that my visit was going to be later in the evening. He immediately called Mum on his mobile phone. Mum called me back on my landline.

"Ah Ayomide, you know it is only you my children that I have. I have no one else. When I was suffering, you were the only ones I saw, you were the only ones who stood by me." Mum's words brought my pain back.

"So why on earth, Mother, were you bent on frustrating my life, when you knew I gave you invaluable support? Why would you stab me in the back and refuse to make amends?"

"Ayo, I did not do all those things, this is the devil trying to destroy this family, don't give him a chance, don't allow him, please."

My eyes welled up with tears, not because I bought her soppy story but because she had caused so much damage to me.

"Mum, this is you; this is your doing, not the devil."

Sometimes I wondered if the devil has the opportunity to go to God. He probably would be reporting God's children to him saying, "God, your children are framing me for things I did not do."

As I was on the phone to Mum, Pastor Enoch and his family arrived. I wrapped up the conversation and left with them.

I had another enjoyable Christmas day with Sister Lydia and her family. We got up to leave and Pastor Enoch headed for Guildford. I was alarmed. They had talked about going to visit a friend in Guildford, but I had presumed they would drop me off first. He and his wife were disappointed. They said we had had such a good time together that they thought I was going to spend the rest of the evening with them. I apologised for any confusion and explained that I had promised Mum I was going to visit her.

I got home and quickly changed my outfit to something more casual while I phoned Mum to ask Olalekan to pick me up. I was not going to speak to him after his unpleasant behaviour in the morning. On his arrival, I said hello to him as I got into his car and kept quiet for the rest of the journey. I got to his house and there was not much happening as usual. It was gravely silent for a Christmas evening; there was a strange unease in the air. Olalekan was trying hard to break the ice with a conversation about the outfit I wore earlier. Wouldn't it have been nice if he had given that compliment in the morning while I was still wearing the outfit and not thrown a hissy fit because I said I was not ready to join them in his house?

Sitting there in Olalekan's living room, it was as if four strangers were put in a house together, even strangers would make the effort to try and get to know each other better. Mum was dozing off on one couch and I fell asleep on another. Ibidun woke me up and asked if I wanted to go upstairs to sleep. Apparently Mum and Ibidun had stayed with Olalekan overnight, so Ibidun ushered me to her bedroom. I was deep in sleep when I was woken up to come downstairs for dinner. At first I couldn't figure out where I was. The room was dark. Ibidun had not switched the light on when she came in; her figure gradually emerged out of the blackness of the room, almost like a strange dream. I got up and walked down the stairs with a little stagger.

The table was set. I sat down still struggling to open my eyes. Olalekan brought out his camera to take some photos,

I didn't want him taking a picture of me in that state but he insisted. I thought it was distasteful to insist on taking someone's picture when they were having a very bad hair evening and they were only half-awake. I really couldn't eat much so I excused myself from the table to continue my sleep. Olalekan went up in arms. He started his torrent of abuse: how selfish I was and how he had sacrificed for me all day and I was throwing it back in his face.

"If not for Mum I would not have bothered to come and pick you up the second time," he claimed as he literally threw his arms up and down in anger.

"You would have been doing me a favour, you know. I didn't want to come here. I was having a perfectly good time where I was."

Olalekan insisted I was not going upstairs again in his house and ordered me out. The whole exchange rapidly descended into an ugly scene. I picked the phone to call a cab. He grabbed the phone from me and said I had to get out immediately. I was not allowed to call a cab. His outrageous behaviour got to me and I gave him a piece of my mind. Mum was beside herself, she was begging for calm.

Olalekan finally calmed down and became overbearing in his attempt at reconciliation, he was now going to carry me upstairs. I had had enough and would have left his house that night if I had driven there myself. I was persuaded to stay the night, which I did, and took the opportunity the next morning to announce to them that I was moving out of London to start my new job.

I was due to start work in the middle of January. On the first of January, God ministered a word into my spirit, found in Deuteronomy 11:10-15

"For the land, whither thou goest in to possess it, is not as the land . . . from whence ye came out, where thou sowedst thy seed, and wateredst it with thy foot, as a garden of herbs: But the land, whither ye go to possess it, is a land of hills and valleys, and drinketh water of the rain of heaven . . . I will give you the rain of your land in his due season, the first rain and the latter rain, that thou mayest gather in thy corn, and thy wine, and thine oil. And I will send grass in thy fields for thy cattle, that thou mayest eat and be full." (KJV)

I couldn't believe God was speaking so distinctly about a choice I made out of my need for a career. Especially with what Jack, the pastor of my church, had said. A part of me had believed I may not find a job as he had said. I had to ask God again what situation the word referred to. I asked Him, "Lord, are you referring to this move to Bath, or are you referring to something else I have in mind?" I knew deep down in my spirit that God was referring to my move to Bath.

A few days before I left, Yinka called and I informed her I was moving. Yinka and I had become pretty close over the years since meeting in church. She seemed to have refrained from our friendship for a while when I had problems with the pastor but then began moving a bit closer at the time that coincided with me leaving London; I had started to get my close friends back, it seemed. Yinka rang again the day before I left and said she was praying and God gave her a word for me, the word she received for me was in Deuteronomy 11:11—part of the same set of verses that He had shown me earlier.

It was such an exciting time, albeit mixed with the anxiety of starting a new life away from the familiar. It was a Sunday morning that I moved from London to Bath. Jide came with me. It was nice to have a friend to share my exciting journey with. As I drove past the final turning on the A4 and hit the M4, I almost screamed for joy, telling Jide we were headed for The West as though he was unable to read the signs.

PART IV

GOD HEALS

20

JOURNEY TOWARDS HEALING

I walked through North Parade to my first day of work in Bath and the beauty of the city unfolded before me. The horseshoe-shaped Pultney Weir came into view as it whipped up the waters of River Avon into a white whirl. My excitement of the previous day faded into a reverent appreciation of my new city. I felt the peace of its quietness, but also the eerie feeling that it might be the first day of a lonely routine life. I had no family of my own to be with and I was not sure of my prospects of meeting an eligible man in this small English city.

I looked down from the street level into Parade Gardens, a small park by the riverbank, which despite the dreariness of winter had maintained a dignified beauty. I took my right turn, walked past the old Empire Hotel with its striking Victorian architecture: the castle, the house and the cottage—I later understood the intricate design of the roof to represent the upper class, the middle class and the artisans. The building dominated Orange Grove like a gateway to the City. I eventually came to the humble building that housed my office, slightly reminiscent of the contrast between the Faculty of EDM and the rest of the academic area in OAU.

Work went well; I was in before my boss, which I thought showed diligence. I was given a quick guide of the intranet and there were plenty of suggestions on house-hunting from colleagues who were keen to help me settle into life in Bath. I met Diane, the other junior surveyor in the development team and struck an acquaintanceship with her. She had stayed in the same bed and breakfast where I was staying when she started work a week before me. Her own journey to Bath was a little bit longer than mine as she had travelled down all the way from Ireland. Diane and I were able to compare notes on more than university experiences as we swapped stories of the journey to Bath, the bed and breakfast experience, and house-hunting challenges.

At the end of my first week in the city, I left my bed and breakfast on Saturday morning and went into town to do some reconnaissance for a suitable church to attend on Sunday. I found one church, but could not find any sign indicating their services times. On Sunday morning I decided to take a drive towards Bristol to find a church there. As I was heading out on the A4, I saw a number of people hurrying along the road; I guessed they were going to church and stopped to ask if there was a Pentecostal Church around that I could attend.

"Dad! Do you know any Pentecostal Church in Bath?" the young lad I was talking to called out to his father who was walking fast, well ahead of the rest of the group.

The father gave his reply as he walked back briskly towards my car. "Sorry we don't know of any but you could join us in our church, it is an Anglican and we are blessed by it."

It was a different experience, but nonetheless an enjoyable one. During the week I looked through the various adverts posted by staff on the intranet and found information about a Christian fellowship. A few Christians at work had got together to form the fellowship, which met in the town hall. Feeling part of a Christian group mattered much to me and I felt a great relief at being able to locate the fellowship.

At the meeting, there were three men and one woman in attendance, all seated along the perimeter of the room on one side. A man of medium build with a thick white beard rose up from his seat. He approached me as I walked in.

"Ayo? Hello, I'm Aaron, the person you exchanged emails with."

"Hi Aaron, nice to meet you and thanks for your reply to my enquiries."

He was the leader of the group. He introduced me to the others and we had a quick chat about me. I suppose it was natural for them to want to know more about their latest member. Peter, one of the other two men, told me about his church.

"Judging from what you've said about the mode of worship in your previous church, you may feel at home at Bath Christian Centre."

I was willing to try the church out and agreed to look out for Peter the following Sunday. The fellowship meeting itself was short and we had some more chat afterwards. Aaron had visited Nigeria in the past and recounted some of his experiences, the cultural differences and way of life. Some of the stories he told were quite fascinating—actually, it was more his reaction to the events that I found quite funny. He recounted the day his host family were taking him for an evening revival meeting and as their car was about to pull out of their front court, extended family members arrived for a visit. The fact that the visit was unannounced was surprising for Aaron and when his host family decided the best course of action was for the guests to come along to the meeting, he was shocked. I almost felt like rolling on the ground with laughter that someone would find the Nigerian approach to hospitality that shocking. Having grown up there, that culture was the norm for me and the difficulty, many times, was trying to adjust to the more reserved English culture.

The following Sunday, I attended Bath Christian Centre and sat next to Peter, his wife, Jenifer, and their daughter Ella. The auditorium where the church met used to be a one-screen art deco cinema that had been refurbished and brought back to its former glory by the church. Most of the images on the panels that crowned the side walls seemed to have been inspired by biblical stories or the city's ancient Roman history. But there were also two sculpted lions' heads with horns, facing each other on the respective side walls near the stage; they were ghoulish and distracting. We sat to the left of the auditorium, where parents with young children sat. There must have been over four hundred people there, singing and praising God; the sound of a throng singing praises to God downed any sinister appearance the carved animal heads could have; it was such an uplifting worship. The word that was preached was good, and my heart was very much stirred by the whole service; Peter was right, I did feel at home at his church, and thus my search for a "spiritual home" came to a successful end.

After almost two weeks of living in a bed and breakfast while still house-hunting, I started to crave the normalcy of cooking my own food and generally having a place that I could call home. The service at the B&B was great—their tasty full English breakfast filled me up so much that I needed to skip lunch in order to have space for supper, and my room was cleaned without me having to lift a finger. Nonetheless, there didn't seem to be a place like home.

I managed to find a newly refurbished Victorian terrace house in the heart of Weston village, on the northeastern edge of the city. The centre of the village was just at the top of the road from the house. Its back looked directly out to the Royal United Hospital, redolent of my childhood homes in Ife and Ilesa. It was dark when I drove up to have a look at my potential new home and I had a job trying to get there. I hit the one-way system in the village from the wrong direction and couldn't figure out, from the map I had with me, how to get back into the correct traffic flow. I parked by the roadside opposite the hospital and walked the long way round to the front of the house. The streetlights illuminated the surroundings, revealing a pretty dowdy terrace. I feared the interior of the house may be just as bad and considered turning round and heading back for the car, but the landlady had sounded very friendly and civilised on the phone—not like someone who would invite others to live in a house that was old and tatty—so I decided to give it a try.

One of the existing householders opened the door for me and I was pleasantly surprised as she ushered me in. The corridor that led away from the door was finished with nice, embossed wallpaper and spotlessly painted over with white emulsion. I noticed two black and white pictures on the wall; they provided an elegant contrast to the white paint. The living room was fully laid with a brand new light brown carpet, and its walls were painted in matt magnolia. A sandstone three-seater sofa sat against the near wall of the living room, and there was another armchair to its left. There was a folding dining table by the kitchen wall. The single-storey extension behind the living room, which formed the kitchen, had a large roof light that gave it a feeling of openness.

"Your room is on the ground floor at the front," said the lady, who had introduced herself as Mariana. I looked at the tiny built-in wardrobe in my otherwise very large room and wondered how I was going to fit all my clothes in there. Luckily the bed was a divan, with storage underneath.

"This will go some way in helping with storage," I said to Mariana with a wink. There were two very large rooms on the first floor, one of which belonged to Mariana and her fiancé, Gareth; the third room was spare.

I moved into the house four days later and barely got to know Mariana and Gareth when they announced they were moving out. A friendly Indian couple replaced them. Mahesh, the husband, was a quantity surveyor and Amrita, his wife, was a nurse who worked at the hospital opposite the house.

About three weeks after I moved into my new home, Peter and Jenifer invited me to their house for a Sunday lunch. After lunch, Jenifer mentioned I might want to go along to a course that was designed for newcomers, as an introduction to the church. The course was called "Power for Living".

"It would be a good place to meet other members and intended members of the church," she explained.

At Power for Living, I met Mary, the wife of one of the church leaders. A tall, slender lady with short, brown hair, she had a gentle voice and there was an air of grace about her. She came over to introduce herself to me and asked what brought me to Bath.

"Just the job," was my reply.

She gave me a searching look.

"I think it is more than just the job," she said. "I sense there is a greater purpose," she reaffirmed.

"Really?" My response was more of a rhetorical question.

"Hmm, yes," she said, nodding her head; she bore a pondering expression on her face. Even though I had carried on with the conversation rather blithely at the start, I became suddenly overwhelmed by God's generosity towards me. It was not enough that he told me before I left London that He had some good things in store for me; He decided to remind me that He had a purpose for my move to Bath. And He chose this lovely woman to give me that reassurance.

I wondered what the purpose could be and thought, whatever it was, it was welcome. As long as it was the purpose of God, it would always be greater than anything I could muscle my way through. I'd just have to wait and see what the plan was.

Zach, the leader of the course, came up to the pulpit after a short period of powerful praise and worship.

"Now, let's release the *freedom fighters* to go and do their thing," he said.

A group of happy looking men and women stood up and gleefully headed for the door to the left of the ballroom. *Wow*, I thought. *I'd like to do that; I'd like to be part of that group.* I had made a presumption. The emphasis with which Zach talked about the "freedom fighters" caused me to assume they were the church's intercessory group, praying as we went through the course. Not that I thought their prayers were solely for us, but by nature of what I thought they did, they would have been interceding for something or another and that mediation must be effective for Zach to give it such enunciation. I love breakthroughs—I love to pray and get results but I needed to complete the Power for Living course before I could join any group within the church. It gave me another motivation for completing the course.

The weeks went by and I received the result of my exams and my certificate. I had been awarded my master's degree, and the graduation ceremony was planned to take place in April, about two months later. I thought about how I wanted to celebrate the graduation. It would be good if Mum, Olalekan and Ibidun came with me to the ceremony. I thought it would be nice to celebrate with friends as well; I would go out with them in the evening. I emailed Olalekan the next morning to tell him I was graduating and invited him along. His reply came rather quickly. He was otherwise engaged that day.

A few days later, I phoned Mum to tell her about the graduation. Mum was not only keen to attend; she wanted to invite her friends as well.

"Ehm, Mum, I'm not so sure about that. The invitation cards are limited and if I want more, I'll have to pay for them."

"How much are they? I will pay for them," Mum replied.

"Actually, Mum, I wanted to invite only close family and some of the friends that supported me through those trying times. I really don't feel up to a big celebration."

She was not having it and the haggling and bargaining began. I eventually got fed up of the argument and conceded that she could invite her friends to the party at home with us, but not to the ceremony.

On thinking it through, I realised it was still not what I wanted but I did not have the emotional strength with which to fight Mum, because I knew she would have got upset. Some days later I summoned up the courage to reject her proposal and phoned her up again.

"What I really want is for us to go to the ceremony together, come back and have lunch and then in the evening I would get together with my friends," I told Mum.

Those few friends of mine had encouraged and supported me through my time studying. It had got to the stage that, as a result of all that was happening with my family and the aftermath of my broken relationship, I felt not only emotionally but mentally drained, feeling as though I couldn't gather the strength to continue. My friends and one of my lecturers were the only ones who knew about my struggles. Shewa, in particular, was passionate in her encouragement; she was the cheerleader I needed at that crucial point in time. But Mum was insistent on having things her way. I realised I needed to take a stand. I told Mum I could not stop her from inviting people to her home, but I could choose whether to be there or not. She ignored me as usual.

On my graduation day, we went to the ceremony, came back and Mum started cooking in readiness for her guests' arrival. I made preparations to leave. Mum became angry and had an outburst, insisting it was her right to be able to invite people for my graduation. I felt guilty, but I had a strong feeling that I was doing the right thing and left.

A few minutes after I left their apartment, Ibidun called me to say Mum was crying. Bless my sister's heart; she was trying to broker peace. Her role was no longer as clearly defined as it had been the night I confronted Mum about her attitude towards the relationship I had with Rex. Ibidun was now torn between her loyalties towards her mother and her sense of what was right for her to do.

"Ayo, you need to come back and stay for Mum's guest."

"No, Ibidun, I don't need to do anything."

"Okay, please, I am asking you. Look, she is crying, can you not hear her over the phone?"

"But she wouldn't need to, if she considered respecting my point of view for a change."

Ibidun decided it would not be right for her to come out with me and my friends that evening; she would prefer to stay with Mum. I felt slightly disappointed but it was not going to spoil my evening. We went and had a great time.

I travelled back to Bath the day after my graduation and life carried on as normal. Power for Living was coming to an end and I was looking forward to joining the Freedom for Life group. My waiting was soon over, but oh! the disappointment I felt when I realised it was not actually the church's intercessory team meeting but another course, a sequel to Power for Living. Its focus was all about forgiveness and emotional healing, and it lasted eight weeks.

A few weeks before I started Freedom for Life, there was a conference in church that was also about emotional freedom. There were sessions throughout the weekend on forgiveness and inner healing. I sat on the balcony inside the church as the preaching went on during the Saturday evening. The wrongs that I had done to other people kept coming to my mind, especially the people whom I had one form of authority or the other over. I felt sorrow within me for the sins I had committed against the people and repented before God for them. I asked God for His forgiveness, praying blessings over each person that I remembered that night. It was probably in preparation for what was to come.

After asking God for forgiveness, I was moved within me to pray for a marriage partner. I asked God to open the way for me to meet the man I would marry and I heard His quiet and gentle voice saying to me, "You have tried that . . . why don't you try me?" I wasn't sure what "try me" meant, but I felt a deep sense of peace within me.

When I went on the Freedom for Life course, my sorrow was not for what I had done to others, but for what had been done to me. The pain of Mum's offences resurfaced as I sat there week after week, being quiet, mostly; it all came back to me in a new way. It was like the tide coming in and eventually pushing back. My eyes were shut and I felt myself drifting with that tide. There was a gentle tap on my right shoulder. It was Jenny, one of the two women facilitating my progress through the course.

"Ayo, you are very quiet."

"Yes," I responded.

"Okay, we will lay hands on you and pray quietly for God's love to soak into you."

"Thank you."

After the fourth week of attending Freedom for Life, I was shopping in Marks and Spencer on Stall Street when the week's teaching re-emerged in my thoughts. I had been taught that forgiveness was the key, and when I forgave my pain would be healed. Right there in the store, without moving my lips, I started to forgive Mum for the wrong she had done that caused me pain, at least those wrongs that occurred to me at that point in time. I took myself through the steps we had been taught on the course. I repented of the ways I had judged her because of her behaviour and asked God to forgive me of those judgements. I recalled all the times, in the past, that I had thought of my mother as cruel and had called her names in my mind. I realised I didn't want to condemn my mother; all I wanted was for her to change and for me to live a peaceful life. Over the final weeks of the course I became familiar with this type of intrusion into my daily thoughts, and I was glad the course was making a difference.

I finished Freedom for Life thinking it was all done with, but my facilitators were convinced there was still a lot there that I needed to address. They tried to encourage me to take the course again, but I resisted. I had dealt with the issues, I said to myself. There was no point going over past events again—it was necessary to move on. So I got on with my life.

I did not get a lot of visits from London and I usually looked forward with eagerness when a friend or a member of my family said they would visit. I particularly looked forward to Mum's visits; the desire to be close to her was still as strong as ever, despite our troubled relationship.

The first time Mum came to Bath it was for a long weekend. She arrived on a Thursday afternoon and left on the Sunday. She had initially said she would be coming a month before, only for me to prepare and she did not turn up. When she eventually came, it was nice to have her around. I picked her up from the train station and on getting home went straight into the kitchen to make supper as it was getting late. I turned round to get some stock from the chest freezer, which was just behind the kitchen door opposite the dining table. I saw Mum, through the living room door, as she emerged from my bedroom. She was abrupt and irritable. I decided to ignore her but I couldn't help wonder what it was that changed her mood so quickly. As the attitude began when she went into my bedroom, I went into the room a while later to check what might have sparked the reaction. There were my graduation photos. I had received them and did not send her copies. The decision not to send them yet was not in any way to spite her, but I was used to Mum taking offence; it did not surprise me that she reacted the way she did.

Mum didn't say anything about the photos, so I decided not to mention them either. The attitude went on for most of the weekend until I had had enough. By the Saturday evening, I decided to throw a big strop of my own.

"Are you not going to rinse the rice grains before you boil them?" Mum snapped.

"No, I will do it my own way, I will parboil it," I snarled back. "Can you give me some space in here? Go sit in the living room or somewhere else."

I made sure I behaved awkwardly enough that she felt uncomfortable. I decided I was going to throw in a little bit of aggression as well, for her to see how well she liked it when she was treated the same way. She mellowed. Mum was so biddable, it was almost unbelievable.

After she left, I realised I had overreacted, and the Holy Spirit was there to give me those gentle convictions that helped me realise I needed to apologise to Mum. Jide came to visit me two weeks afterwards and I got a lift back to London with him to apologise to her. It was as though my penitence gave Mum the moral high ground. Rather than make peace for her own part in the unfortunate exchange of bad attitude, Mum said she had been waiting for when I was going to come to my senses because she was sure I would see sense in the end. I wanted to point her to her own behaviour but I decided to let it go. Naturally, she became reluctant to visit again.

I decided that if Mum was not willing to come to Bath, I would make it a point of duty to travel to London once every month to visit her. I scheduled a day off one Thursday and took the train to London. After spending some time with Mum, I wanted to buy some goat meat in the market to take back with me. Mum, too, was on her way out, so we travelled together and then she decided to come with me to the butcher's. Once we got there Mum created a scene; she insisted on choosing the piece of meat that I should buy but I wasn't having it. The butcher looked confused, probably not knowing which of us the costumer was. He got angry at being messed about. In the end I paid for the meat I liked as Mum walked off angry and upset. I later found her elsewhere in the market and she wouldn't even talk to me. Sulking, she walked past as though I was a stranger.

I think I managed the monthly visits twice.

The lack of success with my monthly visits to Mum appeared to be a major blockage on the way to healing my relationship with her, but I knew it was possible for me to move on with my own life even if I couldn't establish a close relationship with her. I concentrated on building a good life for myself in Bath.

Life was great. Mahesh and Amrita, my housemates, were a joy to live with. Mahesh enjoyed cooking and I was always offered Indian curries to eat. I got to have a taste of it every now and then and they would sometimes have a taste of some of my Nigerian food. I loved their version of the pilau rice in particular; it was slightly different to the one served by restaurants in town. They added a rich array of ingredients to the curried rice, including sultanas and cashew nuts. I was bowled over by their generosity; according them, their culture demanded that they invited me to eat whenever they cooked on a large scale for themselves or for their friends. Amrita even bought me a Salwar kameez, the Indian tunic and trouser, during one of her trips back home. We just had to take a group photograph to celebrate my novel outfit.

Towards the end of summer, I decided to take a holiday and went to Germany. There, I spent a significant amount of time praying and seeking God's face. I was walking through a little park in the centre of Mannheim one afternoon when the whole issue of Yetunde visiting Rex's parents came back to my mind. I thought again, *God, how could she?* I was angry and agitated. I wanted to phone or write to her immediately to let her know what I thought and how I felt about her visit, but I felt God saying, "Leave Yetunde to me." I allowed God to prevail over my anguish, and yielded.

I returned from holiday and got on with business as usual. Lawrence and Emma, who led Freedom for Life, asked if I could be a prayer support for the course. For two terms I went along to the meetings, sitting at the back of the church auditorium and praying as participants were taken through the same process I had gone through some months before.

As I listened to the various speakers talk the participants through the different stages of the healing process, I got an understanding of why my facilitators had suggested that I went back on the course. I decided to heed their advice. This time I was more active, and a lot more open. I knew what to do with my pain; I went straight into pronouncing forgiveness over Mum for whatever hurt came to my mind. There was more than enough to forgive her for.

Later that year I bought the audio recordings of another inner healing conference. As I listened to them, they prompted me to start to forgive my parents for the childhood traumas they had caused me, especially after their separation with the endless journeys I had to make to Dad's house to collect money. As the conference unfolded on the cassettes so did my memory of the experiences of all those years. I realised how, in their fight against each other, I became the battlefield on which they met to exchange fire, and how difficult it had been for me to see Mum get hurt when Dad's retaliation came back fiercer and stronger. I would acknowledge my feelings and go on to pronounce the gift of forgiveness over both my parents.

I woke up one morning, some months after listening to the conference tapes, and on my way to the bathroom I felt my stomach churn. Like an epiphany, I realised that despite over two years' worth of forgiveness, I neither loved nor liked my mother. My stomach had churned, not in hunger, but in dislike of her.

I got to church and told Emma. She suggested that I go through a three-hour prayer and deliverance session called "Issue-Focused Ministry", which is part of the Restoring The Foundations Ministries (RTF)[1]. It uses the foundation of forgiveness, repentance and renunciation through the Blood of Jesus to deal with one particular generational problem, including the deep-rooted hurts that it might have brought.

I got a different understanding of deliverance.

When I became a Christian in Nigeria, the understanding of deliverance that was passed on to me was the type that got rid of demon possessions, whether witchcraft, idol worshiping or other demonic activities that the individual was involved in or had been dragged into by others. However, my new understanding was that even though a Christian may not be possessed by demons; they may be influenced by demons and their activities. Deep hurts like bitterness and resentment have demonic influences, as does control and manipulation. Deliverance from these influences would be necessary.

As I read the notes on the ministry session and the Bible passages that came with them, it seemed there was still so much in my life that needed attention, and it seemed they were all crying out in dissonance, desperate to get noticed. I became overwhelmed and so confused that I completely forgot why I wanted to undergo the ministry in the first place. I veered off course as I tried to complete the application form that accompanied the notes.

Caron and Georgina, two church members who were going to facilitate the prayers, came to have an initial chat with me. We sat down with cups of tea in the living room as they talked me through the process, and I discussed my reasons for wanting to undergo the prayer session. Talking to them clarified my mind a little, but not completely. Once they left me on my own the confusion returned.

On the day of the prayer session, I met them in Georgina's house on the other side of town; it was an early morning start. The first half of the session went fine. During the second half I was asked to wait on the Holy Spirit to show me the root of my hurt. That was a difficult one. My mind kept wandering, and when it eventually settled, what arose was the memory of Mum telling me that she had been praying to God that He would destroy my relationship with Rex. Caron was not convinced that was the root of the hurt. She explained to me that she felt the incident I was describing was like a branch of a tree, and the way I was approaching the tree was picking off the leaves and breaking off some of the branches. She said I wasn't really digging the root out to completely remove the whole tree. After waiting a while longer for more clarity to come, we rounded off with a prayer. We were finished by about midday and had time for pleasantries afterwards.

"How do you feel?" Caron asked.

I thought about it for a minute and answered, with assurance, that I felt free. There was a strong sense of freedom, I knew something had happened but I could not quite put my finger on it.

I went back to work on Monday. Everything seemed pretty much the same as it had been the previous Friday. I, however, noticed a slight difference; my understanding of emotional issues had increased. I was able to put name to some of the unhealthy ways that my parent had related with me. I now understood what false responsibility was, and how it had been piled on me in my childhood. I had always known that the way things happened in our home was not right; I might have even stretched as far as explaining how things should have been in the ideal world. However, being now able to define them in precise terms seemed a clear step towards correcting them. The Single Issue ministry had been like a diagnostic session—and that diagnosis felt like freedom.

21

HEALING—

UNRESTRICTED, INCLUSIVE

The summer of 2003 was approaching. I took my picnic mat to Victoria Park and lay down to bask in the rarity that was sunshine. I could see the south of the city from my vantage position at the top of a slope on the park lawn.

Hang on . . .

I sat up to the take in the views better.

Do you know what? Bath is surrounded by hills!

The city sits in the Avon Valley; much of it is built on the slopes of the hills. The house where I lived was at the bottom of the highest of those hills. Not that I had not noticed the hills when I moved to Bath. In fact I had been fascinated by the height of the one near my house, during my early days in Bath. I was on my way back from a meeting in church one evening when I decided to venture beyond the village in Weston and see what the surrounding roads looked like. I parked my car at a convenient spot and took in the beauty of the night. I noticed, through the darkness, flickering, small lights suspended high in the atmosphere in the far distance.

The lights moved downwards a little and disappeared, only to re-emerge at the top.

I was astounded by this strange phenomenon that was unravelling before my eyes, and peered as much into the distance as it would allow me. That was until I realised the lights were indeed the headlights of cars travelling down the surface of a hill. A visit up the hill further unearthed the mystery. The cars appeared through the thickness of the trees at the top and disappeared as they made their way down the meandering road.

But now, sitting in Victoria Park, the penny finally dropped that God was not simply using an abstract metaphor when he told me about the land of hills and valleys. It was a physical sign of what was going to happen in the spiritual realm.

Another gobsmacking moment with God!

I was being healed of the past, but neither Mum nor Olalekan had changed. It occurred to me that if they changed, things may be a lot better in the family. I decided to invite Mum and Ibidun to one of the programmes in my church.

On the day they were meant to arrive, Mum dragged her feet so much that Ibidun had to leave her behind in London. Mum did not arrive in Bath until almost midnight. I couldn't go to sleep because I was expecting her. I sat up on the makeshift guest room, the sofa bed, trying to fight off my drowsiness. I knew being woken by the telephone after a short sleep was going to knock me for six. I was already succumbing and nodding off when the phone rang; Ibidun was sound asleep in my room and I could hear her snoring. I found it frustrating that Mum was throwing the "big opportunity" I was giving her away, throwing it back in my face.

All throughout that weekend I was desperate for them to "catch the vision" and get healed of their emotional baggage, but they didn't seem to get it. First, on the Sunday morning,

Mum decided she was going to sit away from us, and then Ibidun made a fuss about wanting to sit at the edge of the row.

What a mess, I thought to myself.

After the service, one of my church members told me how she saw Mum sitting on her own and she went to sit with her. The look on the lady's face was giving me the message, *I couldn't bear your mother sitting on her own.* I explained to her that Mum had chosen to sit away from us and that she had two children in the congregation she could have sat with. Mum did the same thing later in the evening; Debbie, another church member, described the way she watched Mum bounce to the front to sit. She thought the confidence Mum displayed in a strange environment was remarkable; I couldn't argue with that, could I?

By the Sunday night when the programme ended, I was emotionally drained. Not only by their actions, but also by my frustration that they were not getting healed of their emotional hurts. I am sure if I could have force-fed them the healing at that point I would have. I was at my wit's end when the Holy Spirit intervened. I realised I was taking over his work in their lives; I was struggling for the control. I had to submit to God there and then. Perhaps it was the fact that I had wearied myself trying to get my family healed, and the relief I must have felt at not needing to carry that burden any longer, or the fact that surrender wasn't palatable and was not always easily achieved, or a combination of all those factors—I couldn't say what exactly it was that came over me but I found myself bursting into tears as I relinquished control and handed it over to God.

Caron must have seen me crying. She came and placed a gentle hand on my shoulder. After I had had my fill of crying I explained the frustration I had just experienced to her and she ministered to me. She prayed God's peace over me and gave me a comforting hug. From then on my battle became about how I could restrain myself and not try and force my family to get healed of their emotional pain. It was difficult standing by and not giving in to my impulses. It was a daily walk with God that I had to embark upon in order to continue in that place of self-control.

About six months later, Mum phoned to tell me Yetunde was in London for a holiday. The last time we spoke was when I was told she visited Rex's parents. She was still not keen on speaking to me and I seemed to have come to terms with it.

Yetunde's birthday came while she was in London, so I sent her a birthday card. She phoned a few days later to say thank you and told me she would be leaving the next day, still rather brusque. I felt in my spirit that the time was right for me to confront her. When I did, she was almost in tears.

"Someone is lying . . . someone is lying," she cried.

Apparently, she never went to Rex's parent's house. He invited her, she declined, and that was the end of the matter. That evening, I forced Mum to apologise to me for the anguish she had caused. It was a reluctant apology, as she initially insisted that saying she was sorry was not going to change anything, and that she may say it and not mean it. Nonetheless, I needed to hear it.

I felt ashamed of the feelings I had held against my sister and felt I needed to apologise to her. I was in tears myself; she couldn't understand why. She seemed to have found it a bit embarrassing that I was sobbing.

"How can my mother do this?" I asked Amrita, who must have been overhearing my loud telephone conversation from the kitchen, where she was with Mahesh, cooking a curry.

"You don't let anyone upset you," she said with emphasis.

Easier said than done, I thought.

Mum then, for some strange reason, took on a new form of resilience. She seemed to have discovered a new determination to be defiant and show no respect for however I desired to be treated. I was asleep one night when the phone rang. It was Mum calling for no apparent reason. A week later there was another late-night call. The late-night calls were particularly difficult as I struggled to get back to sleep. But, despite pleas to Mum, the calls did not stop, so, having gained a new level of emotional balance and confidence, I decided to create a rule. I explained to Mum: eight in the evening was the latest I wanted to take calls. If she called later than that, as long as it was not an emergency, she would have to call back the next day because I would refuse to engage in conversation. She probably thought I did not have the courage to carry it through.

The next time she called me late at night, I asked her what it was she was calling about, she said she wanted to say something but couldn't remember what it was. I told her to call back the next day before eight in the evening. Every time she called late I gave her the same reply, as long as there was no emergency. She would stop for a while, maybe a couple of weeks, sometimes months, and then she would do it again.

"Oh, is that the time?" Mum would say when she realised her defiance had not gone unnoticed.

It became crystal clear to me that the problem I was having with my mother was not one I could solve with one or two ministry sessions; there was more to it than meets the eye and I was determined to get to the bottom of it. I requested the RTF ministry a second time. I then went on to be trained to facilitate ministry sessions, in the hope that I could use the understanding I gained from it in my own prayer time.

"A curse is defined as an empowerment to fail," said Pat, the lady who led the training session.

My heart fluttered.

255

I had always known the potential danger of curses and their effect, but somehow that evening a veil was removed, a new perspective was revealed, and a new understanding emerged—I had been empowered to fail. Each curse, every negative word that mother had pronounced over me, was setting me up for future failure. I wept in sorrow. How could I break free from these curses? It then dawned on me that I was in the right place for Mum's curses over me to be broken. I was on a course that was teaching me how to help others break free of curses! It dawned on me that Pat did not mean an empowerment to fail was a permanent state. If it had happened in the past it was possible to break out of it. I was relieved, and prayed frantically for all curses over me to be broken.

It was a joy that I was getting more insight into the spiritual implications of some of the things that had happened to me both in my childhood and adult years. I was gaining a better understanding of the limitations that some of my experiences posed, as well as the solutions to them. I prayed fervently to God for help each time fresh understanding came to me. I was desperate to get rid of the toxic legacy my experiences had left me. But despite all my successes, there were many times when I felt my prayers couldn't reach further than the ceiling of my room. I was expecting significant shifts and I was not seeing those shifts manifest as I had hoped. The understanding of some of my problems and the resolution to them sometimes did not come swiftly enough despite prayers and following the steps in my manuals. I felt confused, and worse, I was not sure what was confusing me.

I talked to my close friends about the challenges I faced. I talked freely on the phone to Busola about my feeling, which could be summed up with two words—"messed up". I needed a channel through which I could offload my burden, and I poured it all out to her. I did not realise I was jumping ahead of myself and ahead of her. I expected her to understand where I was without her knowing where I was coming from. I had gone from being the strong-minded, focused Ayo, to wobbly, crumbly Ayo who spat out nonsense about her mother and the rest of her family.

I had so much in my brain that there was no space to think about how I was presenting the information to her and whether my expectations of her were rather too high. I could sense Busola becoming unsympathetic towards me as she seemed to increasingly expect to see the otherwise well-composed Ayo back on form.

I had, to all intents and purposes, turned my friend into an agony aunt. The friendship that started as a sharing of each other's strengths and interests had become one-sided emotional support. Whilst I would do the same for her in her own time of need, and I have done so to a large extent, she never seemed to be in need of so much support for problems emanating from family relationship breakdowns. Thankfully, God was not overwhelmed by me. He knew exactly what I needed and he made provisions for those needs in the appropriate way.

There was another seminar happening in church; a different ministry was introducing their work. They were called "Freedom in Christ Ministries". They organised a two-day event. The first day was to train people who were leaders of small groups within the church. The trained leaders would then take other people through what they called "Steps to Freedom in Christ". The application to attend the training had to go in with approval from the church leadership. I went to one of our leaders for permission. His answer and the expression on his face told me I must have appeared very desperate in my request.

"Of course, Ayo, you can attend the seminar. I will approve your application, don't worry about it!"

On the first day of the seminar, we were told about the steps and how to help people through them. The person leading the meeting gave examples of people she had taken through the steps and what immediate transformations had happened in their lives. I wondered why I couldn't experience such instant change—be free once and for all. She talked about there being others who were more like onions. Their issues were in layers, and one layer after the other would be peeled away as they persevere on the journey to freedom. Considering the amount of time and effort I had put into this healing process, there was no doubt that I was one of the onion people.

The next day, we were taken through the steps for first-hand experience. Before the session started I went to speak to the minister who would be leading the day's events.

"I don't seem to be able to feel love for my mother," I told him.

He mused a little and told me to go through the steps and see how it goes.

"Come and speak to me afterwards," he said.

I sat in a corner of the auditorium and followed the steps. A memory started to come back to me. It picked up pace and I remembered the event as though it was happening at that moment in time.

I was about eleven years old; my cousins were living with us in our apartment opposite the health centre in Ife. Mum employed chauffeurs for a while because she could not drive, especially during the period when she ran the licensed bar and for some time afterwards. They would sometimes take us to school in the morning and pick us up again in the afternoon. They ran errands for Mum and took her to the market and other places that she needed to go. There was a particular chauffeur who was very good; he was personable and we regarded him as part of the family, like an older brother.

On the fateful day, my younger cousin, Tosin, and I went with him to fetch some drinking water from the university campus; he filled the kegs and lifted them into the boot of the car, while Tosin and I played nearby on the rugged terrain and gravel-finished paths around the empty river dam offices.

Something transpired between Tosin and I and I decided I would not share the sweets I had on me with her. Tosin was upset and sulking. Despite being upset that she wasn't going to get any sweets, she was not prepared to apologise for what she had done, which I obviously felt very unhappy about. The chauffer, brother Biodun as we called him, intervened on the way home and I explained that Tosin had hurt my feelings and she was unwilling to say she was sorry. He asked her what she had done wrong and she said she had done nothing. Brother Biodun seemed to have taken it to mean I was lying (or so I thought) and tried to coax me into giving her the sweets. In a bid to convince him I was not lying, I quoted a saying, which Mum had quoted to us several times, especially when Yetunde was upset and we claimed we did nothing to upset her.

The saying, which was in the Yoruba language, when translated, goes something like this: *He (or she) does not get upset unnecessarily, the bastard would have done something to cause it*—upon which brother Biodun became mad at me and claimed I called him a bastard.

"No I didn't!"

I was puzzled by his reaction.

"Is it Tosin you are calling a bastard then?" he asked.

I thought, *What, is he trying to be difficult?*

I couldn't understand why he said I had called them bastards. Even I, a child, understood that the saying was an adage and therefore should not have been taken literally. I thought he needed to recognise that fact so I set about trying to make him understand.

"Brother Biodun, what I am saying is that the proverb means if Tosin had done nothing wrong, I would have had no cause to be upset and not share my sweets with her. You know, it is something Mummy had said to us on numerous occasions without causing us any upset, it did not mean Mummy thought we were bastards. You ask Mummy when we get home."

"Are you saying your mother instructed you to call me a bastard? I will definitely ask her when we get home!"

I realised the whole conversation was getting rather more difficult and I told him the bottom line was I was not giving my cousin any sweets. He was still furious and said I could do whatever I liked with my sweets but we would have to see about calling him a bastard.

On getting home, he reported me to Mum, and I went to face her with the confidence that she would understand what I was saying and that I did not mean either of them were bastards. I boldly explained to Mum exactly what happened at the dam and on the way home. At the end of my explanation I paused with eagerness, expecting that Mum would in turn explain to brother Biodun that he had misunderstood me and that I would never call either of them bastards. But to my utmost shock, it was as though Mum didn't hear a word of my explanation; she took issue with it all. She said if there was a bastard anywhere, I was the bastard.

During the ministry, the Holy Spirit showed me that, at that point, a wall of rejection and separation came down between my mother and me. It was not difficult to see how or why it would have happened when a mother tells her eleven year old that *she* is the bastard if there was one around.

The pain of the incident became fresh to me again; it was something I had not remembered in about two decades and there the Holy Spirit was, taking me back to one of the reasons

I was unable to feel love for my mother. The hurt was too intense and I found it difficult to forgive Mum at that very moment; I just wept. I went back to speak to the minister leading the event. He looked perplexed when I told him the story. He comforted me and reassured me of my place in my heavenly Father's family.

"Be clear on this, there are no bastards in God's house," he affirmed.

I told him I was not able to forgive Mum there and then, and he looked at me with understanding, encouraging me to work through the hurts and make sure I forgave her for everything. We had a brief discussion about some of the other problems I had with Mum and he asked me what my relationship with Dad was like. I explained, and he asked how it compared to his relationship with the others in the family. The thing was that, even though Dad had displayed an aggressive side, he had a soft spot for me in comparison to my other siblings. At one point I was the only child he could get along with. He would indicate his preference for me in not so subtle ways. For example, one afternoon we were in Dad's car on the way back from school when he stopped at the petrol station to fill the tank. There was an ice cream machine sitting next to the kiosk, staring us in the face. As Dad settled back in his seat Ibidun dug her right elbow into my left side.

"Ask daddy to buy us ice cream," she murmured. "The new coffee flavour," she added.

"Daddy, can you buy us the new coffee flavour ice cream please?" I asked.

Dad reached into his pocket, turned around from his front seat and handed me twenty five kobo. "Go and buy yourself a cone of ice cream," he said.

Of course, I had to share it with Ibidun, who wanted the ice cream in the first place.

He gave me a birthday present once—I had never seen him give birthday presents to anyone else in the family. It was after he and Mum had separated. He dropped by our house as he was passing, which in itself was unusual. The excitement of the moment overtook me and Ibidun. I frowned at him for having forgotten my birthday which was about a week before. His compensation was the gift. After he gave me the present—ten naira—Ibidun took the opportunity to ask him for some money for a few school books. Shockingly, Dad refused! The joy of me getting the money from him diminished considerably at that point. I felt bad on behalf of Ibidun.

Dad's preference for me seemed obvious even to non-family members and extended family. Aunty Dunmola once pointed out that I was Dad's favourite. The minister at the workshop then told me what I had come to realise for some time, which was that my mother may be jealous of Dad's love for me, and that was probably the reason behind the difficulty I specifically had with her.

Before the workshop, during my personal prayer times, I had thought back to the times when things were really bad between Mum and I. There seemed to have been a pattern: she had exposed me to Dad's wrath, while protecting the other children from him. After a while Dad noticed I was the only one coming to visit him and to collect money. He would ask for Yetunde, telling me to bring her the next time I came. Dad had a volatile relationship with Ibidun; he was never too keen on seeing her so Ibidun couldn't go in my stead. But Mum would insist Yetunde must not go with me. This would annoy Dad, as he read between the lines even though I would make up excuses for her not coming. Dad insisted he would stop giving any money at all if other children did not come, at which point Mum reluctantly allowed Yetunde to go with me. Yetunde went once and couldn't be bothered to go again. At least then I was able to tell Dad it was Yetunde's decision not to come. She was generally treated with a lot more respect; she was never forced to do anything she didn't want to do. It was their way of spoiling her as the lastborn.

Mum's protection of the other children had been a cause of concern for me. Looking back, it would seem she did it partly in resentment of the fact that Dad held me as a favourite child, no matter how minute the favour was.

Deep-seated bitterness serves as a blindfold and spreads. Mum seemed to have extended her resentment to other male figures in my life. This resentment appeared to have been at the root of her actions when she insisted I must not go to church without Yetunde. My relationship with God at the time was special to me; it gave me comfort and provided some soothing for the pain I felt inside. God was Father to me. His love was helping me through and she would not have me access all that love alone, someone else had to share it with me.

The concluding factor for me was that all the while she kicked up a fuss about me meeting a possible future spouse, Mum had never met him—she knew next to nothing about Rex or his family. It was not about me choosing the wrong man or going about choosing a man in the wrong way, or even disrespecting her in any way with it. I took sound advice from people she respected and did everything the right way I could think of. If there was something specific about Rex, from what I had written, that had alarmed Mum, a rational approach would have been to want to know more about it. But she simply was not interested in getting to know him, whoever he was; she didn't want to hear it.

Her claim that she thought I had been to Rex's family with Aunty Dunmola and had the traditional wedding done was clearly a woeful attempt to cover up her misbehaviour. During a traditional wedding, the man and his family are the ones who go to the bride's house to ask for the girl's hand in marriage. It is impossible for the bride and her family to go to the groom's house; it is just not done. Also, with all the supplemental "ears" and "eyes" of the church members that Mum requested to keep an eye on me before she left the country, I think someone, somewhere, might have hinted to her something like that was about to happen. Whatever was going on in her mind, in all the various episodes, the common factor was a relationship with a male figure, the kind of love and care she was not able to get from Dad and perhaps other people in her past.

This understanding, even though it wasn't a completely new one, stirred up more anger in me and I developed fresh resentment for Mum. It was as if she had been out to rob me of whatever happiness I could get in life. Why would a mother determinedly want to wreck her daughter's joy? Why couldn't she be glad that the love she didn't have was within her daughter's grasp? Perhaps if she had, she would have realised that the love she coveted so much was not without its challenges.

22

FORGIVENESS

Forgiving Mum took a while.

One evening in August 2004, almost four months after the Freedom in Christ seminar, a friend called me.

"Ayo, are you going to London for the Gathering of Champions? I wondered if you could give me a lift." She said.

I thought, *Gosh, I can't face going all the way to London for a conference when there's always one conference or the other happening in my church.*

"No, I am not planning to go."

But she seemed to have planted the idea in my mind—about a week later I concluded that I would indeed go to the conference. I booked a bed and breakfast for a couple of nights and set off after work that Thursday. I drove into West London as the sun was setting, having left the journey a bit late to make the most of the longer summer days. I went straight to my accommodation and spent the evening unpacking and settling down.

The next morning after breakfast, I knelt down to pray. I read Matthew 5 until I got to verse 44. I had read it several times in the past, but this time it was different. The verse read:

> *But I say unto you, love your enemies, bless them*
> *that curse you, do good to them that hate you,*
> *and pray for them which despitefully use you.*

It stopped me dead in my tracks. *Lord, what could you possibly be saying to me?* I enquired of him. *Are you asking me to forgive my mother? My mother cursed me, told me I was the only bastard around, if there was one, and I am required to bless her? She has been so spiteful and I am supposed to do good to her?*

I could feel the answer inside of me—*Yes, that is what I require of you.*

I argued with God as I knelt there explaining to Him how difficult a requirement it was for me to fulfil, but somehow, within me, I knew he couldn't tell me to forgive if it was impossible. My heart was softened and I agreed with Him. I tried to pray for Mum but I was tongue-tied; I wasn't sure what to pray. It seemed it was my justification for not forgiving—I simply didn't know what to pray about. It was not a tenable excuse; I had been on Freedom for Life and Freedom in Christ courses and I knew what to do to forgive. I prayed to God and asked Him to help me and give me the strength and willingness to forgive Mum and be able to pray for her. I immediately felt some peace. I got up and headed for the conference.

The speaker at the conference that morning started his talk by asking the congregation to think about the person who had the greatest impact on their lives. Such a question would have made me think about the person who helped me the most to succeed in life. For me the answer would have been my mother, had the question been asked about seven years before. She struggled to ensure we got a good education and were not wanting for our basic material needs. She enrolled me for evening classes and I went from term time school to summer school to make certain I was up to scratch with my education.

This time, my take on the question was different. The answer, though, was still the same. I had no doubt that the person who had the greatest impact on my life was my mother, but for different reasons—she had inflicted the greatest pain on me. She had torn my heart apart. The preacher confirmed my answer that the person who had the greatest impact is the person who has hurt us the most, because that, more than any other good that was done, tends to stick. At this revelation, I burst into tears. The woman who was meant to care for and support me had been the one that damaged me most. I grieved in tears for a few minutes and felt calm afterwards. At the end of his message, the preacher prayed for us and asked us to forgive whomever it was. There was a lot of whimpering and weeping in the large auditorium as it seemed others were remembering the pain of their past as well.

I returned to Bath in the afternoon of the Monday bank holiday and went back to my daily life. It was a busy time as I was preparing to move houses, and I moved about a month later. Oldfield Park, my new area, was not as quiet as Weston, though not noisy either; it had a right balance that made it a lively place to live in. The High Street was one of the city's local shopping areas with variety of shops: there was the Woollies at the end of the road, the large pet shop, the DIY place, the British butcher and a number of banks. They all kept the area vibrant, especially on Saturdays. To top it all up, Oldfield Park was nearer to work and it took me about forty minutes to walk the two miles distance.

I settled into the house pretty quickly, sharing with Holly whom I met in church. Holly had been on similar courses as me, as had a lot of the members of the church. Sharing a house with someone who had the same level of understanding of life issues was a blessing.

A few weeks after I moved in, I set out of the house and headed to work. It was a bright, slightly warm autumn morning. The sun was high in the sky and the ground damp from the morning dew. Slugs and snails littered the paths as I walked through the back alleyways into town. Mum was not far from my mind. Thoughts of her replaced the busy house-hunting and moving arrangements that had swamped my mind in the previous few weeks. As thoughts of her emerged, my heart jumped for fear. I noticed some resentment had started to creep in. *Where is the forgiveness I gifted her with?* I asked myself.

As I turned left from the path overlooking the back gardens on Old Park Lane, a light was turned on inside me. I realised that during the various courses and ministry sessions, I had forgiven Mum for a lot of specific offences, but there were still a lot more that I hadn't forgiven her for, particularly the "bastard" incidence. Also, during the conference I had forgiven her generally for the things she had done—a sweeping prayer which didn't really go deep into the root of the offences. Not by design; it was simply the way the meeting flowed. In a large conference with several thousands of people in attendance, there is not usually the time to address every detailed event of life.

Whilst Mum remained forgiven for everything I had forgiven her for, I needed to address the specific offences that I hadn't touched on. That revelation itself sent shivers down my spine. There was a part of me that didn't want to address those specific horrors that were sneaking into my thoughts. As I walked into work that day, further realisation came to me that it wasn't just the fear of remembering the offences that held me bound. There was also the fear that if I did find a way to forgive Mum for all the things that she had done, she herself would be able to justify her own actions. And perhaps, through this justification, she would never find a way to change her behaviour for the better.

A lot of other people had hurt me throughout my life, and I had always been able to forgive them. But it is harder to forgive where I felt unable to impact my relationship with the perpetrator. It was thus difficult for me to consider completely forgiving Mum's systematic offences. Yet, somehow, this was the challenge I needed to face.

There was no time on the road to pray too long a prayer, so I asked God to give me the grace to forgive her for everything I needed to forgive her for. When I got back home that evening, I remembered some daily devotional entries on forgiveness that I had read about a year before. I went on the internet and searched the archives of Word for Today to print off the entries. Throughout the following week, I went into the Bath Abbey every lunchtime to pray and forgive my mother.

It was difficult opening my mouth and saying the crucial words, "I forgive my mother." I knew it was the bondage of fear that I felt, so I forced myself to say those words as many times as I needed until it sank into my spirit and I actually believed it. I held my stomach as I forced the words out of my mouth. It was like inducing a vomit to extricate a foreign object from the stomach.

After a few weeks I noticed how the thought of my mother no longer repulsed me in quite the same way as it had done before. It was then that the Holy Spirit took me to another level. He reminded me of the passage in the Bible that said, ". . . pray for them which despitefully use you" (Luke 6:28, KJV). I told God it was enough that I was able to forgive her, but to ask me to pray for her was going that little bit too far. I then remembered a line from the Bible that read, "Vengeance is mine . . . says the Lord" (Hebrews 10:30, NKJV™). I was afraid of God's vengeance. I told God I would rather punish her myself than have Him punish her. But again, I had to come to the understanding that God knows how best to handle all of us, after all He created us and loves us the same.

The Holy Spirit then showed me specific prayers I could pray for her, which was that she would one day come to understand the saving grace of God and receive the love of God into her heart. Then she would know who she is in Christ and let His love heal her pain, whatever the root of that pain was, whether the pain of not being given the love she desired, or the pain of not being cared for or supported by the significant people who had that responsibility towards her.

23

MOVING ON

A fter that breakthrough in forgiveness, I thought I was finally going to be free of all the emotional baggage I was carrying, but that freedom still seemed as far away as it was at the beginning.

I felt there were still hindrances in my way and I couldn't figure out what they were and how I could overcome them. I had physically stayed away from Mum, but psychologically she was still there, inflicting pain. My own close friends, whom I had expected understanding and comfort from, condemned me for abandoning my mother and isolating myself from the rest of the family. I felt hurt that my friends did not understand me. Nevertheless, I still held them in high regard.

"How are things between you and your Mum?" they sometimes asked.

Initially, their asking lured me into a false sense of security and I would tell them about some of the challenges I still faced in the hope of a sympathetic view from them. I would wake up to reality when they expressed the same view they had always held, that I was unforgiving and aloof. There were times that I doubted myself and wondered whether they were right. I wondered whether all my emotional turmoil would end if I patched things up with Mum, behaving as if none of the problems had ever occurred and that she was the best Mum in the world. Somehow I knew it was not the answer. As far as I was concerned, Mum in many respects had always been a great Mum but it did not stop her from hurting me and breaking my spirit. There must be a better solution. I decided I was not going to get my friends involved in my family feuds anymore. If I needed comfort, I would pray and trust God that He would bring comfort to me one way or another. They still brought the subject up more often than I wanted.

"So when did you last visit your Mum?" Shewa demanded.

Like a reproached schoolchild I answered, "I actually haven't seen her in a while."

"Ayo, you have to forgive her and move on. What has happened has happened."

Her harsh tone disquieted my spirit. I felt intimidated but remained obstinately quiet. It was Busola's turn next. She just about fell short of throwing Exodus 20:12, where it says honour your father and mother, in my face.

"I'm really not going to say much . . . you know what the Bible requires . . . hmm, anyway."

Each time, I felt like telling my friends to mind their own businesses. Why couldn't they let me be? If I was angry and bitter, it was with good reason. What I needed was their comfort and encouragement to get out of that bitter state (which I wasn't in anyway). I didn't need them beating me over the head with what the Bible says or what I should do, not when I had put so much effort into forgiving Mum. I'm not sure there is any other human being on this planet who had spent so much time and effort forgiving their mother as I had done. All the same, rather than defending myself and asking my friends to keep their opinions to themselves, I directed the conversations away from my family.

Despite my calm approach to my friends' meddling, and regardless of the fact that I knew I had forgiven Mum, their words, their challenges and insinuations stuck in my head like mud. They became heavy, disjointed layers and I couldn't think how I would pull the layers away. I battled with voices in my head telling me life was not going well because I was at odds with my mother. I felt cursed all over again: either my previous plea for God to break every curse over me was not effective or my friends' judgements of me brought the curses back to life again. There were times when I could not pray because of the unwelcomed murmur planted in my thoughts by the allusions from my well-meaning friends. I was sure I had forgiven Mum for what went on in the past, even though some of the memories still brought me pain, but the confusion of my present situation was even more painful.

I sat down in the front room one Saturday morning and read John Arnott's book on forgiveness.[1] There was the story of Carol, his wife, at the back—the story of the problems she faced with her mother. Somehow, it occurred to me that it was the day-to-day relating with Mum that I was finding difficult. The grind of that relationship was taking its toll on me. I realised I was in a better place than I had been when I started on my journey of wholeness, but it was still not the right place to be. I needed help with how I could handle her late-night calls when my strategy didn't seem to be working, how I could deal with her continued attempt at control and manipulation in such a way that I would not get wound up.

I spoke to Holly, who was also one of the church's administrators. I asked her if there was a facility within the church set up for someone to give me some practical advice on how to handle these day-to-day issues. She suggested I spoke to Rosemary, the care leader. Rosemary in turn directed me to a couple who, I understand, were trained counsellors.

The first evening I met Dave and Gill, I tried to explain to them how I got to the place of needing help with my relationship with Mum. They seemed to have misunderstood me. Dave, in particular, told me that I had been rebellious towards my mother and I was now facing the consequences. Their judgemental attitude increased the hurt in me. I left them that evening feeling a need to forgive them.

The battle in my mind grew stronger. I reached the nadir of despair and there seemed to be no one else to turn to for help. The following Sunday morning, I got up to have my quiet time, but pressure mounted inside me and reached its peak. I could find no words for God so I got up to go into the bathroom and get ready for church. As I entered the bathroom and stretched out my hand to grab the toothpaste, I felt a gush inside me. I held my stomach and everything in there felt heavy. I focused back on God but my endeavour to communicate with Him turned into weeping, and then the heaviness in my stomach came out of my mouth as words. I couldn't cry out loud; I couldn't bear Holly hearing me downstairs where she was. I wailed silently with lamentation to God. I told Him that my accusers were not without their own sins and that His word said if He (God) should mark iniquity, who could stand? (Psalm 130:3)

I went back into my room and curled up on my bed. As I cried to God, a moment came and in that moment everything around me seemed worthless. There was a surge and, for a split second, I felt like turning away from Him, but something inside of me turned that idea on its head. And then, worse still, I reached a place where my life felt meaningless and there seemed to be no reason for me to keep going. In that instant, I felt I knew exactly what must have been going through some people's minds when they decided to end their lives. Something needed to give way—would it be my life?

At that point I got myself out of the house and went to church.

I met Margit at the door; she was glad to see me and asked how I was. I explained to her that the problem with my mother was getting me down. She had her own issues with her son to talk about. I asked Margit if she would apologise to her son for the things she may have done wrong to him, but she seemed a bit disinclined. She later told me how she had written a letter to him, shortly before he got married, telling him how much she loved him and how sorry she was for some of the things that had not gone quite well. She said she didn't want him going into marriage without realising how much he was loved. I tried to give her some encouragement, telling her there was nothing better she could do than make right whatever she might have done wrong.

At least I was out of my mental decline. My mind was back at work. The immediate problem was alleviated, but it still felt as though there was a ball and chain holding me back like a prisoner. The most important thing to me, in my world as it was, was to be completely free. I was desperate for help. I had been on a number of healing and deliverance ministry sessions but I would not hesitate to attend another one if it meant my thirst was quenched. In my desperation I walked over to talk to Phoebe, a friend in the church, who was honest enough to tell me she really did not have an answer, but that she would pray. She prayed, and we went together to lunch.

At lunch, I met another friend of hers, Irene. Irene had a lot of comforting words for me. She gave me real pearls of wisdom. She had the heart of a mother, even though she was neither married nor had any children. Later that evening, Phoebe called round to drop a book off for me. It was titled

Boundaries.[2] As I read it I felt liberated. Through reading the book I realised I had suffered from guilt—unnecessary guilt. This is not the same guilt as I felt when I had genuinely done something wrong—that was remorse. The guilt that was affecting me was that when anything went wrong around me it always felt as if it was my fault, regardless of who was to blame for the incident. It is one of the reasons I was affected by what people said to me, especially when their words were condemning. I took the guilt to God and asked Him to deliver me from it.

I gradually started to learn more about boundaries, even though it contradicted my way of thinking. My guilt mentality told me that it was cruel to set boundaries, but my new self knew it was the only way out and the right thing to do. I was getting practical understanding of how to deal with the day-to-day encounters with Mum. I didn't need to cry to my friends for help anymore. It occurred to me that they may never come to understand where I was coming from and what made me the way I was. They were only acting and talking from their frustration at having a friend who seems to always have an enormous weight on her shoulders, who had had bizarre life experiences, by the standards of their own experiences, and whom they were at a loss to help.

It was always good to get answers such as this. The problem was that they still only went so far in helping me to resolve the issues I was facing. I continued to feel oppressed by my mother. She did not give up. I was on my way back from visiting a friend in Bristol one Sunday afternoon, two weeks after I had started to read *Boundaries*, when Mum called. I found somewhere to park to take the call.

"What is your breast size?" Mum asked in a rather undignified manner.

"What?!" I screamed.

"What is your bust size?" Mum replied in a stammer.

I asked her what on earth she wanted my breast size for. She told me she was travelling to Nigeria and she got me a lace fabric that she wanted to sew for me while she was there.

If you bought someone a fabric that needed sewing, you wouldn't just phone them and ask them for their breast size; they would not wear the outfit on just their breasts! You would tell them that you had got them the fabric first and *then* ask for their body measurements—and that would be if they wanted the fabric in the first place! *What have the breasts got to do with it?* I wondered. Somehow I thought it may have to do with the fact that during her first visit to Bath, Mum had seen a fabric in my room and insisted on sewing it for me when next she went to Nigeria. I had refused. Her now impending travel to Nigeria was the first since that incident.

Whilst, in the past, I had adored her resilience, knowing her fortitude kept us going as a family and prevented us from buckling under the strain of single parentage, it was getting to the stage where that resolve was working significantly against me.

Mum felt in control when I was growing up because she was the provider; that probably fuelled some of her negative behaviour. Now, in my adult years, Mum still wanted to have the same type of control, but changing roles are natural and unavoidable. It is often said that change is part of life, and I have heard some people describe it as life itself. I believe we all need to learn to grow with change, even though it is challenging and scary sometimes. Mum's own need to be in control was so great that she couldn't see a way through the change. Being needed gave her a sense of purpose. She had rightly chosen her career. She probably would not have been fulfilled doing anything other than nursing. The desire to be needed, however, should have a limit.

I took after Mum's generosity, but I realised soon enough that there is a limit to generosity after I was taken for granted by some of the people I was generous towards. I almost became an object of provision rather than a human being seeking relationships with fellow human beings. Mum, on the other hand, seemed to regard this understanding almost like an enemy; without being needed she felt she was stripped of her sense of purpose and inherent value. She always required her actions to save her children's day, and she felt a great sense of achievement when it did.

We all want to be heroes in our own ways—God knows I share this desire—but I realised that aspiration needed to be placed under control lest one became an attention-seeking adult. The irony was that Mum did not bring her children up to be dependent on her or anyone else for that matter. Her approach to childrearing told me as a child that I needed to stand on my own two feet. What she did not work out was what her relationship with me would be when that happened. She didn't quite think her strategy through. When you train a child to mature and be successful in life, the side effects are that the child becomes independent of you and you will need to find a different role besides being the primary provider for that child. They will no longer look to you to provide shelter, clothing, food or anything of such major significance. The fact that parents of such children still have a part to play in their lives would stem from any positive relationship they have been able to establish. Mum still wanted the position she had occupied; not having that job was not good enough. The child she made had come through dependence and now chose her own interdependencies. I had to—the way she had tried to make us dependent on her and then showed us up for it meant we all knew we had to make our own way.

Whilst it seemed easy enough for a parent to claim they do not wield control over their adult children's lives, the reality is often a different story. With Mum, there was a force with which she fought change to the last, until the other person was either broken or pushed to the wall and they fought back like a bull shown a red rag. My mother's resistance to letting me go and become the person I should be meant I was thrown into a dark and confusing state all the time, feeling bound and hindered. It meant I was constantly looking for ways to heal from the cycle of control and rebellion that Mum and I were in.

I went forward for prayers in church the Sunday after my telephone conversation with Mum and three weeks after my encounter with Dave and Gill. I explained I had a difficult relationship with someone and I needed some prayer support to get through it. I did not reveal the identity of the person, because I didn't want the people praying with me to judge me for having a difficult relationship with my mother. I was well acquainted with one of them, but did not know her well enough to trust her not to judge me. They prayed and were very supportive. Somehow my acquaintance had an inkling it was my mother and gave me some nuggets of wisdom. Apparently she'd also had some difficult relationships within her immediate and extended family members, so she understood my frustration.

She brought some tapes for me to listen to. They were talks by Chip Judd, an American pastor. He talked about how to set boundaries in relationships. The tapes were such eye openers for me. For the first time, I realised *all*, not just some, of my feelings were part of my boundary definitions. If I felt angry or sad and something external was denying me the ability to express these feelings, my boundaries were being violated—albeit if in the expression of those feelings I hurt someone else, I would then be breaching their boundaries. If the person I hurt was the person who violated my boundaries in the first instance, it *might* be okay, depending on the details of my reactions and the circumstances within which they occurred.

When I had felt sad and hurt in the past, especially during the difficult days in London, I would sometimes call a one-woman pity party. I would cry and feel better after crying. I would feel sorry for myself and tell myself what a cruel world I lived in. Once I had my fill, I would turn back to the Bible and prayer for some soothing until I was ready to get going with my daily life. I did not share my pain with other people. Whether they saw it in my eyes or not, I was not particularly bothered; I owned my pain and unconsciously kept my boundaries well secured. All that I wanted from the people I related to was to enjoy the time we shared with each other. But there was only so much crying, so much pity and sorrow for myself I could feel. To get a lasting result, God knew I needed to travel back in time to deal with the root of the problem.

My new understanding of boundaries encouraged me to revisit some aspects of the RTF ministries that I had received. An important part of the ministry was about identifying and changing the negative beliefs I held in my conscious and subconscious mind. The teachings of the RTF ministry gave me the understanding that with the hurt, pain, and disappointments of life come negative or ungodly beliefs, to use the terminology of the ministry. These could be ungodly beliefs about oneself, about other people, about God and about life in general. It occurred to me that these beliefs would have particularly gained ground in places where my boundary definitions were blurred or non-existent. If my feelings formed part of my boundary definitions, then these beliefs that I held may themselves become boundary definitions, because what we believe usually determines how we feel and act.

It turned out that the hidden ungodly beliefs that I had numbered well over a hundred. I would have continued to live with them and would not have seen them for what they were, nor would I have realised their effect on my life. In fact, I did not consider that some of them, which I expressed in words many times, were negative beliefs; that was until the Holy Spirit convicted me of them. In many cases, they just seemed like the fact of the case.

One of these beliefs was that my mother needed to use me as a guinea pig to learn to deal with whatever relationships my siblings may enter in the future. My thought at the time it all started was that, because I was the first child to enter into a committed relationship, my mother was not used to the idea and she needed to get the shock (or whatever the problem was) out of her system and then learn to incorporate it into her family life.

Nothing could be more wrong, but subconsciously I continued to hold on to this belief for years until the day God pointed it out to me. When I thought back to how the belief came about, it was clear how easy it was to allow lies to be established. It was one of the subconscious reasons I continued to appeal to Mum's better judgement on the hurt and pain she had caused me.

Another strong negative belief that increased my desire to appeal to Mum came from the various criticisms I received from other people, especially those from my close friends. Their insinuations that if I did not phone my mother every week, every Mother's Day, or visit her every month, then I was somehow dishonouring her became the belief within me that I was not progressing in life the way I desired because I was at odds with my mother. Of all the beliefs, this seemed to have been the strongest in its effectiveness. It kept me bound for a long time. As someone who was "in recovery" from hurt, it was another battle I could have done without.

God, in His mercy, spoke. The first thing He showed me was that I was never at odds with my mother; it was my mother who was at odds with me. Whether this fact was apparent to observers or not did not make it any less true. The most liberating part of His message that day was that He would not hold me back because of my mother. He reassured me that all the criticisms I faced were set up by the unseen enemy to hold me bound in the belief that I was not progressing. This belief, if not dealt with, would then have become a self-fulfilling prophesy. After that, I learnt to deal with such criticisms pretty quickly.

Another negative belief that came out of other people's criticisms and their "encouragement" for me to get over my problems was that I was an unforgiving person. I realised people judged the pain and hurt in my heart as being unforgiving. It is one thing for us to forgive, but healing comes gradually. What I needed was healing and an understanding of how to set boundaries so that I was no longer violated by my mother's torrent.

I listened to some other messages on what healthy relationships are like, how unhealthy relationships are formed, and the destructive power of shame. I began to learn how to value and appreciate myself even more and reject any projections contrary to those values that anyone might be advancing towards me. I learnt to own my pain and sadness in a new way. I would not be put down for having issues. I had to understand that I did not choose to have those issues because I did not choose the life experiences that had led to them—not most of the experiences, anyway.

Joyce Meyer was preaching on boundaries and walls one day, prompting me to clarify to a large extent what boundaries are. There are different types and definitions of boundaries: a wall could define a boundary. The wall could be made of brick; it could be made of timber. A wall is impenetrable, but when there is a door in the wall others can be allowed in at the appropriate time and in the appropriate way. An emotionally healthy person will always knock on your door and wait for you to open it. They will not crash in. If the person knocking is unknown or unwanted, the door is kept shut, and they will leave unless they are deranged.

In a house, there is the front door and, for a lot of houses, the back door as well. When a friend comes around, no matter how close they are to us, they knock and we let them in. Once they come in, there may be areas within the house where they do not need to knock before entering because we have mutually, whether verbally or by mere familiarity, agreed to it. They may follow us into the kitchen without knocking; they may enter the dining room when invited expressly or impliedly. There are other rooms where they will still need to knock. They would normally ask permission to use the bathroom and if the door is shut they may need to knock before entering. If they are an overnight guest; they may knock on our bedroom door for a good reason.

I believe the life of an individual is like a house: there are areas where one can enter, because we are familiar with each other and there is an unspoken or spoken agreement to do so. There are other areas where, out of courtesy, we need to knock by way of asking before we enter or interfere. This fosters mutual respect and honour. The Bible talks about "*in honour preferring one another . . .*" (Romans 12:10, KJV). A big part of boundary recognition is that it is not solely about respecting oneself but also about having consideration for other people. I learnt to appreciate and honour others more. Sometimes it is difficult. As they say, old habits die hard, but with practice and a conscious effort it is possible. I allow others to be themselves better than I had done in the past. That way I can grow out of my need to control them.

My need to control others stemmed from wanting to ensure that my needs were met. The fear was that if I didn't make them comply, my needs would go unmet—whether a need for company, help or the need to be respected and valued. I am able to accept that sometimes some of those needs will not be met the way I want them to, but I can look to God, who is the provider for my needs, to meet them as He deems fit. I do not have to resent others for not being there when I expected they would be. If others resent me for not being there for them the way they expect me to be, I can resolve it with them if possible. If not, I can keep away from them as appropriate.

24

A VERY LAST CHANCE

M um did not visit for a long time.
Her last visit to me was only for a few hours and that was eighteen months earlier, in 2005. She had picked up on my determination that I would not be controlled in my own home and she had retreated. Only, her retreat felt more like a rejection. I would have preferred if she came to visit and just let me be, not snarl cooking advice at me and try to order me here and there. I was not too sure why I still allowed thoughts of her offences to fill my head, but I was coming to realise that I missed not having close-knit family; it had created a form of isolation for me. I loved my family so much that I wanted things to be different. Even if we were not overly close, I at least wanted for us to interact civilly. We had been part of each others' lives for so long and my upbringing was such that families always stuck together. The gulf that now existed between us was sometimes difficult to cope with.

Notwithstanding any loneliness I might have felt, I was not prepared to go back to the abusive and manipulative relationships I had with them. I could only hope that one day they would gain better understanding and things would be different.

Mum rang me early in June to say she was coming to visit me two weeks from Saturday. I was pleasantly surprised. I waited for her phone call the Saturday morning that she said she was coming and when I didn't hear from her I phoned her about noon to ask when she would arrive. She could not say because she had not thought about it yet. By mid afternoon, I decided I needed to go out and do my shopping. I phoned Mum to see if she was on her way. She still hadn't left the house, so I suggested to her that perhaps she should not bother coming, as by the time she got to Bath it would be time for her to go back.

"Is there no room for me to stay over?"

Even more surprise!

"Err, yes, there's plenty of room. It just didn't occur to me you might want to stay."

I explained to Mum that I wanted to travel to Bristol to do some shopping. I wouldn't like her to have to wait at the station for very long before I picked her up and that was the reason I wanted to know when she would be arriving. She said she was happy to wait, and she sounded honest in her response.

I went off to do my shopping in Easton area of Bristol, where one could find some Afro-Caribbean and Asian shops, and then I headed to Asda in Brislington. I was pushing the trolley into the checkout when my phone rang.

"Ayo, I am here in Bath."

It was over an hour before I got to Mum, but true to her words she looked happy enough when I met her. I was the one stressing unnecessarily about having left her at the station for an hour. At home, I made a nice meal of fish stew and spinach. After the late meal, we settled down comfortably in front of the television. It was then Mum told me she wanted to stay over because she needed talk to me, that she needed my help on something that was going wrong—my younger sister's relationship with her fiancé. Oh dear.

She had fallen out with Yetunde over issues relating to the relationship. This time she was not telling her not to marry, but still there was a falling out. I listened intently to what was bothering Mum as she poured her heart out. We did not go to bed until two-thirty in the morning. I promised her I would call Yetunde and speak to her the next day. I was happy to help wherever I could; I did care for Yetunde and I had been on the receiving end of relationship fallout, so I was prepared to help both of them in any way I could.

The next morning was fine. Mum and I were getting on well; she was happy to have received the support and assurance she needed. We got back from church and I tried to get hold of Yetunde but she was not picking up her phone. I promised Mum I would speak to her during the week and I went to make lunch.

I was eager to make the best of the opportunity that was laid out before me and Mum to forget all that had gone on in the past and just enjoy each other's presence for that one day. I thought a nice comical family DVD would provide a focus for us as we ate. We could make commentary and have a relaxed time laughing. I needn't have bothered; Mum didn't seem that much interested. She became irritable, and no amount of effort to make it a pleasant bonding time worked. She was in a hurry to get her train and get to London early. At first it was quite frustrating, as Mum had always preached to me each time I tried to talk through our differences and effect the necessary change in how we related to each other. She would quote what seemed to be her favourite Bible verse in Isaiah: 43:18, where it says, "Remember ye not the former things, neither consider the things of old.", (KJV). In other words, she was telling me to forget about the past and move on.

I thought now was the perfect opportunity to do just that, but Mum didn't seem to be able to get past whatever it was that was preventing her from having a good relationship with her daughter. It was starting to be clear that where there is an offence, the best thing would be for all parties involved to confront and resolve it. If not, someone will always find it difficult being completely free with the other, no matter how much they tried. It appeared to me that when Mum quoted me the verse, what she was doing was trying to bury the past when it was not dead. Perhaps it might have served us both well if she didn't read just her favourite verse, but also the preceding ones and those after.

The subsequent verse to Mum's seemingly favourite says, "Behold I will do a new thing; now it shall spring forth; shall ye not know it? I will even make a way in the wilderness and rivers in the desert." The story of the passage was that God was asking the Israelites to follow him and stop turning their backs on Him. He laid out what we could call His resume, asking them to remember the great things He had done for them in the past. In truth, according to the Bible, He had led them out of their slavery in Egypt and parted a whole sea for them. He rained food from heaven and water came out of dry rocks for this small nation when they were in the wilderness. He now told them to forget about all those big things He had done, because He was prepared to do new good things for them. If this was a passage that was relevant to burying the hurt of the past, then, in effect, what my mother was saying to me was that I should forget the bad she had done because more was on the way. And in truth that was what was happening; she has never been able to allow herself to behave in the right way towards me.

I was no longer enjoying Mum's presence so there was no need to persuade her to stay. I dropped her off at the station and she left. From then on, there were copious reasons that she was unable to visit me.

25

I CAN INFLUENCE MY
OWN DESTINY

"In your passage through life, you want to be fully in charge of the route, the events, and the destination: in order to do so, you need a clear view of where you have been. The amount of control you have depends on whether you live your life as your own person or allow another person within you to direct your energies and thoughts . . . your 'inner child of the past' that retains the burdens of your early days."—H Norman Wright[1]

I t felt as though the past had been finally laid to rest; it was time to move into the present and look forward to the future. Perhaps it would be time for me to meet a good man that I could marry. I started the year of 2007 with thirty days of prayer and fasting and had a prophetic dream every night of the fast. In one of the dreams I was hanging out with a bunch of people, some of them old classmates from my secondary school. I was handed a bouquet of red gerberas by one of my friends. When I woke up I prayed that God would reveal the meaning of the dream to me.

The dream was apparently telling me that I had residual anger inside me towards Mum. I had thought I got rid of all the negative emotions towards her. I knew I had been previously angry with her; in fact I had been livid and felt fully justified. But clearly, deep down inside, I was still very much infuriated and the dream was pointing that hidden negative emotion to me.

About two weeks after I had the dream, I went to church for the worship team meeting. We, the backing vocals, were having an interlude while the worship leader worked with the guitarists to perfect the guitar chords for a song we were rehearsing. Kimberly, one of my friends, and I started chatting. As if to confirm what the dream was telling me, she talked to me about my anger towards Mum. Kimberly had seen me with Mum when she had visited in the past and seen how I had built a wall of defence up against her. It was my way of protecting myself from further hurt after forgiving her. When she refused to visit, I put emotional barriers up so that her rejection did not hurt me. When she visited and wanted to control me in my own home, I built up a wall of anger as a counter attack.

When I got back home that night, I decided it was time for me to surrender my anger to God. I asked Him to deliver me from it. The next day, I drew up a strategy for releasing the anger and wrote down my newfound philosophy. I printed it out and hung it on the kitchen wall as a constant reminder.

About four weeks after I had hung my newly acquired wisdom on the wall, Tunde, a friend of mine, came round for lunch. I watched him as he read my "expose". I wondered what he thought of it as I was beginning to get a little nervous in case he found it strange, but he smiled and nodded in acknowledgement of the sentiment. After that, quite a number of people came into the house and they had similar reaction to Tunde.

I had already come to the understanding that anger is one of our God-given emotions which helps us to understand when our boundaries are being breached by someone else. There are passages in the Bible that support being angry—Ephesians 4:26 says, "Be angry, and do not sin: do not let the sun go down on your wrath" (NKJV™). I believe this simply means do not be angry for too long—resolve it before your anger turns into bitterness, because in another part of the Bible it says, "See to it . . . that no bitter root grows . . . to cause trouble and defile many" (Hebrews 12:15, NIV).

I learnt to be friends with my emotions, especially my anger. When I am angry, I welcome it and work with it to help me determine the root of the anger so that I can deal with the cause as well as the symptom. When I was growing up, I repressed my anger, thinking that it would go away after a while and that life would go back to normal; after all, for me as a child, this seemed to be exactly what happened. Someone would offend me and I would greatly resent them for it for a few hours or days and then it would fizzle out and we would become friends again. Of course, a lot of that anger was never actually resolved, it was only muted. I realised that the anger my dream referred to was deeply rooted; it belonged not only in the present, but had origins from events that had taken place in the past. Now I am mature enough to face the issues that caused my anger: its root in the past and its trunk and crown in the present day.

After the fasting, I still had a nagging feeling that there was some unfinished business somewhere. I felt restless and kept trying to look for a solution. I went for some counselling with Pastor Olu. I had the opportunity of meeting and seeking counsel from him during the difficult days in London and now, in another moment of need, I thought I'd go to see him again. He is a very busy man, but I had a brief chat to him after a Sunday service in his church. He asked me to book an appointment to see him at a more convenient time for a longer chat. I did not get a slot in his diary until about two months later.

The day of the appointment finally arrived and I travelled up to London. Unfortunately a wider church matter was taking up his time, but he left his meeting to pray with me briefly. Even though the prayer was short, I felt much of a divine authority and the presence of God in the room. I came out hanging on to every word of the prayer as if it was the last breath that would save my life. I had been worn out and needed the faith of others to carry me through.

The next day, there was still an urge within me; the momentum had changed from restlessness to a steady driving force. I surfed the internet for inspiration and it occurred to me that what I needed might be professional counselling. I searched for Christian counsellors and found one that also offered Christian life coaching. This inspired me to find out more about life coaching as a concept and I contacted the various Christian coaches I found on the internet.

One of them, named Joel, phoned me back almost immediately. He sounded very enthusiastic and took the issues seriously. It felt as if I had found an ally in my journey towards wholeness and fulfilment. I made an appointment to see him the following week. He was based in London and we agreed to meet in Paddington where my train from Bath terminated.

When I met Joel in person, I explained more about why I wanted some coaching. He asked me about my childhood and I told him a little bit about some of my experiences.

Eventually, he asked me if I realised that I had actually been abused as a child. I looked at him and the response was clear in my mind. I may not have defined my challenges in those terms, but clearly that was what they were. He said he could see a little child in me who had been abused but longed to be re-affirmed and loved, a child who was seeking the attention and approval of others in a constant bid to gain that love and re-affirmation. His words struck a chord.

He pointed out that when I try to seek approval, I sometimes grabbed the attention for myself. What he was saying was not difficult for me to see, even though my thought would not have journeyed along that direction if someone else with that level of insight had not pointed it out to me. My actions seemed perfectly justified; many people around me do the same and even worse. He then went on to challenge some of my wrongdoings.

"Why do you try to control others?" he asked.

I did not have to think deeply to find the answer.

"It's not that I want to control others, but if I need help and it seems the person may let me down, I try to make sure that they don't. I've become aware of that tendency and I keep working on it."

"Good," he said. "Make sure you keep working it through."

I did not feel judged by Joel; it felt more like a truthful friend correcting me in love. Therefore, knowing I had faults and that they were apparent to someone else was not shameful for me, and it certainly was not annoying or upsetting that he was pointing these faults out to me.

We had sat down talking in the lobby of the Hilton for about an hour and a half when he told me what the time was. I was astonished; it felt like we had only been there for thirty minutes. After our first meeting, I spoke to Joel every week for a month.

In one conversation, I remember, I ranted about Mum a little.

Joel was quiet, almost as if he had dropped the receiver. I paused for breath and continued. Eventually I stopped. Still, there was no answer from Joel. I was going to check he was still there, and then he spoke.

"You are still pining for your mother's love, aren't you?"

"Well, what is wrong with that?" I could feel another round of ranting gathering pace within me.

"There is nothing wrong with it. It is a natural feeling," Joel responded. "Do you think you will get that love you desire?"

It hit home. I answered, "In all honesty? I doubt it."

"Then it's time to stop looking for it, don't you think?"

It sounded reasonable enough, but it wasn't that easy.

"Everybody needs and deserves to be loved and cared for by their parents. Why should I lack the most natural affection of all?"

"You are not going to lack it because you are going to get it in a different way, from a different source," he said.

The conversation was getting quite interesting. What alternative could there be for a mother's love? Could other older women step into the breach? I thought that to some extent in my adolescent years, some of the men in my church had provided some fatherly input at one stage or another. Maybe something similar may happen here. But that was not the case. Joel had a completely different idea.

"I think you will be the one to mother yourself and provide the love you crave."

"What?"

I gave a loud laugh. He surely must be joking. He really couldn't have meant that.

"How am I going to do that?" I asked, questioning his wisdom more than seeking clarification.

"You need to love yourself in a healthy way."

"But I already love myself."

"Not in a healthy way."

Just what I needed to hear! was my sarcastic thought.

"Ayo, if a child was to be crying, what would you do to that child?"

"I would give him or her a cuddle and try and give some comfort."

"Why don't you start mothering yourself by giving yourself the comfort and understanding you need?"

It all sounded quite cumbersome, but I thought I had no option but to accept what he was saying. Maybe one day I would come to understand how I could comfort and care for myself.

Coaching was extremely helpful, but it became too expensive for me to afford. It wasn't just the cost, I couldn't figure out what to do with the crush I'd had on Joel from the first day I met him. We must have been less than half an hour into our first meeting when my feelings went haywire. That was my first ever crush, and at the age of thirty-four!

I had always been ruled by my head, even in my tender years; there were guys I liked and who I could see myself dating but there were never strong feelings involved. Joel was clearly not interested in me in that way and deep within me, I knew it was not the type of relationship I desired, but the feelings were extremely overwhelming and arose quickly. I had never felt anything like it before. It made me re-examine myself and question what was wrong with me this time, why I was falling in love with a man I would not necessarily choose. My friend Leticia called it lust. I did beg to differ with her; there was something about him that I found irresistibly attractive, and that was that he connected with me in a way that no one else had ever done before. He was not trying to be intellectual or flaunt any form of physical attractiveness. He touched something deep down within me. There was a need in there that was exposed and started to be met by my interaction with him. Any physical attraction was secondary.

It was at this time that I decided to try counselling; life coaching was more about achieving life objectives, while counselling seemed to be about overcoming effects of past bad experiences. I contacted several Christian counsellors and felt I should try two of them: a man, Paul, and a woman, Jane, to see which one of them God would lead me to go with. I ended up taking counselling from both of them at the same time.

Once I had explained why I wanted counselling, Paul asked me to tell him about Dad and from there on he focused on my relationship with him. He said the problem was that as a girl, I would tend to choose a marriage partner that reflected who Dad was. This revelation had an inauspicious ring to it. There had been one or two things about Rex that had made me think, . . . *hmm, that is just like my Dad*. He seemed to have had the same outlook as Dad when it came to certain issues. I did not like those viewpoints, and they were some of the reasons I had concerns about the relationship. However, I had never thought or heard before that the two could be connected. It would not have occurred to me that I was searching out "Dad" as a marriage partner. I had been previously aware, from the ministry sessions I went through, that a mother's relationship with her children affects the children's ability to build other relationships. Paul throwing Dad into the equation was new, and I struggled with understanding how it could happen that I would look for my parents in a man. However, the evidence was there before me; I could sense that it had actually happened. I decided to accept it and not worry too much; after all, it was very possible that when I chose someone to establish a key relationship with, I chose someone like my parents.

Jane naturally veered towards issues about Mum. The good thing about the counsellors was that they were professionals and tended not to judge. There was a level of insight that they had, which seemed to have helped them avoid jumping to the wrong conclusions about me. Issues with each parent were dealt with in detail and for as long as was required to fully address them.

Jane was tender in her approach. I seemed to have found the mother that I had been looking for in her. It was obvious that several times she felt my pain, even where I had become numb to the pain myself. Paul, whom I corresponded with by email, gave a touching reply to one of my messages. He said as he read my account of some of the things that happened in my childhood that he could hear the sound of that child that I was, and he was moved.

Going through counselling, I started to see and understand better how my life and my disposition towards it were shaped by the nature of my parents. But I continued to feel uneasy about the lack of clarity on Paul's indication that I was searching out Dad as a marriage partner. My acceptance of his principle did not last long. How could I have chosen someone who had similar traits to Dad when I was not aware of the person's intimate character at the time I chose to embark on the relationship? I was restless again. I wanted to understand and do more to resolve whatever issues there were in that area of my life as a result of my parentage.

It occurred to me to read books about the father-child relationship. I bought about twenty books. They were full of insights. There were times while reading the books that I felt like confronting Dad. I realised he was the source of my timidity, with Mum capitalising on it. He had taken my courage from me and I needed to get it back. As it happened, I did not need to confront Dad. In the course of my day-to-day life I came across a man who thought the world revolved around him. I knew I had no choice but to challenge him; there was no other option if I was to get my peace back.

Gary, who was originally from coastal Devon, had asked to stay with us in the house while he attended a four-week course at Bath City College. Tara, an acquaintance of mine, made the request on his behalf as she was aware there was a spare room in the house. Gary was about five foot ten inches tall and heavily built. He would come in late in the middle of the night and stomp nosily all the way up the stairs. He came in one evening and told me he had been playing football and had injured himself, tossing his shirt off to reveal his bruised chest and marching up, right into my face, to show it to me. I had to back off in a stagger as the choking smell of sweat filled the air around me.

"Look at it! Look at it!" he said.

I tried to be polite and not tell him what I thought of his manners. When he used the bathroom and toilet, they needed extensive cleaning and mopping to make them useable for the next person. He had no concept of other people's personal space, nor any consideration for their feelings. Worse still, he believed he was one of the cleanest and most considerate people on earth. Diplomacy didn't seem to work when it came to getting Gary to improve on his manners. I knew I needed to let him know in clearer terms that his behaviour was unacceptable, but I found his brash attitude rather intimidating. When I confronted him, all hell broke loose. He expressed verbal and physical aggression, pushing towards me as though he would attack me. I firmly stood my ground against his bullying and asked him to leave and find a hotel to lodge in for the rest of his stay in Bath. Even though the confrontation frightened me to the core and I could feel myself shaking inside, I was determined to do it. Afterwards I had a good cry to Leticia—we had learnt to be open with and support each other (at the same time, we were also able to tell each other some home truths if need be).

By my interaction with Gary, I had confronted my fear of aggressive men. I didn't expect the fear to vanish immediately after that but I knew deep down that I had taken a very significant first step in ensuring there was an end to it.

With the understanding of my relationship with Dad fully gained, I still needed to understand my relationship with Mum better—and not simply *understand* it, but also deal with its problems and resolve them. Counselling with Jane had opened my eyes to a lot of the dynamics of Mum's relationship with us, her children. We provided emotional support for Mum while she met our physical needs. Mum didn't really give us any emotional nurturing, probably not out of choice but from the effects of her own experiences.

I decided there was more to learn about these relationship dynamics and their effects. I went on to my favourite online Christian bookshop to order some books. To my disappointment, I did not find relevant books about the mother-daughter relationship. Frustration started to set in but was soon apprehended. I reluctantly went to Amazon.com and found scores of books. One of the books was titled, *I Am My Mother's Daughter: Making Peace with Mom Before It's Too Late*, by Iris Krasnow. I was captivated by the title, and thought that if at all possible I would like to make peace with my mother. I was curious to know how I could go about doing this.

On the night the book was delivered, I switched my bedside light on, sat up in bed late and buried myself in the book. Towards the middle of it the author made a very profound statement: she said, "*A mother's hands can build a house of horrors or a house of peace. A mother's fingers shapes the moments with her children and their destiny—whether through a slap, cooking or by stroking them."*[2] My immediate reaction was to question what type of house I was capable of building. It was intriguing that I was not questioning what type of house Mum built. My focus was starting to shift to what legacy I was capable of leaving behind. It increased my resolve to confront any issue that would make me less than the person God made me to be.

In the latter part of the book, the author concluded that friendship with our mothers can come if both mother and daughter are patient enough to meet each other totally and faithfully. I wondered if this could ever happen with me and Mum. I would always meet her totally, and with all honesty and faithfulness. The question had always been, would she? I had very serious doubts of a positive answer to that question. One reason for this was that the picture my mother seemed to have of her children is one where they have no right to any form of respect at all. It is not possible to meet the other person with any level of honesty if respect for them is completely lacking.

I thought back to some of the ways Mum had displayed this lack of respect—the ways she tried to defy my dislike of her late-night calls and the ways in which she tried to turn my siblings against me, and it was difficult to see how Mum could make a U-turn from that path. I could feel anger slowly brewing up inside me towards Mum. I knew there was only one thing for me to do with the anger that was beginning to fester—take it to God.

"Will I ever be free of anger against this woman?" I asked Him.

I felt a reassuring answer within me that the more an issue is exposed the easier it would be to deal with, and what I must not do is stop dealing with it. So I knelt down and asked God to strengthen me so that anytime I feel overwhelmed by anger or other negative emotions towards Mum, I would not give up dealing with it. Dealing with the issues did not mean I would never have another angry outburst or never feel anger towards her again, because if she hurt me in the future I would need to express my anger; it is a God-given emotion. I asked God to help me measure my anger appropriately.

On finishing Iris Krasnow's book, I read another book, which was fittingly titled *Mama Drama* by Denise McGregor.[3] It became clear how my own "mama drama" had unfolded over the years, including the criticisms I took from Mum when I was younger. One of the things she constantly criticised about me was my big eyeballs. If I dropped something it was because my eyes were too big for me to see what I was holding; if she asked for me to bring her something else from her room or the kitchen and I couldn't find it, Mum would tell me that, despite my ridiculously big eyeballs, I still could not see. She derided the eyeballs as though they were the reason I was not the child she wanted.

When I was twelve years old I stood in front of the mirror. I was unaware of the existence of cosmetic surgery, yet somehow the idea of an operation to reduce the size of my eyeballs came to me. It never crossed my mind what other people, apart from Mum, thought of my "ugly" eyeballs. I guess it was just enough that Mum ridiculed them; her scorn settled my own opinion of myself. Therefore, when one afternoon Titi, a classmate of mine, told me I was beautiful, I thought there must be something wrong with her. That day, I stood in the corridor outside my classroom when she came out and stood opposite me. She looked straight into my eyes and held her hands out towards me. She brought them down on my face and gently stroked my chin saying, "My God, this girl is beautiful." I gave her a wry smile. I thought she was either out of her mind or blind. I knew, from her countenance, that she was not joking and she was not mocking.

It was not until a few years ago that someone told me that she had seen my mother and recognised her immediately because our profile was very similar. I was revolted by the thought of looking anything like my mother. I tried to verify the woman's claim by checking myself up in a mirror. I couldn't see what she was pointing out and forgot all about it.

A few months later, over Christmas, a friend of mine called Daren was spending the day with me. I brought out a camera and he got busy taking photos. There were shots of me as I stood in the kitchen preparing lunch. When I printed the photos there were some that had captured my profile perfectly.

Urgh! I do look like my mother!

My eyeballs were more pronounced from the side and they were exactly like Mum's. I had inherited my profile and eyeballs from her. Fancy that! As I read *Mama Drama*, it started to bring home the fact that my mother's criticism was probably not very much about me but about her, because what she criticised most about me was the feature I had inherited from her. The realisation did not make it any easier to bear. I hated my profile after that. If there was a magic wand I could have waved to change it, I would have, but the mama drama needed to stop. I took myself through a gradual process of accepting the fact that I see that side of me as ugly because it's Mum's view that it is ugly. This helped me change my opinion, and I kept working on seeing myself as just me—it proved a challenge but I got better at it.

What I had forgotten was that as a young girl I used to admire my mother's beauty. In my teenage years, indeed, until just a few years ago, I believed Mum was beautiful and I would have been glad to be her exact replica. Her inner strength and formidable spirit shone brightly in her face and any trouble in her soul was obliterated by that light. When she got dressed and combed her hair slightly out on her forehead, under her head tie, she looked a million dollars.

One of the other things that Mum's constant criticism did for me was to push me to strive for perfection and the approval of others. By late spring of 2007, I decided it was time for me to move back to London and I began to apply for jobs there. I applied for one particular post and went in to be interviewed by the woman I would have been working with. The interview started well. Although there were one or two signs that caused me a little bit of concern, I yanked the concern aside and threw myself into the meeting. I had spoken to the interviewer on the phone before then and thought we would get on well together and that I would be happy working with her.

She told me about the organisation and asked me about myself. I told her about me, my career to date and my future aspirations. Towards the end of the meeting, she told me she did not think I was suitable for the job, that the details of my experience did not particularly match what she was looking for. This was the kind of organisation I had longed to work for, and I thought there could be no way that I would be unsuitable for the position. I started out calmly in my efforts to redeem the situation and make sure I let this potential employer know what benefits she would derive from appointing me, but I got increasingly exasperated, wanting to prove myself to her. I was so eager for her to hear me out, to give me a chance, that I blew it in the end. It was classic of the description given by Scott Walker when he said, "*the pain of our woundedness is pressing us to perform, labour . . . to prove ourselves, to self-destruct . . .*"[4]

On my way home from the interview, I thought of how to get my mind off the mishap so I picked up the *Mama Drama* book to continue reading. Needless to say, I got the answer to my disappointment on the pages I read while sitting in a bar at Paddington, waiting for my train. I realised that in trying to please the woman in the interview, I was trying to please my mother.

As I gained better insight into my relationship with my parents, there also came a better understanding of what a family should be like. I was inspired one day to set out, separately, what I believed the role of a father and a mother in the life of a child should be.

I believe that a child gets his or her greatest approval and sense of self-worth and value from the father. This serves as a strong basis of emotional and psychological strength for the child. The father is a guiding force in the child's life. A strong, emotionally healthy father will leave a good emotional legacy for the child and help the child to have focus and a sense of direction in life. I believe that the role of a mother should be one of providing physical and emotional nurturing through meaningful and healthy bonding. This, I believe, creates the security and love that the child needs for balance in life. Emotional nurturing can only come through empathy, understanding and acceptance of a child.

An appreciation that God brought to me some years ago was that, among the complex web of issues that faced my family, Mum had tried to provide the input needed from a father—so much so that she lost any sense of being a nurturing mother. The fact was, she could not be Daddy, and in trying to be Daddy, her own role as Mum went unfulfilled. Having come to this understanding, I was able to further accept some of Mum's shortcomings and forgive her for them.

26

LEARNING LOVE AND BREAKING FREE OF CONTROL

I lay on the settee in the living room, watching God Channel television. My mind had wandered away from the small screen to a new book I had started reading: *Facing Co-Dependence by* Pia Mellody.[1] Not that the preaching on the channel at that point had anything to do with co-dependence; if truth be told, I had hardly heard a word of what was being said. No sooner had I turned on the television than my mind wandered away.

Joel's voice rang in my head—*You need to learn to love yourself in a healthy way.*

How much more do I need to love myself than I already am right now? What does it mean to love myself in a healthy way? These were questions that followed.

I was used to hearing about God's agape love from the preachers in church. I never questioned my understanding of the phrase. It seemed pretty straightforward to me: the unconditional love of our heavenly Father. That is what He gives to us and He expects us to love others too. I learnt to love my family unconditionally and I thought I did the same for myself. They did not have to do anything special for me to love them, and I did not have to make an effort to love them; not loving them just didn't cross my mind. It was natural and effortless for me to care for my family. I might have, at the time, made an exception with Ibidun because of the difficulties I believed she was putting the family through. The question that now seemed to emerge was, did I love them so much that I did not think enough about loving myself?

I had stood by Mum.

Back when she was about to turn fifty, she looked at herself and asked aloud what on earth her achievements were at fifty years of age; she was clearly disappointed with the way life had turned out for her. I wasn't having any of it. I recounted to her all that she had done and achieved—seen three children through secondary school, one of them a graduate with a good job in London, another one on her way to becoming a graduate. Sensible children with high moral standards and no pranks about them; to me she had achieved more than some families with both parents available. That cheered her up to no end.

I never questioned my family's love for me. I questioned their sense of right and justice, but not their love. I was required to carry out chores in the house every morning before school like any other child in any other family. It was a general routine in families with disciplined children. In Olalekan's absence I did most of the housework because Ibidun and Yetunde were excused for one reason or another. That was until I decided to rub Ibidun's nose in it. She would not be scorned—she started making an effort.

After Olalekan left home, I was aware that I was my mother's "favourite" child because I did a lot of the housework. I knew I earned her approval that way. I thought to myself one day that if I went to live with relatives they would take to me because I would help them with their household chores. I soon found out that not everyone based their love on the amount of chores that were completed in their home. It was a mystery to me at first, but I soon understood that life didn't work the way I thought it did. Notwithstanding this knowledge of mine, I seemed to have continued in ignorance as to what true love was and I was blissfully unaware of the fact that I was missing something.

The first time I came close to realising what true love is was when I first got to London. One of the leaders from the main church was teaching about loving someone for who they are and not what they do, and I held the meeting up with my request for clarification. It did not make sense to me because my understanding at the time was that who a person is and what they do is one and the same. An example I quoted at the time was that a person who always attended church, and helped out each time, whether by cleaning the chairs, setting up the musical instruments, or sweeping the church loves God. Whereas, you could say someone who doesn't do all those things does not love God. To which he answered:

"Do you have someone in your life that you love?"

I said, "Yes."

"Do you love them because of the things they do?"

I went quiet. Then I answered, "No."

"That settles it then," he said.

A few months later, the senior pastor's wife, Joanna, did some teaching on unconditional love and I started to get it.

Now, almost ten years later, Joanna's teaching came back to my thoughts. I realised what I had from my mother was love based on strict conditions of me being available to her. Her love for me had a price tag—I had to make her look good; otherwise I was to all intents and purposes a disappointment and potential source of shame until things went back to "normal".

Mum and I had created a co-dependent relationship with each other. She gave me the approval I needed and I, in turn, gave her the emotional support she needed. The approval I got from her was, however, not a healthy one, and the emotional support I gave her was not sustainable in the long term. That co-dependent relationship had a destructive effect on both of us, and I made up my mind that it must stop.

I realised that I had continued to believe that I still needed Mum's approval for me to be successful in life, especially when it came to marriage, but that approval and support was not forthcoming. Mum was not even prepared for me to be a woman, much less a married one. She considered it her duty to control every aspect of her children's lives, and if she wasn't ready for us, we should wait for her. Mum had succeeded in giving direction to our education and spiritual development, therefore it was not inconceivable that she would consider herself the one to control and direct our future with a spouse.

My problem was that I had been so dependent on Mum for directions in the now-thriving areas of my life, that I didn't know how to succeed in the areas where she hadn't laid such a good foundation. I might have been able to somehow eventually find my way, but she was not ready for me to try without her at the helm. If it got out of her control it must be truly out of control, and she had to shatter it. We don't respect what we don't understand. Perhaps a better prayer for Mum to pray, in the days when I took my first steps towards independence by loving someone else and preparing to share my life with them, would have been for God to guide me through those decisions and help me to make the right ones, rather than calling down fire and brimstone.

The truth is that every child needs their parents' blessings to separate and individuate. Dad, whether rightly or wrongly, and despite his threat of asserting himself when the time came for me to be married, talked to me a lot about marriage. He did so especially towards the end of my secondary school days. On those occasions when my visits to him went okay, he would chivvy me on to complete my education by the age of twenty-one so that I could settle down with a good husband. I am not sure he considered himself a role model for my future husband, but I never got the sense that Dad would fly off the handle if I brought a guy home at the age of twenty-two.

When it was time to introduce my "intended" to Dad, I first went on my own because I had not seen Dad for some years prior. I needed to reconnect with him and prepare the ground before introducing Rex to him. Initially, our conversation centred on trying to catch up. That was immediately after I finished my university studies, albeit three years later than he had recommended, and he was asking what my plans were. I was, for some reason, trying to impress him and hide the fact that there was a man in the picture. As I told him about the grand plan I had to do a master's degree and then probably a Ph.D., he leaned forward to get a good look at my face. He gave me a questioning gaze and said:

"That is all very good, but where does a man fit in all these plans?" It was such a relief to hear him say those words.

Dad's adopted approach was in contrast to Mum's unwavering struggle to be in control. She didn't seem to know when it was prudent in her interactions with me to back down. Her energy seemed to be renewed anytime there appeared to be an opportunity for her to dominate. Whilst I appreciated—indeed, thought it was great—that she had set a firm foundation for our lives in various ways, now she seemed unaware that her four young children were grown up and needed to live their own independent lives, and that they may make mistakes, but with God's help they could rectify those mistakes without her.

Clearly, no good parent wants their children to make the same mistakes that they had made, but smothering those children will do even more harm. Standing back a little bit and respecting the children and their choices, even when you don't agree with those choices, is a better way forward. More importantly is for a parent to pause and ask themselves the dreadfully tough question—"Is my desire to control the situation truly in the interest of the child, or is it for the fear and anxiety that I have for myself?" If intervention is required, some level of respect for the child's choice is important if the child is to respect the other point of view.

Trying to get Mum to see reason had always been like banging my head against the wall. She would try all sorts of alternative ways—back routes, side doors, rip the roof out to climb down or tunnel through the ground to crawl in. When I lost my temper and shouted her down, it felt as if the ball and chain re-emerged and I felt trapped all over again. I was looking for her approval of me as the grown up, thirty-something-year-old woman that I really was, not a bullied, abused teenager—and I certainly did not want to be turned into a bully and abuser myself. Mum, on the other hand, was lost without her role as the fearsome mother that she had been and the conflict continued. The control and rebellion cycle that Mum and I were locked into brought me endless frustration. This vicious cycle was one of the reasons I was in a double bind, sometimes feeling as though I was not forgiving of Mum.

Perhaps the greatest revelation I had in my quest for emotional maturity was that it was not Dad I was seeking in a man, it was Mum! It was a Eureka moment when I came to that understanding. It was the final piece of the jigsaw in my pursuit of emotional wholeness, and it was a relief to be able to put it in its rightful position. Mum and Rex (and strangely enough, Olalekan, too, in certain respects) had a lot in common in the way they treated me. When I settled down to think about it, it really was not a surprise. Mum was the primary parent in my life, and she had the greater influence.

The similarities between Mum and Rex in the areas of control and manipulation were clear. For both of them, if control and manipulation did not work, they didn't give up; they tried emotional blackmail and resulted to slander if the blackmail failed. Dad was slightly different: if he couldn't get you to do his bidding by force he withdrew into his own shell. One could easily ignore him and stay out of his war path.

For both Mum and Rex, it was as if there was something in their lives they couldn't quite fulfil and they saw me as the person who would make it better. Because I was not fulfilling whatever it was they wanted, I was criticised. If I still couldn't or wouldn't act out their will, I was criticised more, their frustration coming out in angry outbursts, alienation, and put downs.

Mum and Rex may never have met but they were of a similar breed. With my family, because my experiences with them started when I was young, they had been able to establish their terror at an early age. That terror grew up with me, since I did not have a way of confronting it. Even in my adult years I could not foresee any situation in which I would completely cut them off, although I had refrained from seeing or contacting them as often as I used to.

The understanding of how it could be that I was looking for the familiar in the man I would choose to marry started to crystallise. It was definitely not the similarity that drew me in the first instance. I had read *The Fourth Dimension* by Paul Yonggi Cho and made my list of ten things that I wanted in a man. I had a pretty good idea what I wanted him to look like and the type of temperament I wanted him to have. None of those things that I specified were in any way similar to what one would find in my family. However, once the similarities between Rex and my family began to emerge, I did not consciously understand them as being comparable to some of the negative trends in my family of origin; they were merely things I would rather were not happening. As Norman Wright puts it:

> *"All people do not try to recreate their original families when they marry. Many want just the opposite and look for a spouse who is different. They are trying to escape from their original family and to build some type of new one . . . But often in their blindness they may overlook buried similarities that emerge later on."[2]*

I also believe that when people are attracted to us, they can subconsciously sense some traits that they are familiar with. The same is true of when we are attracted to someone. We may not be able to explain why we are attracted to them, but subconsciously we sense in the person those qualities that we recognise. We feel at home with them. Some of these will be positive traits and some will be negative.

In any case, Rex had claimed that the problems we had in the relationship were because I did not know how to treat a man right—hence his rotten attitude. It was believable. After all, I was the one from a broken family. I even asked him to exercise patience with me, that I would learn how to treat a man better. This was despite the fact that I was never clear on what it was that I was doing wrong (or not doing at all) in the way I treated him. What I later realised was that although he wasn't from a broken home, he was more broken and fragmented than I was. A lot of families repress their emotions; they bury whatever would bring them shame in society at the risk of their emotional well-being.

I did not have the instinct to reject his behaviour and walk away from him. I understand better now that his behaviour was familiar to me; I had lived with similar behaviour since I was a child. Whilst I definitely was not happy with it, I was not able to deal with it appropriately, and in any case not with all of my focus being on appeasing Mum. All the energy I should have put into myself to focus and properly address the issues in the relationship was spent in dealing with my mother's own anger. It was that focus that might have afforded me clarity of mind and the emotional strength to actually walk away from the relationship before things got really ugly, but, like a lamb to the slaughter, I walked further into it.

It became clear to me how some of us choose wrongly and why some people are just "lucky". It isn't luck, per se: it is all circumstantial, circumstances that have become more of a destiny. That destiny, however, is subject to change. It only takes a bit of hard work and perseverance.

PART V

WALKING IN FREEDOM

27

LETTING GO

I bidun called me one Saturday afternoon, in the autumn of 2007, to say she would like to visit me in about three weeks' time. She had been more consistent in visiting and I was a lot more at ease inviting her over. It was always nice to have a family member come to visit, reminding me that I'm actually part of a family and didn't simply drop to earth from the sky.

It was, however, not all plain sailing when my sister visited. Her last visit had tested my tolerance to its very limit and pushed many of my age-old buttons. When Ibidun visited, she seemed to remember our childhood rivalry and set herself up for a competitive few days. I found it draining. All I wanted to do was to spend good, quality time with my sister, not have to fight off competition from her. I decided to confront Ibidun about her attitude. But I had a problem; I was scared of confronting her. I didn't know why or where that fear came from.

I casually mentioned the problem to my friend, Leticia, who encouraged me to phone her and let her know how I felt. The thought of phoning Ibidun scared me so much that

I decided to write her a letter instead. I thought about the message I wanted the letter to deliver: first, I wanted her to have no doubt about my love for her as my sister; next, I wanted her to be clear about how much her actions were affecting me and the impact they were having on our closeness. Finally, I wanted her to know that I cherished our times together and that I wanted them to continue, but that I was not prepared to continue getting together if it meant her old attitude continued. Armed with my goals, I wrote the letter.

I didn't hear back from Ibidun.

Mum called me the following weekend. She sounded weighed down. She groaned a bit and said very little. Her tone and silences told me there was something that I had done which she was not happy about, but she seemed unable to bring herself to challenge me, which suggested that I really hadn't done anything wrong. My instinct told me it was about the letter that I had written to Ibidun. It was not difficult for me work out what Mum must have found upsetting about the letter: for reasons known only to her, Mum never seemed able to confront Ibidun. My writing to her in such a firm, but calm and loving way would have seemed to Mum audacious. While Mum clearly had her hands full when we were growing up, and Dad's violent temper did no one good in learning to resolve differences civilly, it was obvious Ibidun needed a stronger hand. Instead, I had grown up with the fear of the repercussions of challenging her behaviour. I believe this fear was the reason I was not able to summon the courage to speak to her about her attitude, choosing to write her a letter instead.

I thanked Mum for her call and ended it. Mum called again the following week. She was very chirpy, extremely so, in fact:

"Mmm . . . hmm, who was it again that called me the other day and was asking after you. Ah, yes, it was Yewande."

Yewande is my cousin who lived in New York—Mum wouldn't usually give me such messages. I hadn't seen Yewande in about five years; she was as busy as I was and we tended not to call or write to each other, instead catching up once in a blue moon when we met at family occasions.

"She came to visit me a few weeks ago, you know."

"I didn't know," I replied. I thanked Mum for her call and left it there.

A week after Mum's second phone call, Ibidun called me to talk about the letter. When such a letter is written to someone who is not used to being confronted in love, it can dent their pride a little. This came through in Ibidun's response to me, as she initially sounded a bit angry and defensive. But even then, her reaction was extremely mild compared to what would have happened when we were children. The Ibidun that I knew in my childhood would not have taken that letter lightly. She would have gone the whole hog to make sure everyone around felt the impact of her anger. This time, it was different. Her changed self got the better of her and she eventually accepted that she might have been in the wrong, even promising that she would watch out for such behaviour and be careful not to repeat it.

What a relief!

It had taken so much for me to write her the letter, and to have such an amicable resolution was practically heaven—bliss! I was very grateful for the way my sister had accepted her responsibility and I made sure I expressed that gratitude to her.

A few hours after Ibidun's call, the phone rang again. It was Mum. She was not pleased that Ibidun had tried to defend herself and that I had stood my ground—and especially not that Ibidun had eventually apologised. She reproved me for writing the letter at all, explaining that Ibidun had shown it to her. She expressed how disappointed she was at me for sending such a letter, knowing my sister's condition. Even now, in Ibidun's adulthood, Mum still couldn't let go of the age-long excuse for letting her off the hook. I do sympathise with my sister's illness, but it definitely didn't handicap her as much as Mum made out that it did. When Ibidun was ready to do the things Mum said she couldn't do, she did them of her own accord and without prompting from anyone—although there might have been the occasional remark from me.

Mum continued her angry reproach, telling me I didn't know how to talk to people. I am not sure she could ever have imagined what followed because I had my own fit of rage and told her never to confront me over anything that happened between me and anyone else, ever again, much less my own sister. Mum mellowed. As if trying to cover up years of allowing my sister to get away with murder, Mum tried to take on a more assertive tone.

"It is not only you she does it to. She does it to me as well and I have told her about it. In fact, I rebuked her strongly."

Mum's assertion was met with my resolute declaration that I would sort out my relationship with my sister, independent of her. I couldn't help but call Ibidun to ask her to shed some light on what Mum had said. She was unequivocal about the fact that she had not asked Mum to speak on her behalf. My sister was adamant that if I had any problem with whatever Mum said that I needed to take it up with her directly. To be quite honest, I was proud of her for her answer. She was applying the principles of boundaries to the situation, whether she realised it or not! *All we need in this family are boundaries*, I thought to myself.

Apparently, Ibidun had not understood what I meant by some of the things I said in the letter, and she asked Mum's opinion in explaining their possible meanings. Mum then took it upon herself to challenge me. It seemed either the maturity I displayed or the possibility of Ibidun rising to a higher level of maturity bothered Mum. I did not, for one second, believe it was about Ibidun, or that I had done anything that needed to be corrected. It was Mum's need to be needed. Yet as a grown-up, I must sort my own relationships out. I did not need her as I did when I was a child. An emotionally healthy adult should be able to determine when and how he or she needs their mother, as well as when it would be appropriate to ask their mother for help.

In seeming retaliation, Mum left a stern message on my answer phone on Christmas day, about four weeks after the bust up, telling me how disappointed she was that I did not even think it necessary to come to her for Christmas, when the least I could have done was spend the day with her. That was Mum making her own stance known, just as I had done with her and Ibidun.

She talked as though it was the first time I had the nerve not to visit her in London for Christmas—I had not been to Mum's place for Christmas for about six years.

When I got the message, I flipped again.

"Mum, I think you need to ask yourself a question—why does this girl not want to come to me for Christmas?"

Mum yielded. She said she only would have loved it if I had been around, and her message was never in the harsh tone I claimed it was. At that point I had had enough. I thought about the past seven years that I had spent forgiving her and seeking healing for my wounded soul. In that instance I realised that the past ten, fifteen years of my life had been about my mother, and that I was growing old. I did not want to look back in five or ten years time and realise I had done nothing but fight to be free from her. I wrote to her, saying that I did not have whatever it was that was missing in her life that she was looking for. All that I wanted was for her to leave me to live my life however I saw fit, and if she was not going to do that I would walk away from her. Even then, as I wrote the letter, I looked up to God and asked that He would not allow to happen anything that would make me walk away from my mother. I couldn't imagine what life would be like without her, especially as she would, in the not so distant future, be entering her twilight years.

Mum wrote back to me, defiant. I phoned her in response but only got further rebuke as Mum told me I was the one always making accusations and that I was never without my own incendiaries.

"You make out as if your sister is the only one that caused trouble in the house. Remember the day I came back from work and I met you two fighting and Sylvia was telling me it was entirely your fault?"

I was shocked. Not because Mum told me I was a troublemaker in my own right, but that she remembered as much detail as she had revealed. Throughout my years of seeking emotional healing, I had refrained from taking Mum back to events of the distant past because I thought it was so long ago that she would have forgotten it all. I myself had not remembered the particular incident until she mentioned it. Once she did, the details of the fight came back to me.

My anger was rekindled, not least because Mum remembered what she wanted to remember and not what actually happened. The incident she referred to occurred in the days when Ibidun was at home after her O-level exams. Yetunde had arrived home from school before me; she must have been about seven years old at the time. I had walked half the way home in the burning heat of the tropical sun. I came home hungry and tired and slumped on my bed, still in my school uniform.

I overheard Yetunde asking Ibidun to give her something to eat for lunch. Ibidun told her to go and ask me. I wondered *why me when I'd only just arrived home?* To be honest, that day, I could have done with a cold bath and someone who would wait on me hand and foot. I told Yetunde to go back to Ibidun, explaining that I was tired. I again overheard their conversation as Ibidun reprimanded Yetunde.

"Why did you mention my name? Why couldn't you simply ask for your food?" she queried.

I ignored the conversation until I heard her order Yetunde to bring the cane with which she started beating her. She insisted Yetunde had mentioned her name on purpose, knowing it was going to cause trouble. My strength came back to me in a jiffy; I flew out of my room and grabbed Yetunde from her. Ibidun turned on me. I seized the cane from her and beat her as much as I could. Yetunde's screams attracted the neighbours, who came in and saw me beating Ibidun—not knowing what had gone on—and they blamed me for the fracas.

After jogging Mum's memory, she was quiet.

Looking back at the times when I thought I had let Mum down through my fighting with Ibidun, I now take a different view. I no longer think I let her down and caused her grief. We were two growing children trying to iron out our differences and some guidance on respecting each other would not have gone amiss. Although I'm not sure Ibidun would have bought any twaddle about mutual respect at the time, but even then it was not a reason to refrain from promoting the message.

After the momentary silence, Mum went on to remind me that I had brought her shame when I caused our neighbour to criticise her. He had said we were spoilt because we did not have our Dad around to discipline us. Whilst I didn't expect Mum to remember that, too, it was no great surprise to me that she did; I had always suspected that criticism had been the motivation behind some of her drive.

Mum bows to pressure too easily, and the final recipients of that pressure were her children. The neighbour was the only person I knew of who criticised Mum (and if you ask me, I think it was his need to justify his existence in his own family that caused him to make that criticism the day he did). The truth was that all the respectable men around us at the time appreciated my mother for the work she was doing in bringing us up single-handedly. We were surrounded by men who by all worldly standards were successful: there were surgeons, other medical practitioners, university lecturers, Ph.D. holders and many more. Moreover, they were men who had happy and successful family lives. Those who could came to Mum's aid when she needed help, especially when it came to references for our university applications, helping me get onto the right course and generally throwing in one or two words of encouragement.

My mother is not one given to looking at the facts of the case: if someone said it, it must be true, and even if it is not true the fact that they said it mattered more than the fact that it was false. All subsequent actions were then based on what they said, not the facts of the case. The way they see us matters, it matters more than anything else; in fact, it is the only thing that matters! That was The Way to Live in My House Act 1978 c.3, passed by my mother's one-woman parliament. I thought answering Mum any further was not going to yield a positive outcome. I told her I did not want her leaving annoying messages for me anymore and hung up the phone.

After that incident, I noticed Mum started to call me "darling" anytime she phoned. Ordinarily, I would be chuffed to be referred to as "darling", and on the face of it, Mum calling me "darling" may seem natural—but it was not. I knew my mother well enough to understand her "darling". The tone of the "darling" was very belittling, infantilising; it was not "darling" in a loving and caring way. Mum had felt defeated on two counts, the first with the letter to Ibidun and the second with the Christmas day telephone message. She was not going to give up easily; her next strategy was to talk to me like a small child. At least that way she could still feel like my mother.

At first I ignored it. I was tired of fighting her. But then something rose up within me, and I decided I was going to fight to the end. The thought occurred to me that if everything had gone well with my relationship and I was married with kids, my mother would not be calling me "darling". In fact, she would probably still be cursing. Growing up, I couldn't remember Mum calling me "darling" on an ordinary day. If she called out *A-yo-mi-de*, I knew all was well and I would saunter to her with confidence. If she shouted *Ayo!* I would start racking my brains to think what I might have done wrong.

I decided to let Mum know how I felt about her recent use of "darling", and that I did not want her calling me that anymore. She insisted she was not going to change even though I maintained my dislike of it. That was what marked the beginning of the end. I needed peace. I needed healthy relationships, and if she was not ready for that then I would have to keep away from her. I also knew that on the face of it, this was silly because a great deal of tolerance is necessary to deal with others, no matter who they are, especially because we often act as though our close relationships are foolproof and can do without the respect we afford to others we know less well. However, that lack of respect veers towards emotional abuse when we show it repeatedly and deliberately, for whatever reasons.

A few weeks later, Mum called me to say my cousin had had a baby. She wanted to ask my opinion on whether she should pay him and his wife a few days' visit. I felt burdened by Mum, not because she asked for my advice, but for the reason that Mum tried to infantilise me when it suited her and then expected me to step up to the position of a wise adult when she needed my counsel. I was aggressive in my reply.

"You are the mother; I am the one that should be coming to you for wisdom, not the other way round. If you do not know how to relate to your own nephew, then so be it. Don't ask me, I am not responsible for you."

Mum responded with self-pity. "Well, I know my God will teach me what to do, He created me and He will help me."

"Let Him teach you, just don't ask me."

Whilst I realised my heightened sensitivity at the time accounted for my aggression, it did not detract from the fact that I was tired of carrying Mum. I wanted to be carried, too. I needed emotional support and I had to pay for mine. I knew that Mum had a lot of issues from her own childhood that she tried to avoid facing. Those issues were the reasons behind some of her behaviour, and those same issues would drive her into worse behaviour if I allowed her to get away with the small things. I could not continue living life that way. I needed a break.

Mum left a voicemail message on my mobile phone about six months after she insisted she was going to continue calling me "darling". She had said what she wanted to say and, as if she was out to provoke me, she extended her message including an emphatic "darling" somewhere in the middle. I phoned her later in the week and told her that I never wanted to see her or hear from her again.

She cried out, "Ayomide, because of a man?"

Mum now put everything that happened between the two of us down to her belief that I was desperately hurting over losing Rex and that I was both regretting it and blaming her for it. This was over ten years after I had broken up with him, and the fact that I had explained to her more than once that I do not consider her directly responsible for the breakup of the relationship and that I never regretted that it ended. I would have preferred the circumstances of the breakup to have been different, but I learnt a lot from it. If she was to blame for anything, it was praying to God that the relationship be destroyed . . . well, she got what she prayed for. It brought to mind the phrase, "be careful what you wish for". Only, in this case it would be: be careful what you pray for, because if you get it, what will you do with it?

I gave no reply to Mum's cry and hung up.

After hanging up the phone, I took a deep breath and I felt a wave of peace wash over me. Had I just found the peace that I had longed for so much?

28

MOTHER'S BLESSING

"You will be blessed in the city and blessed in the
country. The fruit of your womb will be blessed,
and the crops of your land and the young of your
livestock—the calves of your herds and the lambs
of your flocks. Your basket and your kneading
trough will be blessed. You will be blessed when
you come in and blessed when you go out . . .
The LORD will send a blessing on your barns
and on everything you put your hand to. The
LORD your God will bless you in the land he is
giving you."—Deuteronomy 28:3-8

Five months has passed since I told Mum to stay away;
with each passing day, the peace that I experienced stayed
with me still. I seemed to finally have the life I wanted and
that I had desired for so long.

I sat on the beach in Sitges, Spain, and watched the waves
break over the clear, blue water. It was a breezy afternoon. The
spring sun kept the temperature warm; I could feel the heat
of the sunrays on my hand. I had almost finished writing this

book and left my hotel room for the first time that day to get some air. I played with the fine, golden sand with my toes and gazed into the horizon. *What happens now?* I asked, not quite directing the question to God or myself.

I had woken up early that morning and read Deuteronomy, chapter twenty-eight. That afternoon, as I sat on the quiet beach taking in the glory of the Mediterranean Sea, I ruminated, for the thousandth time that week, on my life with Mum and the roles that different people had played in my relationship with her, particularly my friends. I thought again about the insinuations from some of my friends that I was missing some blessings because of my strained relationship with my mother. Even though the insinuations no longer bothered me as they had done in the past, I couldn't help but question what the blessings were that I might be missing and I wondered where that mother's blessing would come from.

Why was I intent on Mother's blessing anyway? If I didn't get it, what would happen? Do I really need this blessing to succeed? Why do I see Mother as the source of my blessing? Thinking about it, it stood to reason that I would seek a blessing from my mother—she is the person I knew cared for us. I knew she was fallible but I still had faith in her to do right by me. I loved Dad, but Dad didn't know how to sacrifice for love. I accepted him all the same and put everything within me into making life with Mum work. It was hard and we fell short sometimes, but we always seemed to bounce back. There was hope, it seemed.

But now I realise that the resolution we adopted for our failure was a broom that swept it all under the carpet in preparation for the big day of eruption. When I was growing up, I thought I had my mother's blessing, not quite realising it was conditional. When reality dawned on me in my adult years, I felt cursed, and in reality I was. Not by the circumstances of life—they were comparatively easy to overcome—but by the words from my earthly mother's mouth, the bitterness and resentment seated within her.

Trying desperately to gain her blessing, I fought and raged; I battled hard with her until I came to my senses. Her blessing was hers to give as she chose; it was not for me to determine who got it or who didn't.

I had lived decades and watched as she gave part of a blessing and took part away. I then felt partly blessed, but life is no life if partly lived. Anger brewed within me when I realised the depth of my loss. Where would I find Mother's blessing; where would I find my own mother? Those were the worries that besieged my mind.

I searched high and low.

Perhaps the older woman who had been pestering me to be her friend for a while now could be the one to help me find the blessing? Perhaps that was why she had shown such resilience in seeking friendship with me?

Ouch! Not so. She was in it for what she could get.

The woman preacher in the church did not do, either; she didn't want to bear my burden. The "Mother in Israel" tried what she could. I could see she was trying her hardest, but it still was not quite the answer. Then God brought a chosen one and I felt a sense of being loved. I thought I got the blessing, but it was love I felt, a shadow of what might have been. She knew what it was to love another woman; she had loved the one who came from her own womb.

Where is this elusive blessing? I thought. *Why does it keep running away from me? Where will I find it?*

But then I realised that God who made the waves over the water that rush in friendly embrace towards the shore, wetting eager feet with their chilled substance; the substance that harbours life deep within where no eye can see; the life that sometimes springs forth out of the deep to remind the earth of its fearsome existence—the God who made all this a blessing to mankind has the Blessing in His breath.

He said:

Can a mother forget the baby at her breast and have no compassion on the child she has borne? Though she may forget, I will not forget you! See, I have engraved you on the palms of my hands; your walls are ever before me (Isaiah 49:15-16, NIV).

As though that was not enough, He said, I will comfort you, as a mother comforts her child and I will make sure you are comforted[1]. He said, I will nurture you and have compassion for you; because the day you were born, no one cut your umbilical cord, I did; no one wiped the blood and fluid from your body, I did. I did more than help you survive, he said. I clothed you and gave you dignity, the dignity others did not see fit to give you. You were dignified and much more. I robed you in luxury; I adorned you with precious ornaments, bracelets for your wrists and a necklace for your neck.[2]

He said further, I even drew a plan for your life with all the trimmings of riches and splendour. I laid your foundation with sapphire, your borders of agates and your walls of the most precious stones.[3] He is the higher power, who gives all these things and no one can take them, try as they may.[4] He said I am the one you need, no one else.[5]

There are many angry sons and daughters out there who have felt cursed one way or another. Feeling cursed makes one feel stuck; life becomes a hamster wheel going nowhere fast, but if we understand that God is up there raining down blessings, we will stop the anger and walk away from the ignorance of those who curse. For out of the abundance of the heart the mouth speaks (Matthew 12:34, KJV) and like a fluttering sparrow or a darting swallow, an undeserved curse does not come to rest (Proverbs 26:2, NIV).

Scott Walker talked about the various ways we experience our parent's blessings.[6] In the Yoruba culture, children usually kneel down (or prostrate) in front of the elders to be prayed for, but that is not the most important thing to happen. A parent can bless a child without speaking a word; it is all in the action and attitude of the mind towards the child. A parent's blessing comes all throughout the day, the week and the year in both childhood and adult life. The same goes for a curse. A child could be cursed without a word being spoken.

I loved to bless my mother, and it would have been in her best interest to bless me in a true way, but sometimes we are ignorant to our own detriment. I wonder, sometimes, where the contented woman I knew when I was five years old went. I ask myself who can search her out for me. The one that knows to bless her children and, if she has no word of blessing, to keep quiet and keep herself occupied with other productive tasks.

My mother: motivated by her fears, impelled by the bitterness and the pain she feels inside. She may not have nurtured my growing person, and her kindness she might have kept buried within her, but she would die for fear that I should die—it is one of her greatest fears in life, losing a child. I have come to terms with the fact that, for better or for worse, I was my mother's daughter. I shared her fears, partook of her bitterness, and drank from her cup of hurt and pain. There is one difference that by the mercy of God exists between us—I acknowledged and accepted my fear, my pain, and my bitterness, and made every effort to face them. I see no other option than to face those inner enemies, fight my fear and shake off that bitterness. How can I overcome, if I do not step onto the battlefield to fight the good fight of faith, of justice and of a life of peace: peace with myself and peace within me? Would it be in the hope that the enemy will go away if it waited too long, with no response from me, to its torment?

There are some enemies that do not go away but exist deep within; they go where I go, eat where I eat, and sleep where I sleep. I needed to call them out and banish them forever, and so I have done.

AFTERWORD

When I embarked on the mission of putting right whatever had gone wrong in my life, writing about it was not one of the end results I had anticipated. As I continued to pursue the goal of emotional wholeness, the inspiration to write came, grew, and continued to grow until I made the decision to publish a book.

I look back on the healing process, and for me, it is the same as when a loved one dies. You don't dig any old hole and put them in it, in order to get it over and done with quickly. There are feelings involved, especially with someone you had shared a lot with. Death can be very hurtful. It brings grief, confusion, pain, a sense of being alone and much more.

Facing the pain of life is sometimes like facing the death of a loved one; the breakdown of a close relationship, for example, is a major source of pain. It represents the death of a much-desired state of being, and when it happens we go through similar emotions as we do when we grieve loss of life. Norman Wright, in analogous expressions, says that healing is not about digging in the cemetery of our minds, looking for emotional ghosts to come back and haunt us. Rather, it is about filling in the half-filled graves.[1]

It was not until I started to untangle the complexities of the problem I was facing that I started to experience real freedom and feel a sense of direction. There were times when I got tired of dealing with "issues", but when I recalled the alternative to dealing with them, I went for it with renewed verve. At one point, someone suggested to me that I might be obsessive about it, but I knew how long I'd felt trapped and didn't know how to deal with Mum and all her antics, let alone all of the other family issues. I knew that if I didn't continue to address them, these issues had the tremendous capacity to be very limiting in various ways. The longer they were left unresolved, the worse their effect would be. My own experience is enough proof to me, but I see it in others as well. I could not bear being limited in life anymore. As long as I was finding answers to all that was weighing me down, it did not really matter to me that I might be obsessed with getting the answers.

In Bob Gass's "Word for Today", an entry on the 20th November 2008 made reference to Philip Yancey, who said pain is a sign of life and love. If you feel pain it means you are still living, and when there is a deep wound in the body two types of tissue must heal, both the connective tissue and the outer protective tissue. If the outer tissue heals too quickly, the inner tissue does not heal properly and leads to complications later. He said healing takes time in God's presence with his peace and his people. He referred to God's promise in Jeremiah 30:17 (AMP) to heal our wounds—"*For I will restore health to you, and I will heal your wounds, says the Lord, because they have called you an outcast, saying, This is Zion, whom no one seeks after and for whom no one cares!*"

I think moving on without healing is very much like the protective tissue healing first. I have heard people say over and over again to "get over it", "it" being the hurt. What such people do is help the hurt person create problems for the future. When I was seeking counselling, I was continually told that most people don't address some of the issues I was addressing until their forties and fifties. No wonder there are so many individuals who suffer from what we colloquially call a "mid-life crisis", and a lot of broken children and adults who look perfectly fine on the outside. Hopefully, I am done with my own mid-life crisis!

It is never easy to connect with the hurts of our past. There is vulnerability involved; it exposes our weaknesses and our lives could seem all a muddle. An acquaintance asked me to come out to dinner one evening, and on arriving at the restaurant she opened up to me. She said she had always thought that she was normal, and that her family was normal, until God started to help her connect with some of the factors that were affecting her. I reassured her that it was normal for God to help us deal with negative circumstances if we allow ourselves to submit to Him.

It is easy to bury hurts under the guise of getting over it and moving on. I see some people who can't stop bickering. There are others who ooze out resentment, jealousy, insecurities, and fears and I can't help wonder whether these are pointers to other deep-seated hurts. As long as we are able to achieve the usual milestones—get a reasonable job, be in a stable relationship, have children, have friends—there is no impetus to look into the past. Doing so would be disturbing the proverbial sleeping dog, even though beneath these seemingly mundane aspects of our lives often lies the rubble of past and present destructions.

There is a further quest that we embark on that keeps us from looking into some of our issues, and that is the quest of not wanting to blame our parents. If what we call "blame" is seeing exactly how we got to where we are so that we can move to where we need to be, what is wrong in identifying who and what circumstances worked against us to cause whatever crippling we have experienced? If identifying and understanding how they have negatively impacted our lives so that we can be more effective in trying to live an emotional healthy life is blaming the parents, then I say blame them!

Many people my age have children who are growing up fast, and some of my older friends have teenage children. For them, the prospect of their children blaming them for whatever happens in their lives in ten or twenty years time might be scary. The one thing I know about children (which comes from me having been a child myself, and growing up amongst other children—my siblings, cousins and outsiders), is that you will get back in full measure every good thing you give to a child. Children are compassionate.

The truth, that I now realise, is that no matter what my parents did to cause whatever hurt I might have experienced in the past, or that I am experiencing right now, I will not place the responsibility for putting it right in their hands. If they could make it right, it would not have gone wrong in the first place. I know that nobody is perfect. I have made mistakes with my life and with other people as well. But I need to understand what has been done to make me who I am today in order for me to move on to where I need to be. Without understanding what and where boundaries broke down in the first place, I cannot understand what repairs and new installations I need to put in place.

It has been a very long journey; nonetheless, it has been a successful one. Sometimes I look back and I tell God that I would rather have lived without the pain, but I had no choice; the pain was already there before I was born. Now that I have dealt with the hurts, my memory of them has not been magically erased. I would be worried if they had. I still remember them; the difference is that the memories do not cause me so much pain, and, in most cases, no pain at all.

When I remember a particular hurt and the memory is accompanied by a strong emotion, I am now conscious of the fact that the strong emotion means there are still one or more issues that I need to address. Sometimes I may feel the emotions on behalf of someone else, but the resolution is still the same. When our emotions become exceptionally charged because of an injustice happening to another person, the emotion goes beyond sympathy, even further than empathy. Many times it is because we have suffered the same or similar fate in the past, as the person is suffering in the present, and we have not laid that experience to rest by appropriately addressing it.

What I also realised going through the whole healing process is that we cannot separate our level of understanding of the problems we face from our spiritual breakthrough. The more I understood my problems, the more effective the various ministry tools were for me. In Hosea 4:6 the Bible says, "*My people are destroyed for lack of knowledge . . .*", (KJV). I can't put it better than the following verses put it:

> "*For wisdom will enter your heart, and knowledge will be pleasant to your soul. Discretion will protect you, and understanding will guard you. Wisdom will save . . .*"—Proverbs 2:10-12 (NIV)

> "*The beginning of wisdom is this: Get wisdom. Though it cost all you have, get understanding.*"—Proverbs 4:7

> "*Know also that wisdom is like honey for you: If you find it, there is a future hope for you, and your hope will not be cut off.*"—Proverbs 24:14

To say I learnt a thing or two about control and manipulation would be an understatement. Control, manipulation, and abuse all come when we have been mistreated by others at some point in the past and we are in need of a way out of the painful feelings that resulted. As Dan Neuarth says, "We control to the extent that we mistrust the world."[2]

Susan Forward tells the story, illustrated in one of her psychology books, of a man who was bawled out by his boss. When he got home, he displaced his anger on his wife; she then yelled at the kids; the kids in turn kicked the dog, then the dog bit the cat.[3] The story ended there, but I wondered what the cat would have done and what would have happened thereafter. We all look for an easier prey on which to displace our anger because we are too fearful to face the person who caused the hurt in the first place, and we know that the hurt will not simply disappear by itself. As Norman Wright has suggested, we try to use other current relationships to resolve the conflicts of the past.[4] The bad news is that this approach stunts our growth.

I believe three things are important in dealing with the abuse we might have experienced in the past:

The first is the need to accept the fact that the abuser was stronger at the time of the abuse, whether by themselves or with help from other people or surrounding circumstances. If not, they would not have conquered their victims. It is, however, important to also realise that the abuser is no longer stronger, if only for the fact that, as adults, or with better understanding, our respective lives are now in our own hands and we can set their courses as we deem fit. Otherwise, the anger we hold against ourselves for being inadequate will keep the abuse and victim mentality alive. A lot of the anger we feel is against ourselves and not the abuser—the anger of being foolish enough to appear an idiot, the anger of being ignorant, the anger of being tongue-tied when we should have spoken; the list is endless. Our vulnerability makes us feel like the loser and a voice in our head tells us we could have been a lot stronger.

The good news is that we can deal with this anger by learning how to respond to people when they do hurtful things. One of my counsellors told me about the immediacy skill. For a lot of us, not being able to answer with the right words at the right moment causes more anger and resentment than what was said to us. We need to allow ourselves the grace to mull things over and get a better perspective. There is absolutely nothing wrong with going back to that person to challenge them or talk things through with them at a later time. But holding on to anger sometimes seems like the only way we can stay conscious of the need to protect ourselves from further harm. We learn to put up a wall of defence that warns the would-be offender that they are treading on dangerous ground if they try to breach our defence. The emotion of anger then serves as a barrier, not only to the offender, but serving to warp our perspectives on other relationships in our lives. We end up hurting innocent people who share those relationships with us, some of them having been sent by God to help us or be companions for us.

The second important factor in dealing with past abuse is the need for us to understand our worth as individuals. This understanding serves as an eye-opener, showing us where the problem lies and minimising our need to transfer an offence to someone else in order to deal with it. The question, then, is how do we find our worth as individuals? I believe living a worthy and fulfilled life comes from the inside. It is not about the size of the house you live in, or how much luxury is laid out in there. It is about the person you are on the inside. Stripped to the bone; no house, no car, no wife, no husband, no children—who are you? Who are you when none of these people or things are there? Not many of us will dare to think this way, because without those people and those things, we are nothing in our own eyes.

Many of us Christians think, *Of course I know who I am; I am a child of God, born of the spirit, born of water*, etc. However, when it comes down to living out our claim, we no longer reflect the confidence of our words, because we only have the head knowledge of our worth as Children of God—it is the heart knowledge that will take us through.

Shame is a major factor that keeps us bound in low self-worth. It is an emotion that tells us we are not good enough. For a lot of us, shame has been drummed into our lives. We are ashamed of the way we look, the way we dress, the way we behave, our countenance, the way we talk, the way we sit, the way we stand, what we say or don't say and our ability to make friends or not. I found that the people who infuse shame into other people live lives of shame themselves. They are ashamed that they are not doing better, they are ashamed of their family circumstances and more. Acceptance of the situation and working through the issues one at a time is a good way to walk out of shame.

The third important element in dealing with past abuse is the need for us to grow in our walk with God and in our journey through life. Our walk with God is our spiritual growth, and our journey through life is what some people may refer to as personal growth. A lot of this personal growth is manifested in our emotional maturity. The emotional maturity itself has a bearing on the feelings (both positive and negative) that we have when we've been hurt, and it determines how we handle those feelings and how we go about resolving the hurt.

The more emotionally and spiritually mature we are, the better we will value ourselves and the more adequate we will feel. This maturity will help us develop enough confidence to appropriately tackle the various sources of offences that may be directed towards us, and we will ultimately be able to find the right way of dealing with them.

All forms of growth require nourishment. From birth, we grew physically every day until we became fully-fledged adults. In our adult years, our bodies might experience changes, and may expand or contract, but our physical development has reached its apex. There is one aspect of us, however, that needs to continually develop if we are to grow old gracefully: our emotions. We need to make use of the opportunities around us to effect this growth.

I believe the most important factor in our emotional growth is how honest we are with ourselves. In order to be better people, it is important that we admit our weaknesses, especially when we express "weak" emotions like jealousy, fear and envy. It is the first crucial step to recovery; denying them is to keep the pain alive. Pia Mellody and her co-authors put it this way: "*We cannot change our emotions. What we feel is what we feel. In fact it is dysfunctional to try not to be angry or not to be afraid when that is what we feel.*"[5] When it comes to the so-called "strong" emotions, such as anger, we need to understand that there is nothing strong or weak about them. I read that anger is usually seen as a masculine emotion, but the expression of that masculine anger can be weak. We need to accept the fact that these emotions are all there (both perceived weak and perceived strong emotions) as warning signs, like the boards on the motorway, to tell us something, somewhere, is going wrong that deserves our attention. Some of the emotions we feel can be traced back to what we perceive as our own personal failures. The shame of these perceived inadequacies then lower our sense of self-worth and, if we do not address

345

this our perception, we run the risk of additional negative feelings that the shame and subsequent low self-esteem bring.

We need to start to understand that despite our weaknesses we are worthy individuals, worthy of our own love, care, and honour. It is when we learn to care for and honour ourselves that we can learn to truly love and honour other people. It is then that we can see that some of the things we consider failures do not make us inherently defective. There is much to be said for contentment. The Bible says that Godliness coupled with contentment is great gain (I Timothy 6:6). This is not to be mistaken for complacency. I believe in people using their optimum capability and being the best that they can be; that is part of God's plan for us. Jesus emphasised this in the parable of the talents (Matthew 25:14-30).

However, of all the verses in the Bible that encourages us to be wise, to get understanding, to use our talents and multiply them, I haven't seen one that says anything about measuring our achievements against the new BMW Geoffrey got last week, or for us to worry about the fact that Brenda is always more confidently poised than we are. Understanding that we are good enough and more than good enough, just the way we are, is the key. It is that understanding that will help us to take bolder steps towards a higher level of personal growth.

This adequacy that we need to see in ourselves is not because of anything we have done, but because we are created in perfection as *individuals*. If we have no understanding of ourselves, or if we are not in tune with who we are, we will never know or appreciate our areas of strength or how to make the most advantageous use of them. In the parable of the talents, the master gave different amounts of money (or talents) to his three servants. He gave one talent, two talents and five talents respectively to the three men. No doubt some of us would want to be the one with the five talents, because we are ambitious by nature. Nevertheless, what will bring us the greatest sense of fulfilment will not be for us to seek out the higher talent or bury our talent altogether, but for us to understand what we have been given and how we can make the best of it. There surely was a reason for the one talent, just as there was for the five talents.

If we keep darting from what is making the most money today to what may be making money tomorrow, or if we are always keeping an eye out for what Clara is doing today that is more interesting or more rewarding than what we are doing, precious happiness will be lost. In the same vein, if we focus on what we could or should be doing that would ensure nobody would badmouth us, the result would be instability. Telltales will always be telltales, slanderers will always slander, critical people will always criticise. We can choose to get on with our lives or focus on what they have to say.

Asking myself some simple but potentially tough questions helps me return to base when it all starts to seem chaotic. These questions include:

> How am I feeling today?
> What am I finding overwhelming?
> What is the trigger for my feelings?
> What is the solution?
> How can I get back to base?

I spent so many years working to get to a place where I am sufficiently emotionally healthy to establish the appropriate relationships with various people in my life, and build new relationships based on healthy and mature attitudes and behaviours. The more I get to that place of maturity, the more I realise it is a lifelong process. I have not become a perfect person through my quest to resolve my personal issues. What I have found is a new way to live. And this has set me up on a new journey where my life will be different and more importantly, where it will be better.

"I'm not saying that I have this all together,
that I have it made.
But I am well on my way, reaching out for Christ,
who has so wondrously reached out for me.
Friends, don't get me wrong:
By no means do I count myself an expert in all of this,
but I've got my eye on the goal, where God is
beckoning us onward—to Jesus.
I'm off and running, and I'm not turning back."
Philippians 3:12-14 (The Message)

The End

NOTES AND
SUGGESTED READINGS

Chapter 20
1. Kylstra, Chester D., and Kylstra, Betsy. *An Integrated Approach to Healing Ministry: A Guide to Receiving Healing and Deliverance from Past Sins, Hurts, Ungodly Mindsets and Demonic Oppression.* Sovereign World Ltd., 2004.

Chapter 23
1. Arnott, John. *What Christians Should Know About the Importance of Forgiveness.* Sovereign World Ltd, 1997.
2. Cloud, Henry, and Townsend, John. *Boundaries: When to Say Yes, How to Say No to Take Control of Your Life.* Zondervan, 1996. Revised edition.

Chapter 25
1. Wright, Norman H. *Making Peace with Your Past.* Fleming H. Revell, 1997.9.
2. Krasnow, Iris. *I Am My Mother's Daughter: Making Peace with Mom—Before It's Too Late.* Basic Books, 2006. 64.
3. McGregor, Denise. *Mama Drama: Making Peace with the One Woman Who Can Push Your Buttons, Make You Cry and Drive You Crazy.* St. Martin's Griffin, 1999.
4. Walker, Scott. *Driven No More: Finding Contentment by Letting Go.* Augsburg Fortress Publishers, 2001.3.

Chapter 26
1. Mellody, Pia; Miller, Andrea Wells; Miller, J Keith. *Facing Codependence: What It Is, Where It Comes From, How It Sabotages Our Lives.* San Francisco: Harper, 2003.
2. Wright, op. cit.20.

Chapter 28
1. Adapted from Isaiah 66:13.
2. Adapted from Ezekiel 16.
3. Adapted from Isaiah 44.
4. Adapted from Revelations 3:7.
5. Adapted from Isaiah 43:11.
6. Walker, op. cit.

Afterword
1. Wright, op. cit.171.
2. Neuharth, Dan. *If you had Controlling Parents: How to Make Peace with Your Past and Take Your Place in the World.* HarperCollins, 1998. xxiii.
3. Forward, Susan. *Toxic Parents: Overcoming their hurtful legacy and reclaiming your life.* Bantam Books, 1990.26.
4. Wright, op. cit.19.
5. Mellody, et al., op. cit.104.

About the Author

Before turning her hand to writing, **Ayomide Adeniola** previously qualified as a chartered surveyor and has worked on several development projects in the beautiful city of Bath and the North East Somerset area. She currently works in London and continues to combine the art of altering the city landscape with the art of writing. This is her first book.